English as a Creative Art

Literary Concepts Linked to Creative Writing

Linden Peach and
Angela Burton

David Fulton Publishers
London

David Fulton Publishers Ltd
2 Barbon Close, London WC1N 3JX

First published in Great Britain by David Fulton Publishers 1995

Note: The right of Linden Peach and Angela Burton to be identified as the authors of this work has been asserted by them in accordance with the Copyright, Designs and Patents Act 1988.

British Library Cataloguing in Publication Data

A catalogue record for this book is available from the British Library

ISBN 1–85346–368–X

Typeset by The Harrington Consultancy Ltd.
Printed in Great Britain by Bell & Bain Ltd., Glasgow

Contents

Acknowledgements

We should like to acknowledge a general debt to our colleagues and students in the Schools of English at University College Bretton Hall, Goldsmiths' College, University of London, and at the University of Leeds for helping us to define and refine our ideas. In particular, we would like to mention Linda Anderson, Sharon Butler, Terry Gifford, Simon Ross, James Waddington and Rob Watson. Special thanks are due to the staff of the libraries at Bretton Hall and at the University of Leeds for their speedy and efficient assistance. We are also indebted to research and administrative staff at Bretton Hall. In addition, we would like to thank our editor and staff at David Fulton Publishers for their advice and support. Finally, this project could not have been completed without the encouragement, understanding and support of family and friends.

The authors and publishers wish to thank the following for permission to use copyright material: Bloodaxe Books Ltd for 'Black Bottom' by Jackie Kay, reprinted by Bloodaxe Books Ltd from: *The Adoption Papers* by Jackie Kay (Bloodaxe Books, 1991); Carcanet Press Ltd for 'Swinging' from Gillian Clarke, *Selected Poems* (Carcanet Press, 1985); Tony Curtis and Seren Books for 'Dedicating the House of Art' reprinted by Seren Books in Tony Curtis, *War Voices* (Seren, 1995); David Dabydeen and Dangaroo Press for 'Nightmare' from David Dabydeen, *Slave Song* (Dangaroo Press, 1984).

Preface

English as a Creative Art is different from previous works on either creative writing or contemporary literary criticism. It is the first book to bring the two together, demonstrating how concepts drawn from literary theory can be used to enable students to develop critical insights into their own writing. Conversely, it also aims to help students understand contemporary critical concepts and become more incisive thinkers through creative work.

As the first book to demonstrate the creative potential of modern literary concepts, it is intended to be worked through and not simply read. Much of the benefit of the book is to be gained from the writing exercises and the critical activities which have been designed to help students reach a fuller understanding of the issues and problems raised by modern theory for both the critic and the writer. The discussions which follow the exercises are not intended to offer definitive solutions but to stimulate further reflection, activity and debate based on the projects completed.

The practical exercises are based on a wide range of writing including short stories, novels, radio plays, television genre, documentary and poetry. Literary examples have been taken from a variety of texts including frequently studied canonical works, critically acclaimed new literatures in English and works of popular culture. The first two sections – 'Suggestions for Using this Book' and 'Getting Started' – are intended to help the reader, whether an independent learner, a member of a class or workshop, or a tutor, to get the most out of this book.

Linden Peach and Angela Burton
Wakefield, September 1995

Suggestions for using this Book

This book is divided into seven chapters which are subdivided into units. Each chapter contains four main types of material:

1. expositions of key ideas in modern critical theory;

2. critical activities providing students with an opportunity to reflect individually or in a group on the ideas raised or to interpret extracts of selected texts in the light of these critical and theoretical ideas;

3. writing activities and case studies enabling students to undertake a piece of work in response to modern critical insights into writing;

4. our reflections upon what we hope students achieved in the critical and the writing activities.

As we said in our Preface, this is a book to be worked through. It has been written so as to be of benefit to an individual working alone or to be used as a text in the classroom. Many of the critical and research activities may be undertaken individually or as group projects. They may form the basis of formal workshops or provide a stimulus for independent learning. We also hope that they will provide subjects for informal discussion.

Readers who are working through the book independently should not try to do too much at one time and make sure that they allocate sufficient time to the critical and writing activities to complete them to the best of their abilities before reading our own comments.

Introduction
Getting Started

In this section you will find information and advice on:

1. Organizing your life around your writing

2. Gathering data

3. Keeping notebooks and journals

4. Undertaking research.

Activities

You will be asked to work through a number of exercises:

1. A preparatory activity which may be undertaken in a few minutes;

2. A research activity which will require a visit to a library;

3. A brainstorming activity;

4. A research activity in preparation for the next chapter.

Preparatory Activity
Before reading further we would like you to take a few minutes and complete the following statement: 'I would like to write, but...'

Being a Writer

We wonder how many of you in response to the above preparatory exercise wrote: 'I don't have anything to write about'; or 'I can never find the time'; or 'I start well but then I dry up'; or 'Everything I want to say has been said before, and better!' These frustrations are not unique to you. Experienced as well as new writers know what it is like to end up staring at a blank page or computer screen.

In an interview with Nicci Gerrard in *The Observer* (15 January, 1994), the Nobel Prize-winning Nigerian writer and political activist, Wole Soyinka, admitted: 'I go through periods of drought when I cannot function as a writer. Literature often requires reflection and creative space' (p.16). Another Nobel Prize-winning writer, Toni Morrison, whose novels we will discuss in chapter 4, has described in an interview with Claudia Tate (1985) how:

> When I sit down in order to write, sometimes it's there; sometimes it's not. But that doesn't bother me any more. I tell my students there is such a thing as "writer's block", and they should respect it. You shouldn't write through it. It's blocked because it ought to be blocked, because you haven't got it right now. All the frustration and nuttiness that comes from "Oh, my God, I cannot write now" should be displaced. It's just a message to you saying, "That's right, you can't write now so don't." We operate with deadlines, so facing the anxiety about the block has become a way of life. We get frightened about the fear. I can't write like that. If I don't have anything to say for three of four months, I just don't write. When I read a book, I can always tell if the writer has written through a block. If he or she had just waited, it would have been better or different, a little more natural. You can see the seams. (p.120)

Sometimes the only answer to writer's block is to get away for a while and clear the head! There are various relaxation techniques and exercises which might help you before you begin working. You will find some of these in the books listed at the end of this section, but, of course, they are only one solution.

First of all, you not only have to find the time to sit down and write, but you must find the right time and place to do so. You should try to find a space in your home where you can work undisturbed and where every member of the family knows you are not to be disturbed. When and for how long you write will depend upon your own particular circumstances, lifestyle and commitments. You must work to a schedule that suits you and all the other demands on your time whilst enabling you, if you are following a formal course, to meet externally imposed deadlines. There are writers who believe it is important to try to work regularly and for the same period of time on each occasion. Even if you do write through writer's block, you may find that very little is really wasted. You may return to what you have written later, to resurrect an idea, a compelling image or a few astute observations.

If you are to write seriously you will need a regular supply of raw material. Just as photographers are hardly ever without their cameras, writers usually carry notebooks or pocket-sized recorders to catch their thoughts, their observations or snippets of conversations they might overhear. The playwright, Joe Orton, was a renowned diary writer; in fact the biography which followed soon after the sensationalism of his early death was based largely on his own private jottings. He believed that life validated art and his plays drew heavily upon the observations which he made in his diaries.

Keeping a Journal

In addition to the notebook which we hope you will carry around with you, we recommend you keep a journal to record your thoughts, your experiences, the conversations you overhear and information which interests you. Not only will this provide you with useful material, but it may also generate ideas and ensure that you are writing regularly. You can also keep newscuttings, reviews (of books, theatre productions, films, or television programmes) as well as visual images, as stimuli for your own thinking or as models of writing styles which might help you in the development of your own.

You can decide whether you want to keep one or more journals. Having one, even though it will soon run to several volumes, centralizes all your material, but it can be useful to keep separate journals or notebooks. For example, you may want to keep a theatre notebook in which you can record your responses to some of the productions you go to see. This would enable you to observe how your responses have changed over the years; to compare how different directors and companies deal with the same dramatic text; to compile a record of the special effects available in the theatre; and to explore systematically the limitations and creative possibilities of dramatic writing for you as an author. In particular, it would enable you to keep a file of as many of the visual aspects as possible of the productions you go to see. You could then start to consider how many of them you ought to have included in your text if you had been the writer. You should record audience reaction and participation as well in your journal to help you in your writing – what seemed to be well received and what was not. Make notes on how the space was used by the performers as this may be a feature you will need to include in your stage directions.

A theatre notebook is also useful because it helps you to appreciate how writers for the theatre do not work alone but as part of a team composed of the director, the theatre's artistic director and the technical experts involved. You may find that the original script of some of the productions you see is available in published form. You should try to compare the visual aspects of the production in the writer's script with those you recorded in your notebook.

From our summary of a theatre notebook, you can see the use which may be made of a separate journal. Other journals you may want to keep are a cinema/film/television journal or a reading journal in which you record your responses to books you have read, in the form of a review and/or critical appraisal. You may want to include quotations or phrases in addition to new or unusual words which you found striking or significant.

Journals are also essential for developing your train of thought and recording your ideas for future projects. They are a useful resource in creating a body of existing ideas, notes and rehearsals for your own work. Wilson Harris, a Guyanan writer, has suggested that life is a process of infinite rehearsals in which we never arrive at the final rehearsal. In a sense, writing is one example of this, a process of infinite rehearsals. Often the cut-off point for a writer is an externally imposed deadline, the point at which a piece of work goes to print. If you are following a course, you will have had to finish some of your writing because of a submission deadline. If you are working through this text as a member of a class or writing group, your tutor may determine the amount of time which you are able to spend on the writing exercises. The work which writers despatch to publishers and which students submit as assignments may not be the final rehearsal. Often more could have been written or further revisions made if there had been more time. Even if this were not the case, more rehearsals normally follow a writer's submission of a manuscript. Editors, printers and, of course, readers of the published work normally have a role in the creation of the text's meanings, as we shall discuss later. In film, television or theatre, writing becomes only one part of a complex process of interaction between, in the case of film, for example, the writer, director, producer, actors, camera operators, film editors, critics, reviewers and audience. In these circumstances, the writer becomes a kind of artisan within a collective project.

A journal is a place for us to rehearse both our ideas and our skill in expressing them. Using a journal to engage critically with other people's writing (fiction, drama, poetry, journalism, reviews, criticism, letters to newspapers and so on) helps us to develop our own thinking.

Research Activity

Most writers keep journals, diaries, letters, and write in a range of registers and formats. In some cases, for example Virginia Woolf, you will find among their 'private' writings 'rehearsals' of their famous works or contradictory ideas to those which they have published.

Survey the private writings of an author with whom you are familiar and compare them to the writer's published works. Discuss your findings in your journal.

Obviously, which writer you are able to choose will depend upon the holdings of your college, school or local reference library as well as on your own inclinations.

The Writer as Researcher

This is a vast topic which justifies a book in itself. All we want to do at this stage is to alert you to the extent to which a great deal of writing depends upon preparatory research. If you completed the above activity you will already have undertaken a research project. This is an important kind of activity for you. While the imagination is a primary source of creativity, many writers find themselves engaged in research of one kind or another.

For a writer, the three most important areas of research are those which:

1. contribute a convincing backdrop to the writing;

2. stimulate ideas for plot, character or subject matter;

3. relate to the publishing and marketing of the work.

In this section we will concentrate on the first two of these areas.

Critical Activity

Before reading further, we would like you, either individually or as a member of a group, to brainstorm the range of source material upon which a writer may draw.

Discussion

Your deliberations probably produced a rather long list which may have included: literary sources, travel literature, maps, tourist guides, archives, historical research, news media, dictionaries, language books, oral history, experiential research, observation/fieldwork, interviewing and memory. Keep these examples in mind as you read the next section.

Principal Types of Research

We have already listed the three major areas of research for a writer. In concentrating on the research which provides material for convincing locations or ideas for plot, character and themes, we can identify two principal types of research:

1. academic research

2. experiential research.

Academic Research

Academic research, that is research undertaken in libraries, record offices and archives or relying on a deliberate programme of private reading, is important to a wide variety of authors working with many different types of writing. It is often obvious from the subject matter of bestselling novels that authors such as Jeffrey Archer, Jack Higgins and Barbara Taylor Bradford have undertaken periods of painstaking research. For example, Barbara Taylor Bradford researched working-class life at the turn of the century in Leeds for her novel *A Woman of Substance* (1980) and Jack Higgins researched details of the Second World War for his novel *The Eagle Has Landed* (1975). His daughter, Sarah Patterson, wrote a novel about a war pilot, *The Distant Summer* (1977), entirely based on information acquired while she was helping her father research *The Eagle Has Landed*; she was fourteen at the time! The acclaimed British-Caribbean writer, Caryl Phillips, wrote his novel *Cambridge* (1991), after researching the Caribbean slave trade for a non-fictional piece of writing. He also relies on oral histories collected from members of his own family. John Fowles' novel *The French Lieutenant's Woman* (1977), is impressive in its knowledge of the content and style of Victorian fiction. David Lodge's *Nice Work* (1988) juxtaposes details of factory management with university life.

As you read more widely in literature, you will become increasingly familiar with authors who rely on this kind of academic research. As you are probably currently engaged yourself in a range of academic studies you may like to consider how, as a writer, you could draw on your own reading as these authors have. Many writers take an actual historical event and, focusing on a character who might plausibly have been involved, weave a story around a well-researched background. Other strategies are to take an organization or an institution of power and again personalize copious amounts of research by telling the story, for example, of a particular character's relationship to the machinations of power within it. John Grisham's recent novels *The Firm, The Client* and *The Pelican Brief* exemplify this strategy.

Where and how do we start with this type of research? Should you want to research a political or historical background, an obvious place to start would be the biographies of key figures or expository overviews of key events. Use the bibliographies at the back of books you read to guide you to further material. Newspapers are often available in the larger reference libraries, major newspapers are kept on file either on microfiche or in CD ROM format. Visit your local reference library as soon as you can and try to familiarize yourself with these formats.

This kind of research will help to provide you with something to write about. If you embark on a writing project which requires this type of preparatory research, remember that there are three golden rules:

1. Be methodical: record your findings, preferably on index cards, under headings to which you can continue to add information;

2. Record the source of your material fully and accurately in case you wish to return to it later;

3. Be imaginative: remember that you are not researching for an essay or a thesis. Record idiosyncratic details, observations of life at the time, information which could later contribute to a sense of place or the creation of a convincing character, and interesting anecdotes or images.

Academic research is a skill which has to be learned by experience. You will become increasingly aware of the kind of information which will be useful to you in the type of writing you undertake. Do not expect to use all your information in one piece of work. Some of your research you will file in order to return to it at a later date. It is important that you develop for yourself a clearly organized and accessible filing system.

Investigative and Experiential Research

Often, research is of an investigative or experiential nature. You will find that much of the material you put into your notebook will be of this kind and the preparatory research activities in this book require you to undertake observation and/or investigation. Lynda La Plante spent time with members of the vice squad for her police procedure television series, *Prime Suspect*. Jeffrey Archer's *Shall We Kill The President* (1973), concerned with a plot to kill Edward Kennedy who is the President of America in 1983, employs researched knowledge of the American political system and key organizations such as the FBI. A distinction has to be made, of course, between fiction which draws on experiential research and writing which documents those experiences. Probably the best known example of the latter type of writing is George Orwell's *Down and Out in London and Paris* (1949). John Thompson (1985) records how Orwell first decided to experience for himself life on the streets of London:

> I thought it over and decided what I would do. I would go suitably disguised to Limehouse and Whitechapel and such places and sleep in common lodging-houses and pal up with dock labourers, street hawkers, derelict people, beggars, and, if possible, criminals. And I would find out about tramps and how you got in touch with them and what was the proper procedure for entering the casual ward; and then when I felt I knew the ropes well enough, I would go on the road myself. (p.14)

Orwell was not content with experiencing life as a down-and-out and even tried to experience life in prison! His difficulty was that he had to get himself arrested for a crime which was serious enough to warrant imprisonment. but not serious enough to lead to a rigorous investigation of his identity. Using a false name, Edward Burton, he managed to get himself detained for a day and a night on a charge of being drunk and disorderly, but the magistrates imposed only a fine.

Orwell wrote extensively from observation and research based on firsthand experience. In 1937 he published *The Road to Wigan Pier,* an account of his travels among the people and places of the Great Depression. In writing this documentary, he relied heavily upon his notebooks. In 1984 Beatrix Campbell published her account of a similar journey, based more extensively than Orwell's on collecting oral interviews and researched and written with more reference to women and feminist issues.

Sometimes the most obvious focus of our research may be lying at our feet. Many poets and fiction writers have found themselves on foreign ground and have been able to draw effectively on their personal experiences of travel. At one extreme, this leads to what we usually call 'travel writing'. While impressions of places, their cultures and their peoples constitute the staple of such work, travel writing invariably also involves background investigation. At the other extreme, there is writing which incorporates research into the different locations in which writers have lived and worked. D.H. Lawrence, for example, extracts from whose work we will discuss later in this study, travelled widely, largely because of his health, and much of his later work is based on his experiences in countries such as Australia and Mexico. These experiences are sometimes elided with the results of personal research, as in *The Boy in the Bush* (1924), a rewriting of another person's story which involves a reconstruction of Australia's adventurous past. Romantic fiction frequently relies on exotic locations, so it is hardly surprising to find its writers drawing conspicuously on research into the different parts of the world in which they find themselves. In fact, it helps us to understand how many of the most prolific authors of this type, such as Catherine George who has lived in various countries with her husband, appear to have such a vast number of convincing locations at their disposal! Most professional writers have held full-time jobs and for some, like Ian Fleming who worked for the diplomatic service, this has provided a plethora of experiences upon which to draw, of which travel is but one!

Research Activity

In preparation for the next chapter, we would like you to research two leading critics, I.A. Richards and F.R. Leavis.

Try to discover why they are regarded as important figures in twentieth-century literary criticism, their key ideas, their chief publications and any interesting features about their lives.

Further Reading

Hall, E., Hall. C. and Leech. A. (1990) *Scripted Fantasy in the Classroom.* London: Routledge

A practical guide to introducing fantasy and imagery work in the classroom. The book is particularly recommended here for its practical relaxation exercises which might assist independent learners who find it difficult to start writing as well as workshop leaders.

Sellers, S. (Ed.) (1991) *Taking Reality by Surprise: Writing for Pleasure and Publication.* London: The Women's Press.

This is a basic practical rather than a critical book which readers, especially independent learners who are new to writing, may find useful. It contains advice and exercises from a range of writers and tutors and is recommended here for its basic start-up activities covering topics such as freeing the imagination, discovering a subject, finding a voice and keeping the momentum going.

Chapter One
Writing Meets Literary Theory

In this chapter you will find sections on:

1. English as a creative subject

2. The process of writing

3. Myths about creativity

4. An explanation of what we mean by critical theory

5. Key differences between modern and traditional criticism

6. The origins of traditional criticism

7. The reader's response to a work

8. Realism

9. Experimental fiction.

Activities

You will be asked to undertake the following activities:

1. A preparatory exercise in which you are asked to reflect upon your previous educational experience.

2. Critical activities concerned with:
   - English as a creative subject
   - your impressions of English as a subject
   - particular approaches to texts
   - factors liable to influence a reader's response to a work
   - a summary of how society is represented on television

- an analysis of an innovative piece of writing
- comparing your rewritten passage with the original.

3. An initial writing exercise to help prepare you for the writing activities later in the chapter.

4. Four major writing activities towards the end of the chapter. You are asked to:

   - adapt a well-known fable or fairy-tale as a piece of realistic writing;
   - an analysis of an innovative piece of writing;
   - adapt an episode from a television or radio soap opera as a non-realistic short story;
   - rewrite a passage from a novel by Dickens using techniques developed by a later innovative writer;
   - write a story-line for a television soap opera fulfilling specified objectives arising from your critical exercises.

5. Research exercises requiring access to a library. You are asked to familiarize yourself with the kind of works painted by Rembrandt, a few chapters from an eighteenth-century realist novel, the nature of one or two literary works – *Piers Plowman* and/or *Pilgrims Progress* – written before the novel emerged as a literary form and one or two short stories by the nineteenth-century American writer, Nathaniel Hawthorne.

6. A reading activity which involves comparing examples of criticism that employ different critical approaches,

---

Preparatory Activity

Before beginning this book, you may like to reflect upon the importance which courses you have followed in English have attached to your own writing. How much opportunity has there been for you to use insights gleaned from your study of literature in your own work? What connections have your courses made or have you been encouraged to make between the critical study of literature and your writing?

Preparatory Writing Activity

The purposes of this exercise are to:

1. get you started with your writing;

2. provide you with a project to supplement some of the exercises you may be undertaking for yourself from the Further Reading section of the Introduction;

3. provide you with insights into writing on a topic which will constitute the focus, albeit in a slightly different form, of subsequent writing exercises in this chapter;

4. provide a link between practically-oriented work you may have undertaken on previous courses and the critical, reflective approach of this book.

Read the stimulus material below and write a short prose account of a family meal on a special occasion from the perspective of a young teenager.

The material listed below consists of snapshots of members of their family by teenagers.

'Tom'

Tom

lean, earringed,
swearing, shouting, cheering,
never as tough as he looks,
Tom

'Sue'

Sue,
surly, sleek,
sulking, mocking, smirking,
moon eyes at waiters,
Sue.

'Dad'

Dad,
cross, canine,
barking, snapping, baying,
always touchy at breakfast,
Dad.

'Mum'

plump, pink,
heaving, sighing, puffing,
fights the flab at keep fit,
Mum.

(Baxter, 1989, p.29)

Discussion

Only one of the above snapshots was written by a male and we wonder whether you are able to decide which of them. Obviously the exercise implies that you should think about the members of your family, but you may prefer to invent a family, drawing on characteristics of a whole range of people you know. On previous writing courses you may have concentrated on getting the external details 'right'. Try to go further now. Consider not just people's appearance, but their attitude towards their appearance. What is their taste in clothes? How do they regard their own bodies? How might someone react to their mannerisms? How do they behave differently with different people? Note their accents, tone, use of stresses, favourite words. All this will help prepare you for later sections and exercises in the book.

Incidentally, only the snapshot of Sue was written by a male.

English as a Creative and Expressive Art

There are now many more opportunities for students of literature to pursue their own writing than existed even ten years ago. Although some advanced and degree level courses still only involve reading works of recognized merit, many schools and colleges have more students studying English Language or English Language and Literature courses which, unlike English Literature generally make provision for the students' own creative writing. An increasing number of university and college courses now teach writing as part of degrees in English, Education, Communications and Combined Arts. There are also a number of postgraduate writing courses, numerous writing classes offered in adult education programmes and community-based writing workshops for which the only entry qualification is a willingness to participate.

Students of art have always been concerned primarily with the development of their own work on courses where their personal and student-centred activity would be supported by classes in the history and the theory of art. Students of music, dance and drama have similarly always been concerned with the development of themselves as musicians, dancers and actors. Despite the interest now being shown in writing in schools and colleges, there is still little or no opportunity at advanced or degree level for students of English to concentrate on their own work to the same extent as other arts students are able to do. Peter Abbs, a leading writer on the arts and education, argues that this is because English is not always recognized in schools and colleges as a creative and expressive subject: 'English has been conceived as an analytical subject belonging to the humanities, rather than one belonging with the other arts' (1989, p.76).

Our own research into the writing backgrounds of students on writing courses in higher education revealed a wide range of prior experience. There were many with more enthusiasm than experience, such as the student who admitted: 'I hadn't had much experience of creative writing, but I knew I was particularly gifted with English and so I thought I would be able to apply myself to it'. Others had been writing with various degrees of success for much longer; many of these students confessed to an enthusiasm for writing which went back to their childhoods, but few of them felt they had completed a great deal of work with which they were satisfied. A typical response was:

> I have always been interested in creative writing, from being a school child onwards.
> I have always been involved in writing and telling stories, usually for my own or
> others' amusement. My writing continued through my adolescence. Prior to this
> course I had tackled one short story which I would consider sharing publicly and

several other pieces which were too personal to share. I had written some poems and a couple of short essays. I did English at advanced level (Language/Literature) as a mature student and I had worked in Personnel for twelve years drafting my own memoranda and letters.

Nearly all the students who were interviewed by our research assistants found following a course in writing very beneficial. We were impressed by the enthusiasm with which many of them spoke about their courses, as evidenced in the following response: 'The workshop exercises are brilliant for developing critical/analytical skills because as well as gaining confidence through speaking in group sessions it is good experience to see how other people respond to your work.' Initially, the transition from writing for oneself to writing for a public caused anxiety for many students although the prospect often proved more daunting than the reality. One respondent seemed to summarize the experiences of a lot of students in this respect:

I found the prospect of workshop exercises quite daunting at first. Prior to these I had never shared my work with anyone (except when I was in my teens). My work has always been kept locked away, a secret pastime. So I thought that I would have difficulty with their [the college's] workshops. What surprised me was how much I enjoyed them and how helpful I found them. I now see their help in assisting me to evaluate my own work and revise my original ideas.

Critical Activity I
At this point, we would like you to reflect for a few minutes on how approaching English as a creative and expressive art might affect the nature of a course on literature. You may be a student on a course which already makes provision for you to develop your writing and you may like to see this opportunity extended within your own programme of study. You may be studying writing courses for the first time and may wish to reflect upon previous courses which did not afford you this opportunity.

Discussion

Your ideas probably fell into three main areas. Firstly, you probably thought of revisions to the structure of English courses at advanced and degree level that would allow more scope for writing itself. You may have envisaged a writing programme within the courses consisting initially, for example, of writing exercises from which students might learn basic skills and techniques while acquiring confidence in working with language and leading on to more sustained pieces of writing. You might have thought of students eventually initiating, devising, planning and writing a substantial piece of work under the guidance of a tutor.

Secondly, some of your other ideas may have concerned approaches to literary works themselves. You might have suggested less emphasis upon the ideas and messages within the set texts and more discussion of the techniques and conventions employed. This area of enquiry might focus on the possibilities afforded by the various techniques, the reasons for using them and some of the difficulties and pitfalls involved. You might have wished to see more comparative study of the different ways in which different writers from different periods and writing different types of literature tackled the same subject. Such studies would lead to opportunities for students to practise some of these techniques themselves or experiment with their own approaches to the same subject.

Thirdly, your provisional thoughts may also have led you to question the boundaries between literature and the other arts. A creative study of plays, for example, leads inevitably to dramatic interpretation and performance considerations. After all, plays are written not for the page but for the stage. This consideration becomes especially important when we remember that not all plays are written for the same type of theatre; a play written for theatre-in-the-round, for example, would be informed by specific performance criteria. Involvement in directing, acting or artistic design makes us more aware of the creative possibilities of playwriting than simply studying the content and form of plays in a classroom. Poetry can lead us to music in, for example, the study of ballads, or to performance. Much contemporary poetry is written with performance in mind and there are many performance poets, such as Benjamin Zephaniah, who work a circuit of public venues, schools and colleges.

A creative approach to English can enhance our appreciation of the characteristics of particular types of writing and of writing for particular media such as television or radio. You may have suggested that the traditional English literature syllabus be expanded to include the study of texts in a variety of media. You might have liked to have seen more emphasis on the adaptation of a work from one medium to another.

Writing as a Process

The fact that English has not been recognized as a creative art has inhibited the development of writing courses in a number of ways. One of the most common sources of anxiety among tutors who are new to this area is the criteria for assessment. It seems easier to draw up a list of criteria for marking critical essays than for assessing creative work. Unpublished manuscripts from untried writers seem harder to judge than works in print. Yet the criteria by which we discuss the strengths even of a work of received merit are applicable to all writing. We should be able to recognize, articulate and reward the strengths of any work in terms of our established critical vocabulary.

One of the premises on which this book is written, however, is that writing courses should focus not only on the work which students produce – the writing upon which the assessment is based – but also on the process of writing. An important element in a creative course is the opportunities which it provides for the students to reflect on their own work and their own development as writers.

This needs to be a systematic process recorded in the form of a working log or diary and in a file of drafts, revisions and amendments. Such reflection should form as important a part of the assessment as the actual writing produced. Members of a writing course need opportunities to share not only their work with each other but also their reflections on their own and each other's writings.

Our own research into the expectations of students on writing courses revealed that, despite initial fears, many of them valued the chance of sharing their work with others and of being able to reflect on what they were trying to achieve. The opportunity to experiment with a variety of styles and techniques was generally regarded as essential. Critical but constructive feedback was also perceived as invaluable, especially if it was tailored to helping students find their own voices.

Myths about Creativity

Students are sometimes too reluctant to recognize their own creativity. Abbs argues that 'creativity is not an esoteric power belonging only to a few exceptional individuals, but an innate power, part of our biological inheritance, part of what it is to be human' (1989, p.4). This book approaches creativity as something which is a part of the everyday lives of all of us whether we are fully aware of it or not. Different types of creativity are employed in conversation, in telling jokes or being witty, in telling stories about what has happened to us, in negotiating difficult situations at home or work, in preparing a meal, in pursuing hobbies and so forth.

There are a number of unhelpful myths about creativity. We still tend to associate artistic creation with figures of genius. The word 'artist' is derived from the Latin 'artes' meaning 'skills'. Before the fifteenth century, artists earned their living by their skills, working with others on specific projects. But, after the Renaissance, a distinction developed between the concept of the artisan as a person with skills and the artist imbued with loftier creative and imaginative purpose. Art became increasingly regarded as the product of people, usually men, with special imaginative powers and exquisite sensibilities. In the late eighteenth and early nineteenth centuries, during what we now call the Romantic period, this concept of the artist easily translated into the Romantic stereotype of the isolated writer or painter described by Louisa Buck and Phillip Dodd: 'driven back on his own resources, forced to draw on his own imaginative powers to produce work which the public might or might not want' (1991, p.43).

In the Romantic stereotype which Buck and Dodd summarize there is a further myth which is unhelpful for would-be writers: that writers can work directly from their own experience and immediate sensations without reference to a cultural past or to a series of conventions. Creativity is an act which involves a complex interaction between the inner world (the private, conscious, unconscious and imaginative) and the outer world (the social, cultural and historical). Of course, there is a mysterious element to creativity; Abbs describes the inner world as 'that obscure interior movement that animates, connects and spontaneously creates inner figurative and narrative patterns' (1989, p.23). In other words, the unconscious is a shaping energy in creativity. But we must not underestimate the importance to the writer of what Abbs calls 'the symbolic or aesthetic field' of literature:

> Creativity, in brief, cannot be understood without reference to the symbolic field in which it takes place – that complex magnetic system of allusion, notation, reference, narrative, knowledge, assumption, understanding which we call culture and in their specific contexts the cultures of the various symbolic forms. (1989, p.17)

If the unconscious were seen as the vertical axis in creativity, then the symbolic field in which it takes place would be seen as the horizontal axis. Creativity involves a constant reworking of previous conventions, notations, images or narratives. Abbs, drawing on Einstein's concept of 'combinatory play', defines creative thinking as stepping downwards into the unconscious and sideways out of the track set by logic and convention (p.10). The difficulty that Abbs does not explore fully is that many of the conventions and concepts constituting his 'symbolic field' are regarded in traditional English studies as self-evident, at times almost beyond question.

Critical Activity 2
In a few sentences, try to summarize from your own educational experience what you think English as a discipline involves.

Discussion

Your summary probably included, and may even have given priority to, the study of literature, which you may even have qualified further with reference to the works of great authors or with reference to the study of themes, maybe qualified in turn by reference to plot and character. You probably emphasized working with language, possibly qualified with reference to literary style and technique, and you may have included the study of other media besides literature.

If you reflect further, you may realize how so much in traditional English studies is taken for granted, such as the nature of literature, the subject of major literary works, the activity of criticism itself and many of the terms we use, for example, character, plot, novel, author, narrator.

There is a tendency for us to pronounce confidently and assertively that a particular work conveys particular messages. Moreover, we are often certain that this was the author's intention. Indeed, many essays still pronounce what Dickens, for example, 'says' or 'believes' even though they are only individual responses in a limited number of words to, say, a particular novel, generated by a selective reading of it.

English Called to Book: Literary and Critical Theory

How far English should be pursued as a creative art has not as yet become such a focus for fierce debate as has the role of literary theory over the last fifteen years. Cries of crisis in English studies which were common by the 1980s referred not to the part creativity should play in English but to the way in which many of its basic premises were questioned. The discipline found itself faced with criticisms which it had not previously considered and which cast doubt upon many of its traditional practices. Worse still, these criticisms could not be ignored because they were being asked in some of the new disciplines which developed in the 1970s and 1980s such as Communication Studies and Cultural Studies. Literature gradually lost the privileged position it had enjoyed in the academic discipline of English. No longer placed at the centre of English culture, literature was approached as a cultural form along with other cultural forms. The new disciplines of the 1970s and 1980s raised questions that should really have been asked by English of itself, and they pursued a more rigorous interrogation of the foundations of English studies than had ever been the case in the past.

The traditional organization of English literary study (by period, movement, author, genre), many of the conventional approaches and some of the established methodologies, such as literary criticism itself, came under scrutiny both from within and from without English studies. For example, the notion of a literary canon – a body of works of recognized merit which traditionally every student of English literature was expected to study – was questioned as much for what it excluded – many works by women and non-white writers – as for what it included. The correlation between the under-representation of women and non-white writers in the canon and their negative representation and invisibility in cultural and social institutions raised uncomfortable questions about the way English as a subject of study had been constructed.

The impact of this questioning upon English studies has been summarized by Brian Doyle (1989):

> It may be that the most positive outcome of this prolonged period of crisis in English (in schools as well as colleges) will prove to be its insistent interrogation of the theoretical, political, and cultural bases of social meaning and value...I take the view that 'English' should be reconstituted as the study of how verbal and written fictions have been produced and used, socially channelled and evaluated, grouped together, given social significance, institutionalized, transformed, repressed, and eliminated. (pp.141–2)

If we are to argue for a greater role for students' own writing within English and for the reconstitution of English as a creative and expressive art, then we must be clear that English is a subject which has been, and to some extent still is, in confusion if not crisis. It is a subject which is increasingly dominated by literary and critical theory in which much that was taken for granted and regarded as self-evident is under scrutiny and subject to fierce debate.

What is Literary and Critical Theory?

Webster (1990, pp.8–9) distinguishes three terms:

1. **Practical criticism,** upon which English studies is traditionally based, is the reading, analysis, explication and interpretation of texts that are designated literary;

2. **Literary theory** which is concerned with examining what we mean by 'literature' and 'literary';

3. **Critical theory** which is concerned with the nature of criticism and critical practice.

Literary and critical theory are interdependent. In fact, we often talk of literary critical theory and literary critical practice. Their function is to make explicit, question and develop models at work in potential or existing practices of the subject.

Critical Activity 3
Consider the following model:

Author – Work – Reader

This model represents what Webster (1990, p.17) calls the 'common-sense' attitude to literature. It implies that authors produce works and that these works are read by readers who believe that the ideas communicated through the work originated with the author.

Either individually or in a group, brainstorm some of the ways in which this 'common-sense' model might be regarded as too simple.

Discussion

The history of critical theory can be represented by the shifts in emphasis across this model. Today, much critical theory is concerned with the role of the reader in the making of a text. A work of literature does not exist until somebody reads it. When we read a text, we notice certain details and miss others. We stress certain features at the expense of others. If we could discover what an author intended, we might find that our own view of the text was very different from what he or she expected. Moreover, no two people will read a text in the same way, although in certain areas there may be a high level of agreement; one of these we will discuss in a later chapter. Interpretations of a text which we believe are universal are based on our own subjective responses. Perhaps more accurately, we should talk of 'readers' rather than 'reader'? Individual readings of particular texts may be influenced by a range of factors which may vary from person to person.

Critical Activity 4

Before we go further in this discussion we would like you, either individually or with others, to brainstorm some of the factors that might influence a reader's response to a text.

Discussion

An individual's response to a text may be influenced by any combination of the following factors:

- educational background
- vocabulary
- experience of reading
- cultural background (especially class, race, gender, nationality)
- personal politics
- personal preoccupations
- interests
- life experience at the time of reading
- emotional state at the time of reading
- the physical location in which a text is read
- how a text has been marketed
- the presentation of the text
- whether the text is read for study or for pleasure
- knowledge about the time in which the text is set
- knowledge of the author
- knowledge of previous works by the author.

One of the aims of literary study as a discipline is to teach the skills necessary to make our responses as objective as possible within these constraints and influences. Moreover, the recent emphasis upon the role of the reader in creating a text does not mean the reader is entirely free to interpret a text in any way at all. Our reading of a text is determined, for example, by the way in which it is structured. However, recognizing the creative role of readers should alert us to the plurality of possible responses.

You may have noticed that throughout this discussion we have used the word 'text' more often than the word 'work'. Basically they are interchangeable. However, the word 'text' implies a less author-centred approach than does the word 'work'. The latter was much in vogue prior to the 1950s when criticism tended to be centred on the role of the author and when meaning in a text was thought to originate with an author. The word 'text' better befits a critical methodology which acknowledges that readers as much as authors create what is read.

In the 'common-sense' model, the work to be read and studied is easily identifiable. It ignores the way in which the plurality of possible approaches makes that act of identification problematic. A socialist may see a text differently from a capitalist; a white, male, working-class reader may see it differently from a female, black, middle-class reader. But identifying the text can be difficult for other reasons too.

The 'common-sense' model of literary criticism also ignores the way in which our reading of a text is influenced by the type of text it is. Whether we approach it, for example, as a serious work of art or as a piece of light fiction. This is a subject to which we will return in a later chapter.

When is a Text *the* Text?

It is more difficult to define a 'text' in relation to an author's intentions than the 'common-sense' model suggests. There are three principal reasons for this.

Firstly, a text passes through many hands apart from the author's before it reaches the reader, including editors, publishers and printers. Often works are altered from what the author had originally intended. This makes it very difficult for us, especially if the author was involved in some of the revisions, to determine with complete confidence what the author did intend. For example, editors of Dickens' novels have tended to follow his own edition of his works (1867–68) in which he made changes to the earlier versions. But this version does not necessarily represent what Dickens wanted as the definitive text. He tended only to read carefully those parts of his texts which he wanted to amend. He overlooked many printers' errors elsewhere through carelessness, or because he was not a good proof reader, or because he was too busy.

Let us consider for a moment one of Dickens' novels to which we will refer later in this book. Do we regard the weekly parts in which *Great Expectations* was first published or the first full length 1861 version or the 1868 version as definitive? The 1868 version has misprints that were not in the 1861 edition and some of the spellings which Dickens used in the weekly parts to represent the dialect of two of the characters, Joe and Magwitch, have been normalized. The text which most students study and regard as the definitive edition is an amalgam compiled by a modern editor of these three versions. It is safer, then, for us to talk about the particular text of *Great Expectations* which we are reading than to make assumptions that everything in it originates with the author.

Secondly, a text may be changed as it is reproduced for different reading publics. For example, the first readers of *Great Expectations* could not read it at one sitting as we are able to do. It was originally published, as we said earlier, as a serial in a weekly magazine. Each part had to end in a way that encouraged the reader to purchase the next instalment, rather like a modern soap opera. This made the time which readers had to wait between episodes part of the reading experience. It was a period during which readers could and would surmise, possibly with friends and family, what would happen next. Even an edition of the novel that indicates where each original episode had ended makes it difficult for contemporary readers to recreate this kind of experience of the work.

Thirdly, defining what is *the* version of a literary work is difficult because editors and publishers often persuade authors to amend their manuscripts, sometimes rearranging or omitting quite large sections. The first supposedly complete version of Thomas Hardy's *Tess of the d'Urbervilles* (1891), another novel to which we will refer later, combined the text which had appeared in *The Graphic* newspaper with further episodes not included previously because they were intended only for adult readers. Ironically, it was not complete even then because some pages were overlooked by the printer.

An important issue which the 'common-sense' model does not allow for, then, is which work should be taken as *the* text if more than one version exists. There is a debate about which version of *Great Expectations* we should 'accept' because Dickens wrote two endings to the novel. In the first conclusion to the serial, the narrator, the adult Pip who is looking back on his life, is estranged from the young woman who insulted him as a child but with whom he has always been in love. But Dickens' friend, Edward Bulwer Lytton the novelist, persuaded him to reunite the two characters and Dickens obligingly created an alternative ending. Yet this happy ending sits uncomfortably with the melancholic tone of the passages in which Estella is described throughout the novel. Given that they would have been narrated by the man who is now living happily with her, their melancholy makes little sense.

Origins of the Traditional Approach

Although the traditional approach to literary studies can be traced to Matthew Arnold in the nineteenth century, the biggest debt is owed to two Cambridge University teachers in the 1920s, I.A. Richards and F.R. Leavis. If you completed the research project which we asked you to undertake in preparation for this chapter, you will already have discovered a great deal about them. The first, I.A. Richards, was the celebrated creator of practical criticism through two seminal works, *Principles of Literary Criticism* (1924) and *Practical Criticism* (1929). The essence of his approach is the close reading of texts without allowing knowledge of the context in which they were written and of history to interfere with that activity. In order to appreciate the latter qualification, we have to realize the emphasis that scholars prior to Richards placed on an author's biography so that often the text became the simulacrum of the life. The objective of English studies was to be a conduit of close reading techniques by which readers could recognize many of the features in a text with which you are probably already familiar such as irony and ambiguity. Texts might appear complex and contradictory but practical criticism could produce coherent readings of them. The kind of readers which English studies produced would be able to resist popular culture and tastes.

The second seminal figure, F.R. Leavis, to whose work generations of teachers became indebted, worked under Richards as a tutorial assistant and, for five years, as a lecturer. He followed Richards' emphasis upon the importance of close reading and upon how an education in literary studies could help expose and resist the threats of popular and mass culture. However, his arguments were taken much further than Richards' and, although he was eventually to represent the mainstream of English studies, recognition by the literary academic establishment did not come immediately; initially he was regarded as a maverick figure.

For Leavis, reading works of literature required a special kind of sensibility and through literature one was admitted to a special level of thought, feeling and perception. He was opposed to industrialism and looked back to an older pre-industrial England with, he believed, an organic sense of community. Opposed to the mass media which he saw as a threat to English civilization, Leavis looked to these values as the determinants of 'great literature'. The golden age of English civilization was the seventeenth century, after which it was possible to chart a decline to the moral malaise of the twentieth century.

Reading Activity

Read and compare the two pieces of criticism set out below. Both were written in the last few years; one is in the traditional style of literary criticism whilst the other is more obviously informed by the kind of considerations which we have seen as characterizing the new approach to English.

Both critics are discussing a collection of short stories, *Portrait of the Artist as a Young Dog*, by Dylan Thomas.

Extract A

But in evoking the compassion of the artist this writing conveys Thomas's widening feeling for humanity; and what distinguishes the *Portrait* stories is the humorous, true-to-life yet swift depiction of character and the equally colourful and authentic portrait of their communities. This is illustrated in the affecting, picaresque yet touchingly sad comedy of 'Old Garbo', perhaps Thomas's most realistic pub story. Here compassion for the adult world of suffering, indignity and loss is presented, unusually, through the adult's rather than the child's vision of the world. It tells of Thomas's initiation as a young reporter into pub life, both the pleasures of beery, brief conviviality and the wounds it often hides. We are reminded that the poet grew up in the Swansea of the Depression, and that its poverty, unemployment and misery left its mark on his memory. (p.193)

(From: Ackerman, John (1991) *A Dylan Thomas Companion.* London: Macmillan.)

Extract B

Except in four stories – 'The Peaches', 'Patricia, Edith and Arnold', 'Old Garbo', and 'One Warm Saturday' – the domestic setting, associated with women and the social order of the bowler, is a confining place in *Portrait*. The male sphere – whether the sanctuary secured from Mrs. Evans in 'Where Tawe Flows', the polar night in 'Just Like Little Dogs', the pub in 'Old Garbo', or Rhossilli beach in 'Extraordinary Little Cough' and 'Who Do You Wish Was With Us?' – is the preferred setting in the collection. Male bonding – 'the great male moment' – is also the central positive emotional experience in Thomas's stories. Women characters are often marginalized by Thomas and generally associated with the 'choking houses' . . . fled by the day hikers in 'Who Do You Wish Was With Us?' Women dust the bowler just as they dust their sitting rooms. (p.129)

(From: Rowe, Margaret, 'Living "under the shadow of the bowler"' in Bold, Alan (Ed.) (1990) *Dylan Thomas. Craft or Sullen Art.* London: Vision Press)

Discussion

Although from a recent publication, the first extract contains little trace of the impact of literary theory on English studies and little awareness of the kind of debates which critics with a philosophical turn of mind have generated. It also betrays a number of the weaknesses of traditional criticism.

Firstly, Ackerman takes an approach which is not only author-centred, but biographically oriented. To be fair, *Portrait of the Artist as a Young Dog* is based on Thomas's life. But then that could be said of all writing. Ackerman does not sufficiently acknowledge how Thomas has *recreated* direct personal experience. He might have considered, for example, how Thomas has drawn upon memory, has used observation, has adapted stories from a plethora of different sources, has conflated different incidents and has exaggerated details.

Secondly, Ackerman uses a number of terms as if they are not problematic. For example, what does 'true-to-life' mean? What is an 'authentic' portrait? Ackerman uses such terms as if there is such a thing as objective reality; as if our perceptions were not influenced by selection, prejudice and preconception.

Thirdly, throughout the extract, there is an implicit conviction on Ackerman's part that the meanings he finds in the text are what Thomas intended. He does not sufficiently acknowledge that, as the reader, he is the creator of the meaning in the story. This omission determines the kind of criticism we are offered. Subjective responses – that one story is 'touchingly sad comedy' – are presented in lieu of critical argument. The extract appears to take for granted what constitutes a 'touchingly sad comedy' as opposed to a 'sad comedy' or 'comedy'. This is characteristic of the way in which traditional literary criticism has tended to use terms such as 'comedy' and 'realism' as if they were self-evident and easily transferable from one context to another. We are not told the criteria by which one story, more than any other, is judged 'Thomas's most realistic pub story'?

The title of the essay from which the second extract was taken, 'Living "under the shadow of the bowler"', refers to Thomas's middle-class upbringing, in suburban Swansea. Ostensibly it might have offered another author-centred, biographical reading. However, the extract demonstrates how modern critical writing tries to avoid some of the pitfalls of traditional literary criticism. For example, Rowe avoids speculating about the author's intention, focusing instead upon what we find in the text. You may have noticed that the extract claims that the male sphere provides the preferred location in Thomas's stories. Rowe does not say, for example, that Thomas preferred to use a male sphere for his locations. She also concentrates on how women are represented without drawing conclusions about Thomas's view of women. Moreover, she resists problematic terms like 'realistic' and 'authentic'.

You may have noted that it is a woman critic who has highlighted the different ways in which men and women are represented in *Portrait*. Rowe's criticism of Thomas's work could be said to have been influenced by her own gender considerations, even bias. Yet until a few decades ago, although the majority of students of literature were women, the majority of teachers were men. The agenda for literary studies was set by men and the majority of authors studied were men. Criticism by women academics has changed, and is still changing, the agenda of literary studies.

You may have realized, too, that Ackerman and Rowe approach Thomas's background differently. Ackerman suggests that Thomas was influenced by the unemployment and poverty of the Depression whilst Rowe argues that Thomas grew up 'under the influence of the bowler'. These critical positions are not contradictory but they demonstrate the care that has to be taken in speculating about what did or did not influence a writer and the dangers in using terms such as 'middle class' and 'working class' as if they are self-evident. In the 1930s, Swansea was a town with a strong working-class population but also extensive middle-class suburbs. However, the distinction between the middle and the working classes was not as pronounced at that time as in some English towns. Although Thomas had a middle-class upbringing, and his father taught English in the local grammar school, both his parents came from working-class backgrounds. His mother – unlike his father – was not educated out of the working class and many of her relatives from rural working-class Wales had most to do with the family.

In the next section, we will explore the implications of the kind of analysis employed by Rowe for our criticism of our own work as writers. In other words, how can we become more critically aware of the way we represent particular subjects. It is an approach which can make us more conscious of what we sometimes construct unconsciously.

Being Critical of Our Writing

The influence of Richards and Leavis on the development of English studies is evident in the emphasis which it has traditionally placed on educated, enlightened readers of particular kinds of works with particular features and characteristics which are designated 'Literature'. This stress on the creation of enlightened critics rather than on writers helps us to understand why 'writing' and 'criticism' became separate activities within English studies. Even as late as the 1980s when one of us taught a postgraduate writing course at a university college, it was located in the Department of Communications because the Department of English at that time did not see it as a legitimate activity within English studies!

Although modern critical theory emphasizes the role of the reader, many theorists are concerned with the way in which the structural features of texts help determine the response of the reader, whether by design, convention or unconscious motivation. In other words, they are concerned with the way in which a text 'positions' the reader in response to it.

In the course of this book, we will examine from the perspective of the writer many of the features and characteristics of texts which have been identified in modern critical theory. In doing so, we hope to show that there is more potential for 'writing' and modern critical theory to inform each other than is the case in traditional literary criticism. First, though, we have to acknowledge the need, which arises from modern critical practice, for writers to be aware of themselves as agents in the creation of texts which represent rather than mirror reality. Writing does not look out on the world as though it were a clear window for the reader to look through; it is like a piece of stained glass. Whatever we see, feel and re-create as writers is influenced by our own prejudices, our preconceptions and the selective nature of our perception. Readers similarly respond to our work according to their prejudices and preconceptions.

As writers we must examine critically our textual representations of the world. This means asking ourselves whether there is an obvious bias which we may not have intended? Would a particular bias or emphasis in our work cause some readers to respond negatively to it in ways we did not intend? Dylan Thomas may be a gifted writer, but you will have realized from Rowe's criticism of *Portrait of the Artist as a Young Dog* that women readers or alert male readers might respond negatively to its gender bias.

There are many television dramas which alienate or enrage viewers because of their representation of sensitive subjects. Often the writer is blamed whereas many people are involved in the creation of a television programme including not only the author of an original text on which it may have been based but the scriptwriter, the director, the producer, editors, directors of photography, location directors and so on. Many studies of television programmes have drawn attention to a bias in their content. Even programmes that we may think of as 'realistic' do not give us a view of society as we might observe it. Before we develop this discussion of the need to be critical of representation, we would like you to consider a summary of representation on television.

Critical Activity 5

How far would you agree with the following summary of conclusions from research into how television presents society?

Generally speaking, in television programmes which are produced here and imported from the USA there is an overemphasis upon occupations concerned with the enforcement of law and order compared with the range of employment in society itself. There is an overemphasis upon men and upon middle-class occupations which are generally pursued by men. Non-white people and women are shown in fewer types of occupations than white men. However, both women and non-white people are increasingly represented in high-prestige posts concerned with law enforcement and administration. Some researchers have observed that in American television programmes, black women are more likely to be portrayed in high-prestige jobs than white women. On television the commonest acts of violence are battery and murder, the least common in society. Although middle-class, white people commit violence, working-class people are more likely to do so. Elderly people are more likely to be the victims of violence than young people while young people are more likely to be the perpetrators of it. Non-white people are more likely to suffer violence than white people.

Discussion

In debating the above conclusions with yourself or with others, you probably found that there was not necessarily a correlation between society on the screen and society on the street. However, television does seem to represent the values of society, the privileged position occupied by white middle-class males and the liberal desire to see more opportunities for groups which have not enjoyed access to high-prestige positions in the past.

Realism

We tend to be very receptive to what we think of as realism; as readers and viewers we trust and enjoy 'realism'. According to Watt (1957), the term 'Réalisme' was first used as an aesthetic description in 1850 to distinguish Rembrandt's paintings from the neo-classical style. It was soon applied to literature, but unfortunately also became associated with portrayals of the seamy side of life. Hence some eighteenth-century English novels were regarded as 'realistic' because they included 'low life' in society. However, many of the novels from the eighteenth and nineteenth centuries which are regarded as realistic portray a wide variety of human experience. A novel is realistic not because of what it portrays but in the way it represents it.

Research Activity 1
In order to obtain a clearer idea of what is meant by realism, we would like you to look at some reproductions of Rembrandt's work – your local library should have illustrated books on art history – and to read a chapter or two in an eighteenth-century realistic novel such as Defoe's *Moll Flanders* or Fielding's *Tom Jones* or Richardson's *Pamela*. Make a brief list of some of the characteristics of realism as they occur to you. For example, what kind of details are emphasised? We will discuss some of these characteristics in a moment.

The majority of fiction sold to the general public, as opposed to that studied on college courses, is realistic. It is the preferred mode in our culture. Although, as we said above, realism constructs the world, it also 'naturalises' it so that we believe that we are watching the world as it is 'out there'. One of the characteristics of realist fiction is that it appears to presume its own transparency and does not draw the reader's attention to its own construction. In other words, we tend to think that realistic writing is the most natural and accessible mode of writing. In the latter part of this century, realism has been subjected to scrutiny. We are no longer seduced by its apparent artlessness. What many of us have understood as a realistic form of writing has been exposed as a particular set of writing strategies within a particular type of writing which achieved dominance over other forms in a given epoch of literary history.

Writing Activity I

Before reading further, and embarking on a discussion of some of the characteristics of realism, we would like you to follow up your research with a practical writing exercise. This will give you experience of working with some of the writing strategies that constitute the realistic mode.

Choose a well known fable or fairy story and rewrite it, providing full contemporary details in terms of historical, clock and date time. Use a contemporary setting (including place names you know of), specific characters with plausible names and precise details of all social activities, such as meal-times, places of work and leisure, means of transport and so on.

Discussion

The novel form is one of the most commonly used, and therefore familiar, kinds of writing we encounter in contemporary culture. We sometimes assume that there have always been novels. However, this is not the case. Can you think of a novel written in the fourteenth or even the fifteenth century? The novel developed a few hundred years later, during a particular historical era for a number of social, philosophical and historical reasons.

The *Concise Oxford Dictionary* defines a novel as a 'fictitious prose narrative of volume length portraying characters and actions representative of real life in continuous plot'. You will have noticed that the definition links the novel with the portrayal and representation of 'real life'. The latter is a term to which we will return in the next chapter. We can supplement such definitions of the novel by listing some of its traditional features.

You may like to pause for a moment and consult the list you compiled from the research activity.

Specific characteristics of the traditional novel form include many of the features and strategies with which you worked in the writing exercise:

1. Particularity of time;

2. Detailed descriptions of particular interior and exterior settings;

3. The use of personal names and place names which correspond to the names of people and places which exist or existed in the society at the time in which the novel was written;

4. The use of fashionable ideas and social activities, such as meal-times, work and leisure patterns, current in society at the time;

5. Personal identity perceived as an identity of consciousness through duration in time.

From this list you will have noticed that the two key characteristics of realistic writing are particularity of individual identities and places and the emphasis upon time. Proper names bring to mind one person only. They express particular identities and result from seeing people as individualized identities. Memory of past thoughts and actions is important here as the means by which individuals keep in touch with their own continuing identity.

The novelist E. M. Forster (1927) saw the novel as adding 'life by time' to the preceding type of writing which had been concerned with 'life by value' (p.51ff.). In the novel, time is an essential feature of the physical world; it is the shaping force of individual and collective experience. Pre-Renaissance writing tended to be influenced by the philosophy of Greece and Rome, particularly Plato's thesis that Forms or Ideas which were timeless and unchanging were the ultimate realities behind the temporal world. Everything that was worthwhile, if you like, was regarded as independent of the flux of time. (Watt 1957, p.22)

Research Activity 2

From your college or local library obtain a copy of William Langland's *Piers Plowman* and/or John Bunyan's *Pilgrim's Progress*. Langland's poem was written between 1362 and 1393. Part 1 of *Pilgrim's Progress* was written in 1678 and Part 2 in 1684. The full title of the work is *Pilgrim's Progress from This World to That Which Is To Come*. Read the first ten pages or so of one or both works and make brief notes on how they are different from the novels which you have read.

Realism and its 'Worldview'

If you are to write effectively in a realistic mode, you should understand the 'worldview' which underpins it. You are not just employing writing strategies, you are giving expression to a particular way of looking at things. If you appreciate this, you will develop a more incisive critical understanding of your own work and be in a better position to exploit and/or subvert some of the strategies of realism.

From your reading of *Piers Plowman* and/or *Pilgrim's Progress*, you probably gleaned what Forster meant when he wrote of 'life by value' as opposed to 'life by time'. Both Langland's and Bunyan's narratives function as allegories; an allegory is a narrative in which the characters, events and locations symbolize other things, often abstractions. The journeys undertaken by the poet in *Piers Plowman* and Christian in *Pilgrim's Progress* are allegories for the journey through life, its trials and tribulations. Thus, in Bunyan's narrative, the central figure, Christian, is advised by Evangelist to undertake a journey from his home town, the City of Destruction, to the Celestial City beyond the Wicket-gate. On his travels, Christian wanders through the Slough of Despond, rests at House Beautiful, is tried and tested at the Vanity Fair, negotiates the Delectable Mountains, is captured by Giant Despair and has to cross the River of Death. The narrative is littered with archetypal characters who perform their nominal functions, so Christian is rescued by Help, advised by Mr Worldly-Wiseman, avoids Hypocrisy, parts company with Timorous and Mistrust while resting with the maidens Discretion, Prudence, Piety and Charity.

The differences between these works and many of the novels we read help us to appreciate the nature of realism. The development of the realist novel was the result of a major intellectual change, pivoted around a shift from the generalized to the particular in terms of time, location and character. The generalized representations in the work of Langland and Bunyan are premised on the assumption that the experience of being human is essentially the same across different centuries and cultures. In other words, that the experience of being human, the activities in which people engage and the values in which people are interested are always the same for everyone and remain constant through all historical periods.

A recurring concern in the classical literature of Greece and Rome is the relationship between men and cosmological beings. In the Middle Ages, literature concerns itself with a world of ideals rooted in cosmologies which suggested that the human world was divinely ordained, ordered and controlled. But in post-Renaissance English literature we find ideas rooted in scientific and rational notions of comprehending the world, with 'real' human experiences placed at the centre of this understanding. Of course, the novel arose from a complex fusion of social and economic factors including developments in printing, the emergence of the middle classes, demographic shifts into urban living and the rise of a reading public. However, the impact of the seventeenth-century shift in ideas about the world and humanity's place in it is evidenced in the literary form of the novel in two principal ways.

Firstly, the shift from theologically-based explanations of the world towards scientifically-based interpretations is mirrored in the novel's preoccupation with the immediacy of human life. Secondly, the influence of scientific methods such as empiricism reinforced the idea of a 'real' world which existed outside human experience and perception.

Empiricism is a way of establishing the truth of things by acting on observation and experiment rather than on theory. Empirical observation as a method of scientific enquiry entails closely detailing the frequency at which something can be seen to happen and collecting the data based on such repeated observations. Today we tend to regard the notion of empirical observation with some scepticism realizing that our observations are at best partial, often unreliable and influenced by prejudice and preconception. We are reluctant to entertain the notion of 'capturing' in words or visual images a world that is independent of our perceptions. However, the conviction that the so-called 'real' world could be apprehended, mapped and understood proved crucial to the development of 'realistic' fiction. The importance of witnessing and recording events – of empirical observation – is evidenced in the novel's apparent capacity to document the detailed particularity of existence.

Writing Activity 2

This exercise is designed to help you acquire more insight into the philosophical assumptions underpinning realism. Record (if possible) and make notes on the content of an episode from a contemporary soap opera on television or radio. Focus on a climactic event, noting details of the characters and the setting involved. Adapt the episode by removing all the particularized details (including names, locations and time) and rewrite it as a self-contained short story, using stock or type names such as Vice, Sloth, Virtue, Hope, and so on. Try to retain the plausibility of the narrative.

Research Activity 3

The nineteenth-century American writer, Nathaniel Hawthorne, adapted the allegorical, pre-novel form in writing about the seventeenth-century origins of white American society. Obtaining copies of his work from your college or local library, read some of his short stories. We particularly recommend 'Young Goodman Brown', 'The Minister's Black Veil', 'The Celestial Railroad' or 'The Maypole of Merry Mount'. How particular is his work? Why do you think he chooses to adapt allegory in this way? How successful is this form in pursuing the themes with which Hawthorne appears to be concerned, such as the repressive nature of Puritan society in America in the seventeenth century; the nature of evil; hypocrisy; guilt; Americans' fear of the wilderness beyond the stockade communities in which they lived; attitudes towards women.

From the writing exercise you undertook and from your reading of Hawthorne's short stories it should be clear that there are a number of effective ways for writers to scrutinize a particular culture or society in a particular historical time without recourse to the traditional realist novel. In fact, since its beginnings, the novel has undergone numerous adaptations and changes at the hands of various authors and as a result of culturally and historically-specific literary trends. Nevertheless, a major legacy of the classic realist text is the assumption that a clear transmission of life into art is possible. From your writing and research activities we hope that you have realized the problematic nature of this assumption. Modern critical theory acknowledges that the Cartesian-inspired notion of the world which we discussed above has undergone extensive revision. It is rooted in some of the ideas which have made classic realism problematic, casting doubt not only on the possibility that the world can be clearly apprehended but on the capacity of language to do so.

In literature, as Durrant and Fabb (1990. p.28) remind us, there are three modes of representing society analytically with which, as a student of literature, you will soon become familiar:

1. **Socialist realism:** You will probably already have read examples of 'socialist realist' novels from the nineteenth and twentieth centuries. Writers of such works normally have a commitment to social change and, in depicting society, are concerned to bring out the underlying social forces within it. The term was developed by George Lukacs with reference to fiction by Tolstoy and Balzac.

2. **Non-realistic texts:** Those of you who have watched one of Dennis Potter's television plays will be familiar with this type of text. Various devices are deployed to expose the artificial nature of society. Whereas the socialist realist novel 'naturalizes' what it portrays so that we accept and trust what we are reading, the non-realistic text alienates us so that we are disturbed, puzzled, confused and possibly very critical of what we are reading or seeing. As such, we are presented with fresh insights into society, how it is structured, in whose interests it is organized and the nature of the social forces determining it.

3. **Experimental texts:** These texts were generally written after the First World War which brought into question much of what had previously been taken for granted. We call many of these assumptions the 'Grand Narratives' such as patriotism, belief in God, the conviction that society develops for the better, a faith in history as the linear progress of humanity, the nature of consciousness, and trust in science and industrialism as providers of long term benefits to society. Whereas the non-realist text uses techniques to alienate the reader, experimental texts appear to subvert normal expectations about the relationship between author, text and reader involved in a process of communication. This is not done for its own sake, but to encourage readers to discard their conventional assumptions about patterns of social organization and behaviour and become more original and insightful. Works by Virginia Woolf, T.S. Eliot, Ezra Pound and James Joyce would fall into this category.

Critical Activity 6

Read the following extract from James Joyce's *Ulysses* and, either individually or as a member of a group, consider how the reader may be taken by surprise, disturbed or even confused by it.

Mr Leopold Bloom ate with relish the inner organs of beasts and fowls. He liked thick giblet soup, nutty gizzards, a stuffed roast heart, liver slices fried with crustcrumbs, fried hencod's roes. Most of all he liked grilled mutton kidneys which gave to his palate a fine tang of faintly scented urine.

Kidneys were in his mind as he moved about the kitchen softly, righting her breakfast things on the humpy tray. Gelid lights and air were in the kitchen but out of doors gentle summer morning everywhere: Made him feel a bit peckish.

The coals were reddening.

Another slice of bread and butter: three, four: right. She didn't like her plate full. Right. He turned from the tray, lifted the kettle off the hob and set it sideways on the fire. It sat there, dull and squat, its spout stuck out. Cup of tea soon. Good. Mouth dry. The cat walked stiffly round a leg of the table with tail on high.

– Mkgnao!

– O, there you are, Mr. Bloom said, turning from the fire.

The cat mewed in answer and stalked again stiffly round a leg of the table, mewing. Just how she stalks over my writing table. Prr. Scratch my head. Prr. Mr Bloom watched curiously, kindly, the little black form. Clean to see: the gloss of her sleek hide, the white button under the butt of her tail, the green flashing eyes. He bent down to her, his hands on his knees.

– Milk for the pussens, he said.

– Mrkgnao! the cat cried.

They call them stupid. They understand what we say better than we understand them. She understands all she wants to. Vindictive too. Wonder what I look like to her. Height of a tower? No, she can jump me. (p.57)

Discussion

You probably included the emphasis on Mr Bloom's food as the cooked flesh or organs of birds and animals. There is a great deal of stress on the inner organs which might repel many readers. The effect of eating kidneys on Mr Bloom's palate probably did not go unnoticed! The way in which the narrative shifts between a third person narrator and Mr. Bloom's own thoughts is obviously a key feature. The kitchen is realized through Bloom's own fragmented sense impressions of it. His prejudices are imposed on the description of the objects such as the kettle. You probably observed how the passage is structured around Bloom's activities, his digressions, his spontaneous thoughts and his sense impressions without a traditional sense of organization and direction.

Writing Activity 3

Inventing what additional details you consider necessary for the exercise, rewrite the following account of a Christmas dinner from Dickens' *Great Expectations* using some of the techniques and devices which you noted in the passage above. The story is told by an adult looking back on his upbringing by his sister and her husband Joe, a blacksmith.

We dined on these occasions in the kitchen, and adjourned, for the nuts and oranges and apples, to the parlour; which was a change very like Joe's change from his working clothes to his Sunday dress. My sister was uncommonly lively on the present occasion, and indeed was generally more gracious in the society of Mrs Hubble than other company. I remember Mrs Hubble as a little curly sharp-edged person in sky-blue, who held a conventionally juvenile position, because she had married Mr Hubble – I don't know at what remote period – when she was much younger than he. I remember Mr Hubble as a tough high-shouldered stooping old man, of sawdust fragrance, with his legs extraordinarily wide apart: so that in my short days I always saw some miles of open country between them when I met him coming up the lane.

Among this good company I should have felt myself, even if I hadn't robbed the pantry, [of which the others at the table are unaware] in a false position. Not because I was squeezed in at an acute angle of the table-cloth, with the table in my chest, and the Pumblechookian [Mr Pumblechook is another guest at the dinner] elbow in my eye, nor because I was not allowed to speak (I didn't want to speak), nor because I was regaled with the scaly tips of the drumsticks of the fowls, and with those obscure corners of pork of which the pig, when living, had the least reason to be vain.... They seemed to think the opportunity lost, if they failed to point the conversation at me every now and then, and stick the point into me...

Joe's station and influence were something feebler (if possible) when there was company, than when there was none. But he always aided and comforted me when he could, in some way of his own, and he always did so at dinner-time by giving me gravy, if there were any. There being plenty of gravy to-day, Joe spooned into my plate, at this point, about half a pint. (Chapter 4)

The above exercise required you to rewrite in a more experimental fashion a piece of work which was in the traditional realist mode. In doing so, you should have been able to present fresh ways of looking at the Christmas dinner.

Critical Activity 7

Compare your version of the Christmas dinner from *Great Expectations* with the original. Make a list of the new details and insights in your piece of work. In employing Joyce's techniques, how far do you think you achieved a reinterpretation of the episode?

Reinterpreting what people tend to take for granted is an important aspect of many writers' work, indeed of art in general, which has its origins as an explanation of the value of art in Russian Formalism. Russian Formalism, of which there were two principal groups, flourished between 1914 and 1925. The Moscow Linguistic Circle, in which the key figure was Roman Jakobson, to whom we will return in the next chapter, was established in 1915. The St. Petersburg Society for the Study of Poetic Language, in which the key figure was Victor Shklovsky, was established in 1916. According to the Russian Formalists the defining quality of literature and art was that they had the power to 'defamiliarize'. Shklovsky, as a member of a group called 'The Futurists', shared the belief that culture had congealed to the point of unconsciousness and that it was the function of art to make the habitual once more unfamiliar. The importance of literature lay in its potential to disturb, but the great works of art, too, had to be 'defamiliarized' so that they could reclaim this capacity.

The crux of the Formalists' manifesto is that literature is art because it breaks the routine, the stale and the clichéd. In an important essay, 'Art as Technique' (1917), Shklovsky identified five techniques by which literature 'defamiliarizes' the use of language:

1. The use of sound through, for example, rhythm, rhyme and structure;

2. The use of rhetorical figures, for example, images and metaphors;

3. The use of connotation (the symbolic, figurative, metaphorical, or allusive meanings of words) rather than denotation (the literal use of words);

4. An interest in how a story is told and not just in its content;

5. The use of literary conventions.

Some of these concepts, such as 'connotation' and 'denotation', and the origins of European criticism we will return to later. For our present purposes, it is the concept of 'defamiliarization' as a defining characteristic of literature that is important. There are many things that we look at in our daily lives but do not really see. Many writers try to make us re-examine patterns of social behaviour and the next writing exercise provides you with an opportunity to 'defamiliarize' stereotypical characters and stock situations.

Writing Activity 4

Either individually or with others in a group, watch a short extract (of say 15 minutes) from a television drama, a soap opera or a film with the sound turned down.

Write a story-line (not the full dialogue) for the scene(s) you have watched. You should include in your story-line: who the characters are, the purpose and nature of the exchanges between them and the significance of the locations. Your story-line should encourage people to rethink their conventional assumptions about social organization and behaviour.

After you have completed the preparatory activity below and viewed the programme, but before embarking on your own work, brainstorm the opportunities for different interpretations of what you have seen, or thought you have seen.

How many different interpretations could be imposed on the location and on the interaction between characters?

Preparatory Activity

Before watching your chosen extract, try to brainstorm the kinds of things you will need to notice in order to write your story-line.

Discussion

Your list of what to observe may have included the following:

- the number of characters
- the gender, race, class, age and health of the characters
- the location(s)
- the movement between locations
- the amount of interaction which occurs among the characters
- the nature of the interaction
- the nature of the body language
- the amount of dialogue in the scene(s)
- the way in which the dialogue is delivered (Do the characters engage in long or short conversations? Are there clues from their facial expressions or from their body language as to the nature of the exchanges?)
- the variety of camera angles.

Further Reading

Abbs, P. (1989) *A is for Aesthetic: Essays on Creative and Aesthetic Education*. London: The Falmer Press. Chapters 1,3 and 4.

Abbs argues for the place of the arts and creativity in any coherent curriculum. The particular chapters recommended are accessible to students and provide further reading on the subject of creativity, the nature of English as an arts discipline and the aesthetic field of English.

Belsey, C. (1980) *Critical Practice*. London: Methuen. Chapter 1.

An accessible introduction to modern critical theory and its criticisms of orthodox literary practice. Belsey focuses on how modern theory rejects notions of the autonomy of the reader, the authority of the author and of unitary meaning within texts.

Eagleton, T. (1983) *Literary Theory: An Introduction*. Oxford: Basil Blackwell. Chapters 1 and 2.

Peim, N. (1993) *Critical Theory and the English Teacher: Transforming the Subject*. London: Routledge. Chapters 1–3.

This book provides an introduction to modern critical theory for the teacher of English. Students will not find it very accessible.

Watt, I. (1957: reprinted 1970) *The Rise of the Novel*. Harmondsworth: Penguin. Chapters 1 and 2.

An accessible account of the social, economic and philosophical factors which determined the nature of the novel as a literary form. Particularly good on the reading public.

Webster, R. (1990) *Studying Literary Theory: An Introduction.* London: Routledge. Chapters 1 and 2.

Webster's book provides an accessible and highly readable introduction to the main issues in modern critical and literary theory.

Chapter Two
Language and Meaning

In this chapter you will find sections on:

1. The origins of modern critical theory

2. The differences between English and European criticism

3. The nature of language

4. Language and culture

5. The concept of signs

6. How language works: syntagms and paradigms

7. The importance of detail

8. Deconstruction

9. Multiple meanings

10. Polyglossia.

Activities

You will be asked to undertake the following activities:

1. Critical exercises involving:
   - the comparison of two extracts of comic writing
   - the use of language in *Great Expectations, Jane Eyre* and *Sons and Lovers*
   - a brainstorming activity on binary opposites
   - the use of language in a poem, 'Asgwrn Cefn Y Beic'.

2. Two reading activities in which you are asked to consider the use of language in a poem, 'Swinging', and in an extract from a novel, *The Unbelonging*.

3. A preparatory writing activity and six major writing activities. You are asked to:

- write an account of a character, or characters, based on observation in a public place;

- undertake a piece of writing based on a visual illustration;

- develop an account of an event based on a basic narrative triad;

- in a form of your choice, write an account of an embarrassing or humiliating experience;

- write a fictitious consultation between a doctor and a patient to fulfil specific objectives;

- write an account of an emotional event making use of the range of meanings in a selected word.

4. Three research activities, one involving familiarizing yourself with aspects of a novel by David Lodge, another going into a public place to observe people, and a preparatory research activity for chapter 3.

Preparatory Writing Activity

Choose an everyday event such as making a cup of tea, filling a tyre with air, having a shower, or making a telephone call. Imagine that you have to explain to an alien, who paradoxically understands English, how to complete the task you have selected.

First relate the task, carefully employing precise, rational language. Then redraft your description employing figurative and vivid language.

In the previous chapter, we suggested that the philosophical notions of reality and how it could be comprehended which emerged in post-Renaissance Europe helped determine the nature of the novel as a literary form and its particular style of English usage. During this period English usage itself was standardized and rationalized, a process which led to metaphorical and figurative language becoming subordinate to a more literal usage. As Barber (1993) observes:

> The rise of a scientific writing in English helped to establish a simple referential style of prose as the central kind in Modern English. Other kinds of prose continued to exist...but a rhetorical or poetical style ceased to be the norm and what we may call the *plain style* became central, the background against which other kinds of prose were read [this became a style] found in all kinds of expository writing – history, philosophy, literary criticism, and so on. (pp.214–15)

We also argued that a major legacy of the classic realist text is the assumption that there can be a clear transmission of life experience into text. As both Watt (1957) and Lodge (1990) have maintained, the verisimilitude – that is, the semblance of actuality – of the classic realist text is based on an assumed correspondence between the world inside the text and the world immediately outside the text. In addition, verisimilitude is achieved by the correspondence between the language usage in everyday life and the language usage within the text. One example of this is the mimicry within the novel of non-fictional literary practices, a feature which Lodge (1990) describes as the novel's 'pseudo-documentary specificity' (p.68). Here Lodge is referring to the inclusion within a novel of forms of writing from the lived, everyday world which novelists appropriate and add to the body of their narratives: letters, journals, shopping lists, lyrics, newspaper articles, advertising hoardings and so on. Ironically, these modes of writing are not normally regarded as 'literary' forms, but when they are reproduced within a novel they assume both a literary status and reinforce the novel's claim to 'realism'. Lodge's use of the word 'pseudo' implies that their deployment in the text may be more self-conscious and deliberate than we might have thought. It suggests that the world which these forms of writing evoke is a construction by the author masquerading as a reflection of what lies outside the text.

Research Activity 1
From your college or local library, try to obtain a copy of Lodge's novel *Nice Work* (1988). Read a few of the chapters and consider the different ways in which he incorporates into it the kind of non-fictional writing we have been discussing. For example, on page 17, basic facts about one of the major characters is given in the form of a curriculum vitae.

Origins of the New Critical Approaches

An important plank in many of the new critical approaches to literary texts is the relationship between language, meaning and culture. Their concern with how meaning is created makes them relevant not only to the reader of literature but to the writer.

In the previous chapter, we suggested that traditional criticism could be traced back to the work of Matthew Arnold in the nineteenth century and, particularly, to the writings of I.A. Richards and F.R. Leavis in the twentieth century. The origins of the new critical approaches would take a book in itself to describe fully. Although French and American theorists have made substantial contributions from the mid 1940s onwards to modern critical thinking, the origins lie in northern, eastern and central Europe with the Geneva school of linguistics in Switzerland, and the Russian Formalists from Moscow and Leningrad in the 1920s. Members of the Moscow Linguistic Circle, to whom we referred in our discussion of 'defamiliarization' in the previous chapter, worked under difficult political conditions created by the extremes of censorship in Tsarist Russia prior to the Bolshevik Revolution. Not surprisingly, their work was hasty and provisional, but their ideas were provocative and intellectually challenging, ultimately influencing generations of thinkers.

Before reading further, we would like you to turn to the biographical notes on Jakobson, the founding member of the Moscow Linguistic Circle (p.176).

Many of the seminal ideas of these linguists are usually grouped generically under the label of 'structuralism'. Structuralism is normally taken to refer to approaches which study literary texts as though they had the same structures as language. Put bluntly, a literary text, like a sentence, consist of 'units' which are arranged, like the parts of a sentence, according to pre-existing rules. As you would have gleaned from the biographical note on Jakobson, structuralism, in the early part of the twentieth century, was more concerned with literary form than literary content, with what makes meaning rather than with meaning itself. Whereas traditional Anglo-American literary criticism has tended to be concerned with questions of moral value and with establishing a canon of great writers, the structuralists were concerned with 'literariness', the special kind of language usage which defines literature. As we suggested in our earlier discussion of 'defamiliarization', although members of the Moscow Linguistic Circle believed that the function of art was to see the habitual or the commonplace in fresh ways, they also concerned themselves with the techniques by which literature 'defamiliarized' conventional language usage. At this point, try to remember the techniques listed in the previous chapter by which literature, according to Shklovsky in his essay 'Art as Technique', defamiliarizes the use of language.

The techniques which we asked you to recall are employed frequently by most writers: the use of sound structures, such as rhyme and rhythm; metaphor and imagery; the symbolic, figurative, metaphoric or allusive meanings of words rather than plain speaking; an interest in how a story is told; and the use of literary conventions to express ideas and observations differently from the way in which they are expressed outside literature.

In the 1920s, then, a different approach to literature was developing in Europe from that prevalent in Britain. As we said in the previous chapter, and as you may have discovered from your own research, the corner-stones of traditional criticism were laid with I.A. Richards *Principles of Literary Criticism* (1924) and *Practical Criticism* (1929). About the same time a linguistically-based approach concerned with identifying the units in literary works and how they are combined to make meanings was gathering momentum through essays and books with which you will become increasingly familiar in your literary studies: Schklovsky, 'Art as Technique' (1917); Jakobson, *The New Russian Poetry* (1921); Eichenbaum, 'The Theory of the Formal Method' (1926); Propp, *Morphology of the Folktale* (1928) and Tynjaov, 'On Literary Evolution' (1929).

Among the critical thinkers indebted to structuralism there is much debate and disagreement. In particular, those who are now recognised as poststructuralists – Roland Barthes, Jacques Derrida, Michel Foucault, Fredric Jameson Julia Kristeva and Edward Said – have taken issue with the earlier structuralists. One of the reasons for their dissent is what they regard as the early structuralists' faith in the stability of language, linguistic codes and structures. That is to say that the meanings associated with particular words or signs do not change over time. For poststructuralists, language is not only changeable, but the link between words and meanings often contentious. You may like to consider here how the words 'gay' and 'straight' have acquired new meanings associated with sexual orientation and try to think of other words for a moment which, in acquiring new meanings, have become subjects of contention. Poststructuralists have extended complex versions of the structuralist approach into new political and philosophical territories.

The Nature of Language

The writer and teacher Peter Abbs, to whom we referred in the previous chapter, has complained that the study of literature in schools and colleges, under the influence of traditional critical approaches, has tended to focus on the discussion of literature's messages. Generally speaking, not enough time has been devoted, he argues, to language, traditions and conventions with reference to the creative possibilities of writing.

Many writers, even renowned authors, feel frustrated at the inadequacy of language to express fully their ideas and experiences. But it is very difficult to conceive of us being able to think without language. Although it may be possible to perceive something without recourse to language, as many mystics for example claim, it cannot be articulated without language even if we interpret the word 'language' broadly to include the language of dance, of painting, of sculpture and so forth.

As we have already observed, there is a tendency to think of meaning as deriving from the extent to which a text reflects a world outside itself. Occasionally, too, we still come across language being regarded as the instrument of thought, as if a thought could exist in a naked state waiting to be clothed in language. But language does not simply mirror a world outside itself nor simply clothe our ideas, it shapes and structures them. This is a subject which we need to explore in more detail. In a moment, in the light of the suggestion that language determines meaning, we would like you to consider how 'comic' writing from different centuries parodies the notion of realism. First, however, we would like you to undertake a piece of descriptive writing yourself.

Research Activity 2
Before reading further we would like you to have experience of developing a piece of writing based on earlier observation.

Go out into a public place, such as a pub, a park or a bus station, and observe one person or some people together. Note down your observations about the way they are dressed, the way they carry themselves, the way in which they interact with others, how they speak and any personal idiosyncrasies they may have.

Writing Activity I
On your return, write up your account in the form of a description. You may write in prose or try to write a poem. Make your account as vivid and interesting as possible. If you are able, try to include a comic element.

Discussion

As you tried to develop your description, you may have found that you left your original model(s) behind, exaggerating certain aspects and suppressing others. In other words, you may have found yourself building each time upon what had been written previously and becoming more inventive the more you wrote. With your experience of writing this piece in mind, we would like you to study two examples of comic description.

Critical Activity I

Consider the following brief examples of comic writing. The first is a description of Mrs Gargery, Pip's sister, from *Great Expectations* and the second is a description of a Chinese family in London from *Sour Sweet,* a novel by Timothy Mo published in 1982. What techniques do the writers employ to make their writing vivid and coherent?

Extract A

We walked to town, my sister leading the way in a very large beaver bonnet, and carrying a basket like the Great Seal of England in plaited straw, a pair of pattens, a spare shawl, and an umbrella, though it was a fine bright day. I am not quite clear whether these articles were carried penitentially or ostentatiously; but, I rather think they were displayed as articles of property – much as Cleopatra or any other sovereign lady on the Rampage might exhibit her wealth in a pageant or procession. (chapter 13)

Extract B

And indeed there was an impression of invincible eccentricity about the little group now re-forming on the pavement for the next stage of its journey. Chen appeared unremarkable enough in his black trousers and brown padded jacket; although his trilby hat was a bit odd as accessory to these. The girls, however, having no uniform to provide them with an approximate sartorial guideline, nor a job to get them out of the house, had become rather disorganized about their clothing. One relaxation of convention had led to another. Both were wearing thin tunic suits in a tiny floral pattern…Over these summery suits each was wearing a baggy cardigan of Chen's. Lily's was grey with walnut leather patterns, Mui's olive-green in a chunky knit with transparent plastic toggles. Mui almost filled her woollen but, having shorter arms than her brother-in-law, had been forced to roll the sleeves back several times. Lily, on the other hand, found Chen's sleeves too short, uncomfortably so, even with the cuffs rolled down, so that the top part of the garment acted as a strait-jacket, riding up under the arms and exposing her wrists and a substantial length of her shapely forearm, while around her slender waist the cardigan's elasticated bottom had concertinaed in a thick roll rather like the domed edge of a toadstool…Mui had commandeered a pair of Chen's size 7 shoes, laceless unhappily, in which her own size 3 feet floundered like landed fish. (chapter 10)

Discussion

Although there is some attempt to paint a plausible picture, both passages seem to derive their energy from the juxtaposition of increasingly discordant details. Neither relies exclusively on referring to what is outside itself; both have an intrinsic life of their own, as it were. In both passages, we feel the writer's excitement and sense of fun in combining outrageous features. Both authors use imagery to exaggerate their sense of the absurd. Dickens employs 'the Great Seal of England' and utilizes the incongruous image of Cleopatra, while Mo employs images of a strait-jacket, the domed edge of a toadstool and landed fish. Both writers are presenting a comic interpretation of life through exaggerating the absurdity of social behaviour but for different purposes. Dickens' passage exposes snobbery, pretence and greed; Mo's passage is concerned with the incongruity of different cultural patterns of behaviour and the difficulty of transposing what is acceptable in one culture to another.

The next writing activity is designed to provide you with a basis for exploring how cultural assumptions determine our writing.

Writing Activity 2

Find an illustration to work from: use a picture postcard; a photograph from a book, a magazine or a travel brochure; an advertisement illustration or a reproduction of a painting. Answer the following questions about your response to your selected illustration:

- What was the first detail that caught your eye?
- Where was your eye drawn to next? And in what direction?
- Where was the dominant shade or colour?
- What time of day or night was depicted?
- What mood, atmosphere or feeling was evoked?
- Were you reminded of something, someone or some other place?

Look away from the picture and then look back.

- What do you see now?
- Imagine a person who loves you has brought you this picture. What are they trying to tell you?
- Imagine the picture has been destroyed. What will remain in your mind?

Using your responses to this exercise, write a poem. You may wish to write about your relationship to the person whom you imagined bringing you the picture. Or your responses might suggest a different theme.

Discussion (and follow-up activities)

When you have finished, spend some time assessing how you have made use of images from the illustration. What associations sprang immediately to mind in the first stage of the exercise? What additional associations are evident in the way you have developed the details you chose to focus upon? Do you think most people would have responded to the picture in the way you have? If you think they would, can you explain why? Compare your responses, if you can, to those of other students working on the same exercise. In what ways are their responses different from your own?

Language and Culture

What we see is structured by conscious and unconscious influences, the limits of perception, our own prejudices and preconceptions and our language. As we said earlier, when we look at the world we perceive it as though we were looking through a stained glass window, colouring everything on the other side. One of the 'colours' in that window, perhaps the most important, is language. What we think of as ourselves, as our own thoughts and our own emotions are structured by the language we use. One of America's most influential linguists of the first half of the nineteenth century, Edward Sapir, whose work formed the basis of 'structural linguistics', concluded that there is no such thing as an objective, unchanging 'real world':

> Human beings do not live in the objective world alone, nor alone in the world of social activity as ordinarily understood, but are very much at the mercy of the particular language which has become the medium of expression for their society. It is quite an illusion to imagine that one adjusts to reality essentially without the use of language and that language is merely an incidental means of solving specific problems of communication or reflection. The fact of the matter is that the 'real world' is to a large extent built up on the language habits of the group. No two languages are ever sufficiently similar to be considered as representing the same social reality. The worlds in which different societies live are distinct worlds ... We see and hear and otherwise experience very largely as we do because the language habits of our community predispose certain choices of interpretation. (1949, p.162)

Sapir makes three very important points here. Firstly, that as writers, even allowing for our ability to 'defamiliarize' habitual language usage, we are all at the mercy of the particular language system in which we think and work. Secondly, that the language system in which we work predisposes us to see the world in a particular way. Thirdly, that no two languages structure the world in the same way. These points may be illustrated by an example from a writer working in English in Africa.

The Nigerian novelist, Chinua Achebe, in *Things Fall Apart* describes how in Nigeria the 'polite name' for leprosy was 'the white skin'. In European literature, white tends to be associated with purity and innocence as in the wedding dress and veil. Although it is associated with death – as in references to the death shroud, which was traditionally white, and to ghosts – white is not normally associated with disease and decay. A European reader, then, may be confused by the colour white as it is used in Nigerian writing. A Nigerian reader, on the other hand, may find problematic the association between the colour black and disease and decay – for example, in *Great Expectations*.

The description of Miss Havisham in *Great Expectations* where the traditional bridal colour is associated with decay and disease rather than purity may also confound readers versed in English traditions. The effect is to stress the consequences of what she has undergone. She was jilted at the altar many years earlier and has lived as a recluse in her wedding dress alongside the crumbling wedding cake ever since.

Critical Activity 2

Consider the way in which the colour 'white' is used in this short extract about Miss Havisham. If you are able to obtain a copy of *Great Expectations* read the full account of her in chapter 8.

> She was dressed in rich materials – satins, and lace, and silks – all of white. Her shoes were white. And she had a long white veil dependent from her hair, and she had bridal flowers in her hair, but her hair was white...I saw that everything within my view which ought to be white, had been white long ago, and had lost its lustre, and was faded and yellow.

Discussion

In order to understand fully the description of Miss Havisham, it is important to realize that white as a signifier of innocence is a bridal colour. But, of course, Dickens picks up other associations of the colour white, connecting it with age – Miss Havisham's hair is white – and, by implication here but explicitly in the chapter as a whole, with death. Indeed, the association of the colour 'white' with decay in European culture is so unusual that Dickens has to shift the emphasis to faded white and yellow.

Those of you who are studying or have studied language, communication studies or media studies will be only too aware that language is an arbitrary system. In Welsh the word for white is 'gwyn'; in French it is 'blanc (blanche)'; in Spanish it is 'blanco'. There is no reason why any of these words *should* mean what they do. The association between the word and the thing is one that has to be learned just as the associations have to be acquired. This was first pointed out by the Swiss linguist Ferdinand de Saussure, who was associated with the Geneva school of linguistics to which we made reference above.

If you are studying or have studied communications or media studies, you may already be familiar with the name Saussure. However, before reading further we suggest you read the short biographical note on Saussure (p.178–79).

Saussure's Concept of Signs

Saussure's suggestion that language is an arbitrary system which has to be learned in order for communication to take place has important implications for writers and would-be writers. Using a language involves participating in the larger conventions and the particular associations constructed by them. Saussure saw all language as consisting of 'signs' to which a concept or an image is attached. Thus we learn to associate the sound w-h-i-t-e with a particular colour. But we also learn that this sound is different from the sounds y-e-l-l-o-w and r-e-d, for example, which we have learned to associate with other colours. Thus learning a language involves learning the concepts and meanings attached to particular signs and the differences between them.

In order to summarize the arbitrariness of language, Saussure labelled the verbal or visual signs (or codes) 'signifiers' and the concepts or meanings which we learn to attach to them, as what is 'signified'. These are terms which may already be familiar to you if you have studied the mass media. Books which analyse advertisements, for example, frequently talk in terms of the 'signifier' and what is 'signified'.

No matter how preoccupied a writer or critic may be with the transparency or lack of transparency in their observation, all writers have to be aware, if they care about the quality of their work and the effectiveness of their communication, that the language in which they work is a public language. We have only to try to learn a foreign language to realize how far language and consciousness are interwoven. In English, for example, we might say 'He is hungry'. But in Welsh we might say 'There is need for food on him' ('Y mae eisiau bwyd arno ef'). In each language, the state of hunger is perceived slightly differently from the other. In Welsh, there is a greater sense of how the need for food can afflict us!

Connotations of Signs

All words carry what the French theorist, Roland Barthes, called 'connotation': 'a feature that has the power to relate to previous, subsequent or exterior terms, to other places in the text (or in another text)' (Barthes, 1970, p.14). In the previous chapter, we distinguished connotation (the symbolic figurative, metaphorical and allusive meanings of language) from denotation (the literal or referential use of language, the plain speech referred to in the Barber quotation above – see p.38). At this point, we need to explore some of the implications of this distinction for writers.

Words carry meanings or connotations which are not of any one individual author's making and go beyond any simple sense of meaning attached to a 'signifier'. Thus we learn that the sound w-h-i-t-e is a sign by which a particular colour is signified. But we also realized above that the sign 'white' suggests more than a particular colour and that these connotations may not be carried by the sign for that particular colour in another language and culture. Often the meanings carried by a particular word or combination of words shift according to the context. A fork can mean literally a piece of cutlery, or a division in a road or a false (in the sense of deceitful) tongue.

Barthes is an important theorist and before reading further you may like to read the short biographical account of him (pp.169–70).

We are now suggesting that signs carry different levels of meaning or, in other words, that different levels of meaning are signified by them. Connotation expands meaning beyond the limits of an individual word. Only a sloppy writer would work without reference to this power in language. For example, a simple narrative might be that someone was hit by a car. The sign 'car' (or automobile) denotes a vehicle of a particular type, different from, say, a petrol tanker or a van or truck. Suppose that, instead of simply writing 'a car', we specified a make, maybe a Ford. Fords are common enough vehicles and the detail adds little more than a piece of background information. A lot more is added, though, if we specify that the car was a Rolls-Royce because that would suggest or 'connote' wealth and privilege. If the person who was hit was a child, there are further connotations of innocence. If the child was black and the setting was South Africa in 1980, then the whole incident becomes symbolic of apartheid and racial hatred, especially if the car was a white Rolls-Royce. Should the child be not only black but barefooted further connotations would be added because bare feet can reinforce the suggestion of innocence yet also connote poverty. All this is fairly crude, but it demonstrates that, whereas some of the elements in a narrative which we might regard as fillers may simply provide information, others carry connotations which are often very significant for the argument which the writer is trying to construct, communicate and explore through the narrative.

In working through the creative possibilities in this example, we have moved from a narrow concept of a sign suggesting a particular thing to a suggestion that signs connote quite complex associations. We have even moved beyond this to a much larger structure of meaning in which individual signs participate but also relate to each other.

In our discussion of Saussure we said that, in his view, language involved learning what was signified by each sign and learning the differences between signs. Words, then, not only have an associative aspect but carry meanings that are influenced by words that are absent. Hence the significance of the Rolls-Royce is determined to some extent by the brands of car which we might have chosen to use but decided against. The importance of the child being black is that he is not white; he is part of the underclass not the privileged white minority in South Africa.

Writing Activity 3

Take the event of someone being run over by a vehicle which we have developed in a particular way above and use your own version of it to form the basis of a short story.

You may like to begin by making a diagrammatic plan, as we have below, in which you build up aspects of the connotative dimensions of your narrative. Either write from our recommendations or develop your own. You may need to research some of the details in our suggestions. For example, what is a Triumph Roadster? What do you know about Jersey that would make it a significant location in this context?

person > vehicle > location

1. barefoot black child > white Rolls-Royce > South Africa
2. thirty-year-old man > Model T Ford > South of France
3. man in mid-forties > Triumph Roadster > Jersey
4. Irishman > Chieftain tank > Northern Ireland
5. professional driver > lorry/truck > motorway/freeway
6. four-year-old girl > BMW > small village
7. twenty-year-old woman > Ford Sierra/Sedan > Wiltshire countryside
8. fourteen-year-old boy > Ford XR2/Mustang > school playing fields

Discussion

Even at an early stage, you may have seen some likely directions for a narrative to take based on the connotative function of the words chosen in the examples. Perhaps in examples 1 and 4 the associations worked together even at the outset to generate culturally specific meanings. They both referred to political situations which have changed recently but which are still potentially unstable. From the beginning, both examples require careful handling in order to avoid stereotypes or clichéd narratives. The challenge in these examples would be to remain ahead of your reader by taking their expectations of stereotypical situations and developing them in unexpected ways. Of course, this is an important feature of writing. Remember in chapter 1 we said that art of any kind involves a constant reworking of the established conventions, notations, images and narratives. How successful were you in staying ahead of your reader? You may like to show your writing to a friend or another member of your group and obtain their opinion.

Example 2 introduces connotations of wealth because of the setting which has been selected. It also, but not necessarily, suggests an earlier time period through the model of car. If we change a few of the details we have a different set of connotations. The association of a Triumph Roadster with Jersey in example 3 might lead some readers to think of the man as Bergerac in the 1980s British television series. This example demonstrates how in order to share connotations we must share a cultural context.

Examples 5 and 6 connote an accident and example 8 suggests a joyriding incident in which a youth has stolen a powerful car. Changing any of the details or elaborating them in particular ways will alter the potentialities for meaning. For instance, details on who is the professional driver in example 5 would be crucial. Are we referring here to a man or a woman? How would this be relevant? Is this person a victim? Or is he/she involved in another way, as an off-duty police officer perhaps? What possibilities would be opened up if this person were a minibus driver? Are any of the characters related to one another?

Experiment further with the basic triad of narrative events outlined above. Add further layers of connotative details and consider what each does to the direction which the narrative is taking. It is important to remember that the connotative effects of language should be incorporated into your narrative at every stage of its construction. Every word should work in creative writing; every word you choose should be there because it is being actively and purposefully employed.

Critical Activity 3

Consider the associative aspects of the language employed in the following extract from Charlotte Brontë's *Jane Eyre*, a novel with which many of you will already be familiar. In this extract, which describes an incident to which critics frequently make reference, Jane is punished by being made to stand on a chair in front of the class. Which words seem to carry the most powerful associations? What are these 'connotations'? What other words might have been used in their place? Would they have carried the same associations?

> Now I wept: Helen Burns was not there; nothing sustained me; left to myself I abandoned myself, and my tears watered the boards. I had meant to be so good, and to do so much at Lowood: to make so many friends, to earn respect, and win affection. Already I had made visible progress: that very morning I had reached the head of my class; Miss Miller had praised me warmly; Miss Temple had smiled approbation; she had promised to teach me drawing, and to let me learn French, if I continued to make similar improvement two months longer: and then I was well received by my fellow-pupils; treated as an equal by those of my own age, and not molested by any; now, here I lay again crushed and trodden on; and could I ever rise more?

Discussion

You probably picked out words such as 'abandoned', 'watered', 'molested', 'crushed' and 'trodden on'. The word 'abandoned' is particularly striking because we normally think of someone being abandoned by another. What Jane means here is that she lost control of herself. Yet to express it in this kind of way fails to convey the same sense of isolation and devastation that Jane feels. Similarly, while the words 'molested', 'crushed' and 'trodden on', like 'abandoned', may at first seem rather extreme in the context of what is being described, they do convey Jane's personal sense of victimization.

Writing Activity 4

We discussed above the risks which Brontë took with language in describing the emotional devastation of a humiliating incident. Describe a humiliating experience from the point of view of the person who has suffered in the form of a poem, a letter, an extract from a novel or a monologue from a play.

Language as a System

The relational or associative aspect of language is a key element identified by European linguists and called variously the 'expressive', 'poetic' or 'associative' function of language. There has been a tendency to distinguish 'creative writing' from 'writing' by stressing the dependence of the former on the associative aspect of language, even though all writing by definition is creative. The associative aspect of language tends to be present in writing in the form of metaphor. The European linguist Jakobson, to whom we referred earlier, recognized that the associative aspect of language is present in all types of writing and that it is only when it becomes dominant that we tend to describe it as 'poetry' or 'prose poetry' at one extreme, and as 'figurative' language at the other. While all verbal art must employ figurative language to some degree, prose which contains too much of it can appear to be straining for effect, a common fault in students' early pieces of writing.

Earlier we cited Peter Abbs' complaint that although all teachers and critics are concerned with language and the quality of writing, they still tend to stress content. An emphasis upon language leads us more obviously than an emphasis upon content to how works of literature are constructed.

The way in which we tend to think about language has undergone a number of changes. We have already said that Saussure provided a watershed in our thinking. At this point, we need to reintroduce and stress a further aspect of the way in which he conceived of language. Instead of approaching language in terms of its individual parts, he argued that we should think in terms of language as a system. When we think of a system, we inevitably think not of individual parts but of the relationship between the different parts. Once we approach language as a system, we start to conceive of meaning as something generated by the relationship between the different parts.

Implications of Saussure's Thesis for Writers

What are the implications of Saussure's thesis for the writer? It helps us to realize that the mode of language is fundamentally one of sequential movement through time. Each word has a linear or, if you prefer, horizontal relationship with another. In the account of the event narrated above – a white Rolls-Royce hitting a barefoot black child in South Africa – the meaning unfolds as each word follows its precursor until the final word. From this and the examples in Writing Activity 3 (p.47), we can see that the meaning of any word together with its importance is determined by the total context in which it occurs.

In the extract from *Jane Eyre* which we discussed above, words like 'abandoned' and 'molested' carried a whole range of possible meanings, but the context in which the words were used highlighted a particular set of meanings attached to them. Once taken in context with 'Now I wept', the word 'abandoned' serves to qualify the nature of that weeping. In association with the equally exaggerated 'my tears watered the boards', the clauses 'Now I wept' and 'I abandoned myself' reinforce the extreme nature of her reaction to the punishment and prepare us for the explanation as to why Jane should feel so humiliated. This is provided by the breathlessly cumulative structure of the second sentence which suggests the intensity of her ambitions. Jane does not just want but *craves* affection and admiration. The repetition of the first person pronoun suggests her over-concern with herself and her achievements. The repetitive account of the reactions of others towards her suggests the importance which she attaches to them, conveying her insecurity and lack of self-esteem.

Chains of Associations – Syntagms and Paradigms

As most of the examples we have looked at in this chapter illustrate, the meaning of a word is created through a chain of associations within a text. If you read Barthes' definition of 'connotation' again (see p.46), you will notice that he talks of the power of words to relate to exterior terms or to other terms within the text. The example of the narrative about an incident in South Africa and the subsequent writing exercise illustrate the importance of combining words in particular relationships so as to reinforce and develop specific meanings. The meaning of events in a narrative is provided not by any resemblance that they have to real events but by their relationships within the context of a narrative.

Language, therefore, works in terms of a two-fold process. In order to make a sentence in English, we have to engage in two types of thinking which allow us to combine words 'syntagmatically' and 'paradigmatically'. 'Syntagmatic comes from two Greek words meaning to combine in the correct order. In order to communicate clearly in English sentences, we have to combine words according to English grammar. When we go to our wardrobe to dress, there are rules governing the clothes which we select. We have to wear shoes on our feet and hats on our heads. Such rules conform to syntagmatic relationships. However, when we select clothes we also have to co-ordinate them. So what we choose to wear above the waist normally has to conform with what we select to wear below the waist and on our feet. Thus, thinking syntagmatically may also be compared to the way in which we co-ordinate our clothes into outfits according to rules which we have had to learn.

We have to select our words from a range of possibilities, rather like choosing clothes from our total collection. This is thinking 'paradigmatically'. We may have to select, for example, clothes for the top half of our bodies, choosing from a shirt or blouse, a T-shirt or a sweater. All these items share a fundamental similarity; they are worn above the waist. But we do not always have an *undetermined* choice from the range of clothes we own. Our selection may be determined by the context in which we are going to wear them. At school or at work we may have to wear a uniform, for example. There are similar contexts determining our choice of language. In the course of a week, or even a single day, we may find ourselves communicating something in different contexts through very different language.

Thinking paradigmatically involves making imaginative leaps. If we cannot find the right shirt or blouse we may in a moment of lateral thinking realize that we could choose a different item of clothing altogether. When we choose clothes we normally consider the kind of messages we think they will transmit to others. Sometimes we will reject an item of clothing because it sends the wrong signals. We may also have prejudices about some clothes which are personal to us; we may have a lucky tie or dislike a skirt because someone whom we dislike has one like it.

The clothes available to us are normally determined by the fashion of the day. In much the same way, the language open to us is determined by current intellectual systems. Around the year 1500, our thinking about the universe would have been determined by the belief that the Earth was at its centre. But a paradigmatic shift occurred as astronomers began to accept Copernicus' thesis of 1530 that the Earth and other planets circled the sun. The thesis was not accepted immediately, there being years of dispute – periods when both ideas and variations of each existed together. The meanings which language carries are not always clear-cut, just as the boundary lines between what is in or out of fashion are fluid and debatable.

Most writers seem to be generally well aware of the chain of associations in their texts, although no writer can predict all the chains which the preconceptions and prejudices of particular readers will construct. We may co-ordinate our clothes with a great deal of thought, but be surprised by the way someone may interpret how we are dressed. Some degree of command over the organization of these chains, as is clear from the examples discussed above, is important if a writer wishes to communicate a particular argument.

In *Great Expectations,* for example, a chain of associations is used to convey and comment upon the mercenary and uncompassionate side of society. The novel abounds with images of decay. It opens in a graveyard where the gravestones are overgrown with nettles; one of the first things which Pip sees is a gibbet; Satis House is itself a symbol of decay; Miss Havisham is as withered as her dress; the first impression that Pip has of London is that it is ugly and dirty; and the description of the Thames is dominated by stagnation and mud.

In writing, we need to be able to shift strategically between the two mental processes outlined above – syntagmatic and paradigmatic thinking. Since paradigmatic thinking involves making imaginative leaps we may feel at some points that we would be likely to confuse our readers, in which case we may need to write more cautiously, moving carefully from one step to another. Or we may find ourselves moving too cautiously and, in order to retain our readership, we may need to be more imaginative, be prepared to take more risks.

Semes and the Importance of Detail

From what has been said so far, it should be clear that details which we might regard as fillers in a narrative can prove to be very important. As writers, we need to pay attention to the selection of words within a syntagm, a succession of words determined by the rules of combination or grammar. The smallest unit of communication within a syntagm has been labelled by Barthes (1990) as a 'seme'. Hence, in the account of the car hitting the child, 'Rolls-Royce', 'child', 'bare feet', 'black', 'white' are all examples of semes. Obviously, if we change one of those semes we alter the meaning. For example, if we changed 'child' to 'teenager' we lose the strong association with innocence: older children are better able to look after themselves. If the child is white rather than black we lose the force of the connection with the brutality of racialism.

Before we pursue this issue further we would like you to consider a passage from D.H. Lawrence's *Sons and Lovers*, his third novel, published in 1913. It has an apparently simple story-line covering the period of the courtship of a Nottinghamshire coal miner, Walter Morel, and his marriage to Gertrude, a woman of middle-class origins; the nature of their life together in a mining community and the emotional rift that develops between them; the birth of their son, Paul, his upbringing and his love affairs with Miriam and a married woman, Clara; the death of Paul's mother, his attempts to free himself from her influence and his obsession with her; and his struggle towards achieving a fulfilling relationship with a woman.

Critical Activity 4

Consider Lawrence's use of language in the following extract from *Sons and Lovers*. It is from the first chapter of part two of the novel and is concerned with the first stages in the relationship between Paul and Miriam. The chapter focuses on significant moments during a period of three years from when Paul was sixteen. Here they are together at Willey Farm. What connotations are suggested by the details of the description? Have they been marshalled in a particular way? Is there an argument of some kind informing this particular combination of details?

He set off with a spring, and in a moment was flying through the air, almost out of the door of the shed, the upper half of which was open, showing outside the drizzling rain, the filthy yard, the cattle standing disconsolate against the black cart-shed, and at the back of all the grey-green wall of the wood. She stood below in her crimson tam-o'-shanter and watched. He looked down at her, and she saw his blue eyes sparkling.

'It's a treat of a swing', he said.

'Yes'.

He was swinging through the air, every bit of him swinging, like a bird that swoops for joy of movement. And he looked down at her. Her crimson cap hung over her dark curls, her beautiful warm face, so still in a kind of brooding, was lifted towards him. It was dark and rather cold in the shed. Suddenly a swallow came down from the high roof and darted out of the door.

Discussion

The extract contrasts Paul's energy and enthusiasm with Miriam's reluctance, his spontaneous joy with her brooding presence. The detail of her 'brooding face' is more than a point of information. It suggests the introspection which comes to irritate Paul. The effect that this has on him is anticipated in the description of the shed as 'dark' and 'cold', adjectives which are applicable later to Miriam as Paul sees her. The whole scene could be seen as a metaphor for sexual intercourse between them; Paul's eagerness and her diffidence. A feminist critique of this episode would highlight the way in which it reinforces stereotypical patterns of gender relationships, the active male and the passive female.

A writer, then, has to marshall significant details, with due regard for both their public connotations and the previous ways in which they have been organized. We can employ insights into connotative aspects of language not only to reiterate and affirm received connotative associations, but also to challenge and subvert them. For example, Lawrence's *Sons and Lovers* is set in industrial Nottinghamshire and Willey Farm seems to share the grimy and depressing features of this landscape. In other words, Lawrence avoids the clichéd polarization of the countryside as cleaner and superior to the industrial environment. The farm is more than an incidental setting. It connotes the threat which industrialism in Lawrence's work poses to life. It is part of the environment from which Paul is trying to escape and which here, albeit temporarily, he transcends, as both the height reached by the swing and the image of the bird suggest.

The complexity of some of the ways in which writers use, challenge or develop conventional meanings and associations may be illustrated by juxtaposing Lawrence's employment of the swing and the farm as extended metaphors with their use by two other writers. The swing is a key metaphor in a poem by a contemporary writer from Wales, Gillian Clarke.

Reading Activity

Swinging

At the end of the hot day it rains
Softly, stirring the smells from the raked
Soil. In her sundress and shorts she rocks
On the swing, watching the rain run down
Her brown arms, hands folded warm between
Small thighs, watching her white daps darken
And soak in the cut and sodden grass.
She used to fling her anguish into
My arms, staining my solitude with
Her salt and grimy griefs. Older now
She runs, her violence prevailing
Against silence and the avenue's
Complacency, I her hatred's object.

Her dress, the washed green of deck chairs, sun
Bleached and chalk-sea rinsed, colours the drops,
And her hair a flag, half and then full
Mast in the apple-trees, flies in the face
Of the rain. Raised now her hands grip tight
The iron rods, her legs thrusting the tide
Of rain aside until, parallel
With the sky, she triumphs and gently
Falls. A green kite. I wind in the string.

Discussion

In the last stanza, the to-and-fro movement of the swing is used as in the prose passage by Lawrence to connote the thrusting action of sexual intercourse, in both pieces of writing an anticipated rather than actual event for the moment. But in Clarke's poem, it is a girl who is experiencing the sensation of the swing and in her case, unlike Paul, she is too young to appreciate the full significance of it. Although the girl in the poem does not understand the implications of the action of the swing, the adult narrator of the poem, the girl's mother, does. By implication, the swinging action anticipates the sexually active young woman whom the girl will grow into. Here a familiar assumption of the woman as passive in sexual activity is overturned. The poem is riddled with sexual connotations which arise from the language of the mother-narrator-observer rather than the girl-subject-observed. The subject of the poem on a closer reading is not the girl on the swing but the emotions and anxieties of the mother. Although there is a great deal of literature written by women, women have often been the object and not the subject of art. In 'Swinging', the complex relationship between a mother and her daughter is made the subject of the writing. The mother's increasing awareness of her daughter's developing sexuality and independence is conveyed through connotations which depend upon traditional associations. For example, there are a number of references which may refer to the loss of virginity and of innocence such as the 'the cut and sodden grass', and the darkening of the white plimsolls. The loss of innocence to sexual knowledge is further suggested by the apple-trees, an image redolent of the Garden of Eden, while the metaphoric association of the girl's hair with a flag that is half and then full mast connotes her state between innocence and experience.

Binary Division: Rural and Urban

The conventional antithesis of urban and rural to which we referred in our discussion of the extract from *Sons and Lovers* is subverted in Dylan Thomas's collection of stories, *Portrait of the Artist as a Young Dog*. In the opening story, 'The Peaches', the young Dylan from Swansea spends a holiday at the farm, Fernhill:

The ramshackle outhouses had tumbling, rotten roofs, jagged holes in their sides, broken shutters, and peeling whitewash; rusty screws ripped out from the dangling, crooked boards; the lean cat of the night before sat snugly between the splintered jaws of bottles, cleaning its face, on the tip of the rubbish pile that rose triangular and smelling sweet and strong to the level of the riddled cart-house roof. There was nowhere like that farm-yard in all the slapdash county, nowhere so poor and grand and dirty as that square of mud and rubbish and bad wood and falling stone, where a bucketful of old and bedraggled hens scratched and laid small eggs.

At one level the narrator is trying to recreate the farm as it appeared to his childish imagination, but without the customary idealization or nostalgia for the rural which we find in literature generally. The leanness of the cat and the smallness of the eggs suggest not only a loss of fertility but that the rural itself from the perspective of a native of urban Swansea is somehow a spent force. His prose provides examples of the subversion of conventional perspectives in an attempt to be original which also involve unusual uses of language – see, for example, the application of the epithet 'slapdash' to the county, the use of 'poor and grand and dirty' together and the description of 'a bucketful of old and bedraggled hens'. 'Bucketful' is an effective collective noun, appropriate in describing a farm. It suggests a small number of hens in a way which furthers the image of a run-down place, while anticipating the birds' poor physical condition.

Deconstruction

From our discussion of the ways in which D.H. Lawrence, Gillian Clarke and Dylan Thomas subvert conventional assumptions and expectations, it is clear that language cannot be regarded as embracing an absolute truth. 'Deconstruction' is the critical process by which we seek to unravel what might be taken as absolute truths. The word itself comes from the German 'abbauen' which means 'to take apart' or 'to unbuild'. In some ways it is the linchpin of some of the post-structuralists' quarrel with structuralism and the theorist most responsible for bringing deconstruction to America was Jacques Derrida.

Derrida is an important theorist whose name and ideas you will encounter regularly in literary studies. Before reading further, you may like to consult the biographical note on Derrida (pp.171–73).

Critical Activity 5
Deconstructionists agree with structuralists that language often works through binary opposites. For example, rural/urban, male/female, white/black, rich/poor, work/leisure.

Either individually or as a member of a group, make a list of some of the binary opposites in the English language.

What do you notice about each pair you have drawn up?

Discussion

You probably had no difficulty in extending this list: teacher/student, adult/child, win/lose, love/hate, pure/impure, light/dark, sun/moon, boy/girl, peace/war, First World/Third World. We think you may have noticed that in many if not all the pairs you have written down, the first term is superior to the second. For example, we have already noted that although the majority of people in Britain live in urban communities and they provide the majority of the nation's wealth, the countryside is often regarded as superior to the town. It is generally regarded as cleaner and healthier and is associated with freedom. Males have traditionally enjoyed more power and importance in our society than women.

Deconstructionalism is not content simply to notice the inequality in these binary opposites but to ask why this should be so. This line of enquiry questions the values attached to each term and exposes how each is attached to particular ideologies. Often the opposition is based on power relations and one section of society uses the distinction to maintain its authority and control over another.

Critical Activity 5 (continued)

Before reading further, we would like you to reconsider your list in the light of the above remarks. Ask yourself why the first terms in some of your pairs are regarded as superior to the second.

Discussion (continued)

You may also have realized that the unequal relationship between the two parts of each pair of opposites is not stable and is or has been the subject of dispute. This would be true, for example, of male/female, black/white, rural/urban.

Most writers seem to follow a deconstruction impulse. For example, in *Great Expectations,* Pip has to choose between Biddy and Estella. Biddy is polite, caring and warm; Estella is rude, ruthless and cold. The novel is structured around two places: the forge and the small village it serves, and London. In each case, the first term of the pair would seem to be superior to the second. However, as in many literary works, when we examine the apparent binary organization, it is often more complicated than at first appears. Estella can be seen as much as a victim as a victimiser; she is intellectually superior to Biddy and, her haughtiness notwithstanding, she has more drive. Although the forge might appear to be superior to London, on closer inspection it shares, albeit on a smaller scale, the greed, hypocrisy and cruelty of the capital.

Writing Activity 5

Imagine you are in a doctor's waiting room and you can overhear a consultation between a patient and the doctor. Write up what you can hear in such a way:

1. that it is not consistently clear to the reader throughout who is the patient and who is the doctor;
2. that the patient who finally appears at the door is different – in age, gender and so on – from what we have been led to expect.

Multiple Meanings

Such innovative, sometimes exuberantly innovative, use of the English language as that which we find in Dylan Thomas's writing is not uncommon among Welsh writers who work in English. Although not all these writers are as fluent in Welsh as in English, or not so fluent as to be able to fulfil their obligations to their craft in both languages, the Welsh language often seems to be a liberating force on their imaginations.

The poems in the third section of *Skevington's Daughter,* the first collection by the Cardiff-born poet, Oliver Reynolds, were written while the poet was learning Welsh as an adult and remind us of the interconnection between language and consciousness. The poem 'Asgwrn Cefn Y Beic' is not so much a love poem as a poem of seduction. It derives its energy from the realization that the Welsh term for crossbar is 'the backbone of the bike'.

Critical Activity 6

Consider the language in this poem carefully. You may need to look some words up in the dictionary to be sure of their meaning, eg. 'crenellation', 'castling', 'foraging'. You may also have to research two of the references: *The Third Policeman* and the reference to the Marcher Lords.

      Asgwrn Cefn Y Beic

A while now since he dismounted.
Foraging, his fingers assess
The length of her still-tacky spine.

She is leaning against the wall,
Absorbed in *The Third Policeman.*
One of his knees nudges her seat.

Giving in taut waves, folded flesh
Hummocks above the knuckling bones'
Smoothed and stubborn crenellation.

Castling, he skims the long hollow.
Mated, grinning, she shuts the book.
His fingers, Marcher Lords, push south.

Discussion

A writer's choice of words from the available *lexis,* or range of vocabulary, is conditioned by education, social status and reading. Often in our everyday lives we employ a vocabulary derived from our immediate environment, families and personal relationships. All these combine to produce our, and ultimately a writer's, personal language or *ideolect.*

Reynolds breathes life into what in the Welsh language is a dead metaphor, developing the Welsh for crossbar into an exuberant conceit. Indeed, in the poem as a whole, he treads a narrow line between linguistic playfulness and serious social comment. In using Welsh for the titles of poems in English, Reynolds could be accused of opportunism, exploiting concern with the Welsh language in Wales in order to find favour in the country among Welsh speakers, without making a concerted effort to contribute directly to Welsh-language literature or culture. However, his poems embody a profound commitment to some of the issues of identity and culture in Wales. This poem is especially successful because of the skill with which it suggests what is only overtly declared in the last line, the part conquest of Wales by the Marcher Lords, while keeping to the fore the immediate situation – the seduction of the female cyclist by her companion. Thus the poem begins with the latter making tentative first moves towards the girl's spine, still sticky from the perspiration of cycling, employing the verb 'foraging', which is more commonly used of armies on their manoeuvres. The third verse at one level offers us the physical sensation of the fingers along the spine and a description of the girl's back responding to the kneading fingers. But the language develops the military associations of the verb 'foraging'; 'crenellation' is an apt metaphor for the spinal vertebrae but it literally means 'battlements', anticipating the use of 'castling'. This is a key part of many attacking and defensive strategies in chess – the full significance of the chess conceit becoming evident in the pun that she has been 'mated'. The poem ends on a note of complicity: 'grinning, she shuts the book'. The book is *The Third Policeman* in which cyclists are alleged to become, to varying degrees, like their bikes. The suggestion here is that the Anglicization of Wales was rooted in a process of seduction and complicity since many Welshmen literally sided with the English Lords and in post-conquest Wales sought places at the English court and an English education for their children.

Not all writers develop such an innovative and playful approach to their use of language as some of the writers in Wales, where such playfulness may be an artistic legacy of the Welsh language. You may like to pause for a moment and consider some of the dangers of being too self-conscious in your writing or of being too innovative or too clever. Indeed, in prose writing such an intensity of linguistic innovation would produce an effect of overstraining, as it can even in poetry if not handled carefully.

In writing about Oliver Reynolds's work, Professor Wynn Thomas (1994) has pointed out: 'The eccentric independent life of human language is one of

Reynolds's preoccupations in that volume [*Skevington's Daughter*] from the outset'
(p.516). However, Reynolds's linguistic inventiveness makes a key element of
writing explicit; writers are involved with developing language but language does
not develop in ways which are commonly assumed. With their listings of obsolete
words, dialect terms and etymology, dictionaries – as you might have discovered
in looking up the words above – suggest not only how difficult it is to pin down
the meaning of a word precisely, but also that within the etymology of a word
there is a dead centre. Although a language develops historically, it grows like a
tree. As Harland (1987) explains: 'Ordinarily we tend to imagine – even when we
know better – that a tree rises and flourishes by virtue of some deep and inwardly
hidden source of life. We tend to imagine some single essential centre which was
there in the earliest stages of growth, and which has remained constant under all
later increments. But in fact, of course, a tree lives on the outside, by the
circulation which flows through its green bark and sapwood; and its centre is
mere dead heartwood, endlessly supplanted and left behind' (p.129). Reynolds is
not breathing life into a dead piece of wood, but adding to the green bark of the
Welsh word for 'crossbar' which means literally 'the *backbone* of the bike'. As
Derrida argued, language grows historically and conceptually. Reynolds's poetry
frequently, and more frequently than is usually the case, demonstrates Derrida's
assertion that the development of language owes more to the conceptual than the
historical. Derrida envisaged what he called 'supplements' added on to language
and culture and assuming predominance. Some writers, such as James Joyce in
Finnegans Wake (1939), pursue the ramifications of this to phenomenal lengths
but nearly all writers are excited by 'supplements', pursuing fresh meanings or
implications in language which might have escaped general attention. Within
language and culture these supplements often work in a way which the Russian
theorist Bakhtin labelled 'centrifugal', in other words against normalizing
tendencies in both. Before pursuing this discussion, however, we would like you
to undertake a short reading exercise and a writing activity based on the multiple
meanings of language.

**At this point, we would like you to read the biographical note on
Bakhtin, whose name we are going to meet several times in the rest of this
book (pp.168–69).**

Writing Activity 6
Search a dictionary or thesaurus to discover about six words that might be used to open up
a short exploration of an event charged with emotional significance.

You might choose words such as 'after', 'absence', 'barrier', 'deception', 'envy', 'imprison',
'obsessed', 'rumour'. It is important that you identify words that act as triggers for you.

Retreat to a quiet space where you feel you can relax and think undisturbed. Allow your
mind to wander around each of your words. As we would expect, some will carry more
emotional resonance for you than others.

Select those words from your list that seem to act more powerfully as triggers than
others. Look up each of them in a dictionary. Make lists of the range of meanings of each

word. For example, if you were to look up the word 'watch' you would discover a number of virtually obsolete meanings and a number of 'supplements' which might stimulate you to realize others, some of which might be currently coming into fashion:

watch: remain awake for a purpose; be on the watch, keep watch, be vigilant; look out for opportunity etc.; exercise protecting care over; keep eyes fixed on; keep under observation; follow observantly; take care or precautions; look out, bide, await; small time piece worked by a coiled spring for carrying about the person.

Write a short account of an emotional event in prose or poetry applying, directly or indirectly, the range of meanings of a particular word, so as to exploit the full implications of some of the 'supplements'.

Polyglossia

In recent writing in English a heightened consciousness of language has been fuelled by an increasing realization of life in modern, cosmopolitan, polyglot, multicultural societies. As preparation for our discussion, we would like you to undertake the following reading.

Reading Activity

Read the following extract from Joan Riley's *The Unbelonging* which involves a black teenager who has been sent to Britain from the Caribbean by her family to be looked after by her stepfather who subsequently abuses her. Eventually she is able to leave him for a foster home, but her ambitions are frustrated when she fails her examinations. She decides, as a result, to enrol in the local college:

Hyacinth lowered her eyes, bracing herself. She had expected this reaction, but it was no easier to bear.

'I am going to college', she repeated stubbornly, toes curling in her shoes.

'What college will take you?' the woman sneered. 'Can't you blacks see there isn't any place for you in education? You had your chance and failed. Why don't you give up and stop wasting everybody's time?'

'Keene Fields have offered me a place to do the one-year 'O' level revision course,' Hyacinth mumbled, shifting uncomfortably under the hostile blue gaze.

The woman looked taken aback, but soon recovered herself. 'They did, did they?' she asked frostily. 'And I suppose they just wrote to you out of the blue and asked you to come.'

'I took their entrance exam three weeks ago. The results and the offer came today.'

'How dare you go behind my back and enrol!' the woman almost shouted. 'When did you become a staff member in this house, Miss Williams?'

Hyacinth stepped back, the sick feeling in her stomach increasing. Her father's voice came out of her nightmare, overlaid Aunt Susan's.

'You think you bad? A going to knock the rust off you.'

She closed her eyes tightly, pushing the image back. She was going to go to college, whatever the cost. The skin on her back stretched taut with remembered pain and expectation of punishment...

Discussion

Here Riley is using three different ways of speaking: the educated voice of Aunt Susan who runs the children's home (aunt here is an honorary title to make the children feel at home), the learned speech of the West Indian educated in English in the West Indies and Britain, and the voice of the West Indians who have lived and worked in Britain.

Hyacinth speaks in clipped sentences, each with a subject-verb-object structure, because she is speaking a recently learned syntax and pronunciation, but also because she is fighting hard to resist the intimidation of Aunt Susan who feels threatened by Hyacinth's initiative. She is also trying to suppress what her stepfather has done to her and develop her own sense of self-esteem in spite of it. You may have noticed that the referent of the pronoun 'you' shifts from addressing Hyacinth, an individual black girl, to black people in general, of whom Hyacinth becomes a representative. The effect of this is to emphasize the generic nature of the racism to which Aunt Susan gives expression.

Anybody living in Britain must be aware that the country has never been homogeneous in terms of ethnicity or class and that English, and our own ideolect, is never a single language. People use a mixture of Latinized and Anglo-Saxon vocabulary and 'English' constitutes a myriad of regional and ethnic dialects. The above extract reflects something of the cultural heterogeneity of English as it is spoken in England. But, of course, English is not the only language spoken in Britain. Quite apart from indigenous languages such as Welsh, other British citizens speak Urdu and Hindi. For a term to describe the coexistence of two or more languages in a culture we must return to the Russian critic, Bakhtin. It is a concept which he labelled 'polyglossia'. The multiplicity of voices in a literary work and in society are subjects to which we will return in chapter 6.

Having focused on the way in which a text looks inwards to its own chain of associations, and the way in which language determines our construction of the world outside the text, we now turn our attention to another related area. The type of language which an author employs is determined by the kind of work being written. This is the subject of the next chapter which also introduces our concern over the subsequent three chapters with the way in which narrative is organized and structured.

Research Activity 3

In our introduction, we said that writers often have to undertake different types of research. While this may entail working in a reference library, it could also involve interviewing people. As preparation for the next chapter, we would like you to ask several friends, members of your group or people you work with who have seen the same film at the cinema or on television to summarize its plot. Record their responses, using a pocket tape recorder if you have access to one.

Further Reading

Belsey, C. (1980) *Critical Practice*. London: Methuen. Chapter 5.
An accessible introduction to deconstruction.

Hawkes, T. (1977) *Structuralism and Semiotics*. London: Methuen. Chapter 3.
Hawkes provides an account of early European structuralism which may be difficult for some students.

Peim, N. (1993) *Literary Theory: An Introduction*. Oxford: Basil Blackwell. Chapter 2.
A useful introduction for teachers to the implications of working with structuralist and poststructuralist strategies.

Rice, P. and Waugh, P. (1989) *Modern Literary Theory: A Reader*. London: Arnold. Part 1. Section 2 and Part 2 Section 2.
Contains useful, short follow-up extracts on structuralism and the semiotics of signs.

Webster, R. (1900) *Studying Literary Theory: An Introduction*. London: Routledge. Chapter 3.
A highly readable account of the key issues involved in literary language.

Chapter Three
Writing and Genre

In this chapter you will find sections on:

1. Embarking upon writing a narrative

2. The significance of plot

3. Events and genre

4. Reader expectations

5. Romantic fiction, television soap opera and thrillers

6. Literary styles.

Activities

You will be asked to undertake the following activities:

1. The preparatory exercise described at the end of the last chapter.

2. Critical activities concerned with:
   - decisions involved in writing a narrative
   - plots and types of genre
   - characteristics of romantic fiction
   - characteristics of television soap opera
   - characteristics of various genres.

3. A research activity requiring access to a library.

4. Three writing activities. You are asked to:
   - make a list of details you would use in describing a character and write the first 1000 words or so in which the character is introduced;
   - write the script of a television soap opera;
   - write the opening of a literary genre.

Embarking on a Narrative: Initial Questions

In planning a story around key events what kind of questions are writers likely to have to ask themselves?

Before we begin discussing this very complicated subject we would like to give you the opportunity, either individually or with others, to brainstorm what might be involved.

Discussion

Your list might include some of the following:

1. What are the key events?

2. How are the events connected?

3. What type of narrative am I writing?

4. What narrative perspective is to be employed: are the events to be recounted in the third person or the first person, for example?

5. Is the narrator to be involved in the events?

6. Are the events to be narrated as they happen or are they in the past or the future?

7. Are the events to be related in a strictly chronological sequence?

8. What are the geographical settings of the events?

Obviously all these questions are interrelated, but over the next few chapters we will discuss them under the following topics: the significance of the choice of work, the organization of the narrative, and the point of view from which the story is told. As we said at the end of the last chapter, this chapter will be concerned with how the type of work determines the selection of events and the importance attached to them.

The Significance of Plot

Practical writing exercises and the study of literature undertaken at pre-advanced level often focus upon plot narration. Students are expected to know thoroughly the development of the plots of the works they have read and every stage in the changing relationships between the main characters. At advanced and degree level, knowledge of the plot is taken for granted and other topics such as theme, style and language are emphasized. Nevertheless, in the practice of writing and in the study of narrative at advanced and degree level, plot once again demands our attention. Sophisticated analyses of plots, of their different elements and of the different ways they may be structured, arising out of narratology (the structuralist study of narrative), should enhance, and in turn be enhanced by, our own writing.

The pioneering study in this area was undertaken by a Russian Formalist, Vladimir Propp, who analysed 200 Russian fairy-tales to discover the basic structural pattern of folk-tales. In 1928, he published his conclusions:

1. Different sequences in different fairy-tales can be understood as variations of the same sequence of events manifested in different ways;

2. All fairy-tales make use of the same types of event: there are thirty-one of these;

3. The sequence of events is always identical;

4. All fairy-tales fit into the same basic pattern.

We can see the common structural pattern which Propp has identified in the following examples:

- A tsar gives an eagle to a hero. The eagle carries the hero away to another kingdom.
- An old man gives Sucenko a horse. The horse carries Sucenko away to another kingdom.

The same event may, however, fulfil different functions at different points in the story. Thus a hero may receive money at the beginning of a tale and make a purchase which sets a train of events in motion, or at the end of a tale as a reward for bravery and thus the tale may be brought to an end.

Key Events

You will no doubt have found that all your friends provided you with virtually the same summary of the film even though a film is usually quite long and you might have expected different people to have remembered different elements of its plot. This tells us something about the nature of narrative. All narratives consist of essential elements upon which their structure depends – usually events such as someone failing to keep an appointment or, more sensationally, someone being killed.

Barthes proposed that we think of narrative on three levels: the level of 'functions', which we might think of as the plot; the level of 'actions', the level at which we might analyse the characters in a narrative (whom Barthes refers to as 'actants'); and the level of 'narration', which loosely refers to everything else that comprises a narrative.

Thus, the fundamental events of the film narrative which your friends reported to you are what Barthes calls 'functions'. Many novelists plan their works in terms of these functions before they start writing. Some of them are so essential to a particular plot that if you change one you change the whole structure of the work. This can be illustrated with reference to a text to which we have already referred. The meeting between the young orphan Pip and the escaped convict Magwitch at the beginning of Dickens' *Great Expectations* is obviously a crucial event, as is the later revelation that Magwitch rather than the upper-class Miss Havisham was Pip's benefactor, supporting his move to London and his becoming a 'gentleman'.

Often, however, it is the event itself not the nature of the event that is important. If your plot hinges upon someone failing to keep an appointment, how or why that happens may not be crucial to your story. Should you change the circumstances responsible for him or her not arriving on time, you may not fundamentally change your plot. Similarly, what is important to a plot is often not *how* someone has been killed but the *fact* that they have been killed.

Barthes has sought to differentiate between the different fundamental events or functions. While they may all be important, some would appear to be more important than others! The events which are absolutely essential are variously referred to in narratology as the 'nuclei' of the narrative and called 'kernels' or, in Barthes' term, 'cardinal functions'. Events which occur in the sequence between these, often preparing for them, are called 'catalysers'.

In any narrative there are details, which are sometimes regarded as 'fillers', which do not have a strong function in establishing the sequence of events, but are important in enabling the reader to engage with the text. Many readers enjoy a novel for its description of place or of a particular historical period. These features are known as 'indices'. Although the jargon may be troublesome when we first encounter it, this type of analysis of the structure of a narrative helps us to realize what is involved in constructing a plot around events.

Just as there is a hierarchy of events in a narrative, so there is a hierarchy of indices. As a writer you need to be aware of this for your reader will soon construct a hierarchy, possibly skipping pages which are fillers. In our discussion of Writing Activity 3 in chapter 2, we recommended that every word a writer selects should have a purpose. Indices, then, should be active in the generation of meaning in a narrative. In fact, narratology distinguishes between 'indices proper', which contribute to the creation of atmosphere or provide insights into character, and those which convey ready-made information in the form of a backdrop, called 'informants'. Generally speaking, indices are the connotative, allusive details while informants are the minimal, denotative details.

There are narratives which are constructed primarily around cardinal functions such as folk-tales, fairy-tales and detective stories. There are others which rely far more heavily upon indices. An obvious example in this category would be the 'stream of consciousness' narrative used by some modernist writers – for example, James Joyce's *Ulysses* (1922) or Virginia Woolf's *Mrs Dalloway* (1925).

Before reading further, we would like you to explore the significance of indices through a writing exercise.

Writing Activity 1

Choose a minor character from a story on which you are working. List the details which you are going to make available to the reader. Map out how you think each detail will contribute to the reader's understanding of your character. Write the first 1000 words or so in which you introduce your character, employing some of the indices you have drawn up.

Events and Genre

Why is it important for a writer to be able to think about a work in terms of its main events? On one level, of course, many writers need a map of where they are going with their writing. But there is more to it than that.

Try to remember your friends' various summaries of the film which they had seen. How many key events did their summaries consist of? Now ask yourself what kind of film it was. Do you think that there would have been fewer or more events if it were a different kind of film?

In both film and literature the attention which a writer pays to events depends upon the kind of work being produced. A writer is more likely to be concerned with what we call 'genre' than are teachers and critics. Genre is a French term which describes the division of texts into groups which have common characteristics relating to style or content – for example, 'thriller', 'romance' or 'detective fiction'. Teachers and many critics tend not to be overly concerned with genre because they often approach works of literature as individual texts. However, we have only to examine the shelf markings in bookshops to realize that genre is important to booksellers, their customers, publishers and, therefore, writers. The potential significance of genre to the study of English as a creative art has been identified by Peter Abbs:

> The creative application of genre to English Studies could generate a more comprehensive and a richer practice. If the conception of English as a subject concerned essentially with literature appears to narrow it, then the notion of genre immediately expands it – for literature is a universe made up of many galaxies, all of which require attention and recognition. (1989, p.69)

At this point, we would like you to look back to Writing Activity 3 in chapter 2 (p.47). We asked you to develop layers of connotations on a basic triad of narrative events. Read again example 6. By adding particular details we can alter both the potential meanings and the type of work, or genre, we are writing. For example, we could add details which highlight a seasonally moral dimension:

> Four-year-old girl > knocked down by a drunken driver in a BMW > in her home village at Christmas time.

Or we could emphasize a political dimension:

> Four-year-old-daughter of American President > knocked down by an Iranian terrorist in a BMW > while her family are guests of the British government.

In the first illustration, the connotations would suggest that we have written the story-line of a narrative supporting a public awareness campaign launched at Christmas to combat drinking and driving. The use of the little girl would tug at our emotions while the choice of car might arouse anger towards the driver. The second story-line might suggest a political thriller or perhaps not a work of fiction at all but the genre of a news report.

Of course, writers frequently push back the boundaries of genres and work across the divisions between them. When Gollancz published Angela Carter's *The Passion of New Eve* (1977) they invented a new genre, 'Fantasy and Macabre'! There are many works which are innovative because they include different types of writing. For example, Olive Schreiner's *The Story of an African Farm* (1883), which she published under the pseudonym 'Ralph Iron', contains philosophical, contemplative, polemical and humorous writing. It is a moot point as to whether the invention of television or radio produced new genres or adaptations of existing ones in other media. Dylan Thomas's *Under Milk Wood* (1954) was originally written for radio; you may well have difficulty deciding whether it is a play, a prose work or a prose-drama. It takes place over a day, it is not divided into acts and scenes and very little happens in the conventional sense of dramatic action. It is subtitled *A Play For Voices*, but Thomas also called it 'prose with blood pressure'. In a later chapter, we will discuss the characteristics of radio drama and you may like to return then to Thomas's text in the light of that information to see whether it helps you to determine its genre.

Here is a research activity which need not be completed before you rejoin our commentary, but which will help you to consolidate your appreciation of how innovative particular works can be. We would also like you, before rejoining our text, to have the opportunity to think about the range of genres available to a writer.

Research Activity
Obtain a copy of *The Passion of New Eve* and/or *Story of an African Farm* and/or *Under Milk Wood* from your college or local library. Read as much of them as you have time for (remember that we said it is not necessary to complete this research activity before undertaking the next critical activity) and consider the ways in which they cross conventional genre boundaries. Try to relate the innovative structure to the ways in which the texts challenge you in their representation of individuals and communities and in their subject matter.

Critical Activity 2

At this point it would be useful for you to take ten minutes or so and – either individually or with friends – try to think of as many genres as you can without looking at the list below.

Discussion

We have already referred to several examples of genre in the course of our discussion: thriller, romantic fiction, detective fiction.

To the examples given above you could have added: science fiction, horror fiction, crime fiction, utopian fiction, the western, fantasy, melodrama, soap opera, situation comedy, tragedy, comedy, revenge tragedy, tragi-comedy, fairy-tales, fable, epic, sonnet, lyric, elegy, narrative poem, documentary.

This list indicates our eclectic approach to genre today. It allows for new types of works constantly coming into existence and for the way in which new forms emerge at the interface between existing genres. The creative possibilities of reworking existing genres or subverting traditional expectations are such that to think in terms of categories and then sub-genres, for example, narrative and types of narrative, does not do it justice.

Aristotle defined three genres:

1. **Poetic/lyric:** a text spoken in the first person throughout;

2. **Epic/narrative:** a text in which the narrator speaks in the first person but allows other characters to speak for themselves;

3. **Drama:** a text in which characters do all the speaking.

Such a narrow set of definitions would be impracticable in the twentieth century.

Critical Activity 3

If there are genres mentioned above with which you are not familiar – for example, 'crime' as distinct from 'detective' fiction – you should try to discover their characteristics. You may find it useful to consult a dictionary of literary terms. If you are working in a group, you may like to take a few genres each and report back to the group on what you have discovered about the genres you have been assigned. It is not necessary to do this before moving on to the next activity.

Critical Activity 4

At this point pause and try to summarize in your mind the plot of a popular novel which you have read or seen televised recently, the kind of book which is often called a 'potboiler'.

Discussion

You will realize that such a book is packed with events. But if you try to summarize a different type of book, a classic novel maybe or a popular romance, you will see that there are fewer hinge events. At advanced level, students are generally asked to think in terms of types of plot and are often presented with brief and convenient summaries of those which they are likely to encounter. Coxon and Baker (1983), for example, identify two main groupings. The first is the category of novels which have 'a highly structured architectonic story, with artfully arranged parallels, contrasts, discoveries, shifts of scene and time, character groupings or major character establishment'. In this category, they include several of Conrad's novels, such as *The Secret Agent* and *Nostromo*.

The second main grouping consists of novels 'where there is less concern with "a story" and more with the growth and development of affairs, or the progress of events, as in life' (pp.116–117). Here they include novels such as Virginia Woolf's *Mrs Dalloway* and D.H. Lawrence's *The Rainbow*.

Even though Coxon and Baker also mention novels such as prose-poems which have scarcely any plot, the range of possibilities open to a writer is much more complex than their summary suggests. This is probably due, in part, to the fact that teachers and academic critics in traditional English studies have tended to think in terms of a somewhat narrower definition of literature than many writers. Academics are concerned with works of acknowledged merit, of psychological depth, of social complexity and of sophisticated sensibility. Writers are more likely to be concerned in a much wider sense with the creative possibilities of language, form and content: with how to explore new subjects and present a new perspective on established themes. Hence they often have a much wider perspective on literature than academic critics.

Moreover, authors are often more aware of aspects of writing which in the rarefied world of literary criticism hardly ever receive consideration. In their bread-and-butter world, many writers have to meet the needs and expectations of particular audiences. We have argued that genre is an important element in determining the expectations that a reader brings to a work. Anyone can write as they wish but published writers generally have to work to the demands or preferences of publishers, to satisfy audience taste and to meet the recommendations of literary agents, as well as to satisfy their own creative ambitions. For these reasons, too, the categories of writing with which many authors have to work are wider than those in which critics and teachers like Coxon and Baker generally have to think.

Reader Expectations in Three Examples of Genre

Approaching literature from the point of view of the writer rather than the critic –

even though all writers must also be critics – we have to think in much wider and more complex terms. This can be illustrated with reference to three genres that do not fit easily into the two categories outlined above: romantic fiction, soap opera and the thriller.

Romantic Fiction

In romantic fiction, the entire plot is the movement between two biographical moments: passion between two people and their successful union in marriage. In early romances, what happens between these two moments does not affect their love which is never in doubt; they remain true to each other and chaste. In later romances, however, the emphasis is often not on the lovers' adventures but on how their passion for each other is tested and how they come to know each other better. In other words, the events upon which the plot turns acquire biographical or psychological significance. Romantic fiction is often clichéd or unrealistic yet huge numbers of people read and enjoy it. Even when publishers are struggling in a declining market, Mills and Boon sell millions of copies of their romances. Romantic fiction is read not for the events as such but for the emotions, anguish, issues and problems that entanglement in a love-affair creates.

Mills and Boon romances are an extreme example of how writers are influenced by the market expectations of their publishers. Margolies (1982/83) points out:

> Unlike the traditional image of publishing which assumes the unique value of each book, Mills and Boon romance is presented as a commodity like tea or soap powder. Whereas literary publishers may advertise a new novel stressing the qualities that distinguish it from others, Mills and Boon advertise a general product, 'the rose of romance'. The product is sold in an easily recognizable package assuring the purchaser of standard quantity (192 pages of romance) and consistent quality. (p.5)

Mills and Boon are not part of a cultural conspiracy to instill a particular way of thinking about romance in the population. Writers are not told what to write as such – even the 'tip sheet' for authors is no more than encouragement to provide realistic dialogue and authentic settings, as Margolies reminds us (p.6). But obviously writers have to work within a framework acceptable to the publishers and what the publishers believe the reading public wants on the evidence of their sales.

Critical Activity 5
If romantic fiction was one of the genres which you and/or your friends researched or is one with which you are already familiar, you may like to pause for a few minutes and try to recall its characteristics.

Discussion

We have only to read a handful of these books to realize that even if they are not exactly formulaic, they follow a number of obvious conventions. First and foremost, the goal of the heroine is marriage to the hero. She is usually passive, that is, things happen to her rather than being instigated by her. The hero is someone who makes things happen. He is often mysterious and virile, however, and sometimes even violent. The heroine has no identity and no full sense of self outside her relationship to the hero. In other words, the hero makes her complete. She is often insecure and riddled with guilt over her relationship. She wants sexual fulfilment but, as Margolies says, she is ashamed of having a sexual response (p.11). The work setting is often important in romance fiction, but where the heroine has a romance and a career, she is obliged, sometimes after much soul-searching, to choose the former.

Soap Operas

The Australian soap opera *Neighbours* provides a further example of how perceived audience needs and expectations influence writing – particularly the nature of events. Over the years, it has acquired an increasingly obvious orientation toward young people. As older characters have left the programme, they have often been replaced by younger characters in line with with the age range of the targeted audience. The story-lines, too, have tended to involve issues of concern to teenagers.

In romantic fiction, events are often less plausible because they are only pegs upon which to construct and develop the love anguish of the heroine and the problems of her relationship with the hero. In soap operas, there is usually more suspense and melodrama than in real life because each episode requires a cliff-hanger ending.

Thrillers

In thrillers, events are normally seen from the point of view of the hero while the *status quo*, disrupted by the actions of villains to which the hero responds, is restored by his actions. How the reader views the events is once again influenced by the nature of the genre. We avoid attributing final meanings to events in a thriller because we know that they will probably turn out to have a significance different from that which we are led to expect. We also put up with confusion and perplexity because we know that in the thriller events are usually clarified in relation to the final outcome.

Critical Activity 6
At this point, we would like you to watch an episode of a television soap opera. As you do so, make a list of what you take to be the chief characteristics of the genre.

Discussion

Soap operas began on the radio in the 1920s, so-called because they were sponsored by soap manufacturers. Today the television companies use soaps to capture audiences in the early evening which will remain with their channel for the remainder of the evening. The radio soaps targeted housewives for whom they provided surrogate company and reassuring familiarity.

Soap operas are written with specific conventions in mind. They have an episodic structure, a core of familiar characters and a number of minor characters who only appear for a few episodes. The major characters are usually of mixed ages and backgrounds in order to maximize the number of potential story-lines. Several parallel story-lines are pursued through a number of significant events in order to present a multiplicity of experiences. Sometimes events are used to merge two or more of the plots. The credibility of the characters in most British and Australian soap operas depends on the ordinariness of their stories, their homes, their families and their friends. Soap operas include plenty of suspense and melodramatic action. They are usually located in the present and generally the passing of time mirrors the passing of actual time. Gossip plays a major part in soap operas at the level of action, while also presenting information, ideas and speculation to the audience.

These television soap operas take the same detailed look at day-to-day family life as did the early radio programmes: they centre around gossip, petty quarrels and misunderstandings, jealousy, romance and illness. Nevertheless, soap operas project the good-heartedness of ordinary people and the value of community – perhaps nostalgically in some of the British soaps. Relations between family members often give rise to tensions and crises. But even though the family is not the safe haven it is supposed to be, traditional family norms provide a backdrop for the familial conflict. The family is an important feature of these soap operas and where wider events are portrayed, they are seen through the microcosm of the family.

Writing Activity 2

After completing the Preparatory Activities outlined below, we would like you to write the script for the first fifteen minutes of the first episode of a new soap opera for television. Your script should indicate clearly who is speaking, as in a play script.

You should also indicate locations and changes of locations, but you should not try to provide a fully annotated camera script. There may be some essential sound effects or essential camera angles you would want to stipulate.

Preparatory Activities

These preparatory activities are designed so as to make your actual writing task easier. They consist of a reading task and a planning task.

Reading task

In order to increase your appreciation of some of the issues relating to genre, audience expectation, style and content which you may wish to tackle in your own soap opera we would like you to read – and perhaps discuss in a group with others – the following transcript of part of a discussion about soap operas.

The discussion involves three people who were seventeen at the time, Gabrielle Winston (GW), Robert Sullivan (RS), Teresa Jones (TJ); Preethi Munoz (PM) acts as Chair.

GW: Soaps are almost entirely negative about black people. We are seen as small-time crooks or as good-for-nothings. They reinforce white people's racism.

RS: But that's true of television generally. Black people – especially young black people – don't have many role models they can look up to on television.

TJ: If you ask me, there aren't enough black people working in television. Not enough black writers. If more black people were in control of television programming there would be a more honest portrayal of black people on the screen.

GW: There is evidence to suggest that people who do not come into contact with ethnic minorities on a day-to-day basis have their images of them shaped endlessly by the mass media.

RS: But women as well as black people are stereotyped on television. If there were more women writers, more women in... What did you say?... What was it?...

PM: Control of television programming.

RS: Soaps would have more interesting women characters.

TJ: Not necessarily. Having a woman Prime Minister did not increase the number of women cabinet ministers or advance equal opportunities for women particularly.

PM: Let's keep to television for the moment.

GW: We are being too negative. After all we are beginning to see more positive portrayals of black people in soap operas and more interesting, less stereotypical, parts for women. *Neighbours* once had a young woman choosing to make a career in car mechanics. That's quite advanced – especially for some parts of Australia.

RS: They like their 'Sheilas' [Australian slang for women] in the homes, looking after the men.

TJ: But that's just the point that Gabrielle was making earlier. None of us have been to Australia. Is that right? So we believe the stereotypes we see on television. That's why stereotyping is dangerous. Besides, I don't believe that the role of women in soap operas has changed that much over the years.

PM: You don't think that some soap operas challenge our prejudices and assumptions?

TJ: Of course, it depends what soaps you are talking about. Some do. The women in *EastEnders* are ordinary women, leading ordinary working-class lives. But *EastEnders* is frequently raising social issues such as violence against women; racism; women trying to return to education; how easy it is to get into debt; drug-taking.

RS: So does *Brookside*. And both *Brookside* and *EastEnders* have dealt with gay issues. Both have included a lesbian relationship in their story-lines.

GW: But their lives are so miserable *(general expression of disagreement from the others)*. If my life were as miserable as theirs I'd commit suicide. They [soap operas] steamroller us with social issues. It's as if these soaps have to be topical. Sometimes they deal with the same social issues simultaneously, as if they are competing to see which can be the more politically correct. And they are usually picked up and then dropped. There is never enough time spent on them.

RS: So you are really saying that soap operas are shallow.

TJ: At least they're bringing issues to our attention – making people think. I mean those people who would not ordinarily read a book or watch more serious drama.

GW: I find them [soap operas] paradoxical. Is that the word? They pick up whatever is in the news, but they don't do enough with it – as I was saying about the way they portray black people. Anyway, I think they repel viewers because they are so bleak, so unrealistic.

PJ1: What do you mean by unrealistic?

GW: People's lives are never as full of problems in real life. We might know someone who'll dabble with drugs or hear of someone who gets attacked. But in *EastEnders* and the like, everyone stumbles from one crisis to another.

RS: But you cannot have a soap opera based faithfully on the lives of ordinary people – it would be too dull!

Planning task

Before undertaking this task, we recommend that individually or in a group you discuss the issues raised in the above extract.

Before you start writing, decide which market you are aiming for. Work out your key characters (how they will contrast with each other, to whom will they appeal, how challenging the part would be for an actor) and your story-lines. Think about how you would intend to develop your story-lines after the first episode which we have asked you to write. For example,consider the approaches you are going to take, the extent of your emphasis upon social realism or the significance you are going to attach to location. In *Eldorado,* a soap opera concerned with British expatriates living in Spain, the location was more important than in *Neighbours* which could take place in any Australian suburb.

Now undertake Writing Activity 2 (p.74).

Critical Activity 7

Before attempting this activity, you should have completed Writing Activity 2 and be familiar with the characteristics of the key genres.

Read the following extracts from various genres. Either individually or with others in a group, try to identify the genre of which each is representative. Draw up a list of reasons for your choice. Examine the language and style of each extract.

Extract A

Mrs Vanderlyn swept into the room looking very handsome. She was wearing an artfully-cut russet sports suit that showed up the warm lights in her hair. She swept to a chair and smiled in a dazzling fashion at the little man in front of her.

For a moment something showed through the smile. It might have been triumph, it might also have been mockery. It was gone almost immediately, but it had been there. Poirot found the suggestion of it interesting.

"Burglars? Last night? But how dreadful! Why no, I never heard a *thing*. What about the police? Can't they *do* anything?"

Again, just for a moment, the mockery showed in her eyes. Hercule Poirot thought:

"It is very clear that you are not afraid of the police, my lady. You know very well that they are not going to be called in."

And from that followed – what?

He said soberly:

"You comprehend, Madame, it is an affair of the most discreet."

"Why, naturally, M. – Poirot, isn't it? – I shouldn't dream of breathing a word. I'm much too great an admirer of dear Lord Mayfield's to do anything to cause him the least little bit of worry."

She crossed her knees. A highly-polished slipper of brown leather dangled on the tip of her silk-shod foot.

She smiled, a warm, compelling smile of perfect health and deep satisfaction.

"Do tell me if there's anything at all I can do?"

Extract B

When Sarah saw who it was, she stopped short, her grey eyes widening in shock recognition of someone she hadn't seen for a year and, during that time, had done her best to forget.

Following him into the hall, Tim Ardsley closed the panelled door topped by an elegant Regency fanlight.

'Let me take your coat, Hastings.'

'Thank you.' The tall black-haired man with the unseasonably sun-tanned face unwound a cashmere scarf and shrugged off his navy blue coat. His suit was also navy blue, chalk-striped, superbly cut – or would his broad-shouldered athletic frame have made any suit look good?

In the short time Sarah had known him, he had worn casual hot-weather clothes. This Englishman-about-town persona was a side of him unfamiliar to her.

Tim caught sight of her standing, frozen, on the beige-carpeted stairs, gripping the gleaming mahogany hand-rail.

Extract C

"Don't yu," the puncher rasped. "I'm showin' yu why."

He flipped a silver dollar away from him and by the time it tinkled on the boards both his guns were out and spouting flame. The first bullet struck the edge of the coin, spinning it in the air again, the second drove it down, and the third jumped it a yard further away. Ten shots in as many seconds were fired, and each time the winking target was fairly hit. Then the puncher thrust his weapons back into their holsters and looked contemptuously at the prostrate man.

Extract D

At first she thought it was thunder, but then came the creaking from overhead, and she knew.

Somebody had come into the house. Somebody was tip-toeing along the hall. Was it Sam? Had he come to find her? But then why didn't he call her name?

And why did he close the cellar door?

The cellar door *had* closed, just now. She could hear the sharp click of the lock, and the footsteps moving away, back along the hall. The intruder must be going upstairs to the second floor.

She was locked in the cellar. And there was no way out. No way out, nowhere to hide. The whole basement was visible to anyone descending the cellar stairs. And somebody would be coming down those stairs soon. She knew it now.

Discussion

You probably had little difficulty identifying each genre. The first extract contained a large clue in the name Hercule Poirot. It was taken from Agatha Christie's

Murder in the Mews (1937) and is an example of detective fiction. The second extract was from a Mills and Boon romance, Anne Weale's *Night Train* (1987). The third extract is from a western, Oliver Strange's *Sudden* (1933). The fourth extract might have posed more problems for you. It is an example of horror fiction and the extract is from Robert Bloch's *Psycho* (1960) of which Alfred Hitchcock made his famous film version.

The real challenge lay in identifying the characteristics of each genre in the extracts. The first extract is concerned with events from the detective's point of view, but there is a complication in the narrative. At the end of the first paragraph there is a subtle shift to Mrs. Vanderlyn's somewhat condescending view of Poirot, 'the little man', which later in the extract Poirot notices. We see Mrs. Vanderlyn as she presents herself to Poirot; the repetition of the verb 'swept' tells us much about her attitude towards others and her propensity for drama, evident when she learns of the burglars. Her hyperbolic reaction is contrasted with the more sober Poirot who cautions her, significantly, to be discreet. Poirot's own faltering grammar marks him as an outsider. In detective fiction, the detective is always an outsider, characterized by remarkable powers of observation, and even an outsider in terms of normal sexual relations. Detectives like Poirot are invariably single and this makes their encounters with assertive women such as Mrs Vanderlyn, by whom they are never duped, all the more interesting. In detective fiction, there is much emphasis on questioning suspects; the cut-and-thrust of the dialogue and the importance attached to observation are key sources of interest and tension. We are constantly being invited to scrutinize what people say and to notice non-verbal as well as verbal clues.

Typically of romance fiction, we see events from Sarah's point of view in the second extract. The hero is introduced from the heroine's perspective. Initially, he is often, as here, both attractive and repelling. Romance fiction is essentially fantasy and the hero has an ideal physique. He also has the capacity to surprise. A third perspective, in this case Tim's, is introduced to confirm the impact which the hero has had on the heroine, which she may not wish to admit to herself. As this extract demonstrates, romance fiction presents a particular discourse about women – that they should be attentive to and responsive to men and in a state of constant potential sexuality – and an ideology of masculinity: the men are usually older, richer, wiser and more experienced than the women.

The third extract also presents us with a fantasy. The western is essentially a male fantasy of a world either devoid of women or where men are firmly and unequivocally in control of women. The western tends to stress conflict – this extract is typical in its emphasis upon trials of strength or skill between males. The colloquial language reinforces a fantasy of male prowess where the edges have not been smoothed by civilization, domesticity and women. Such dexterity with a gun, a source of pride and admiration, is again sheer fantasy for no one and no gun, even in the American west, could be this accurate. The western, like the romance, admits the reader into a codified world in which certain patterns of behaviour are taken for granted. But whereas romance fiction emphasizes inner confusion and anxiety rather than events, the western stresses action and plot. It relies heavily on external description and one-dimensional characters. Good and bad are clearly defined and the boundaries between them are rarely problematic.

The fourth extract relies heavily upon presenting us with the victim's point of view. In order for us to experience her sense of fear, we have to be able to identify with the situation in which she finds herself. The questions which she constantly asks herself constitute a key strategy here; we share her uncertainty. Once again, we can see in this genre particular discourses around female and male roles. The victim is more likely to be a woman than a man. From this short extract we cannot tell who Sam is but it is obvious he is someone she can rely on, thus perpetuating the stereotype of female dependency. The ideology of masculinity posits the male as either dependable hero or villain. One of the conventions of horror fiction is that the victim strays into an area of danger. This extract comes from near the end of the novel. The female victim here is Lila whose sister, early in the novel, had strayed off the highway into Bates' Motel which received few guests since they built the new road. At the motel, she is murdered in the shower. In this extract Lila has strayed from Sam and has entered the house of Norman Bates whom the reader at this point believes lives with his mother. The cellar, literally the underneath of the house, symbolizes its dark secrets and also the subconscious of Norman Bates who we learn is responsible for the murders which have occurred at the motel.

Writing Activity 3

Select one of the following sentences, each taken from a particular genre. Use it as the opening of a passage written in the style and language of a different genre.

> I thought I could hear shouts and the sound of sirens, but there was no way of being sure – not with the crackling and murmur that followed me down the stairs.
> (from Robert Bloch, *Firebug* (1961) – horror fiction)

> 'There isn't a single muscle in my body that isn't screaming right now, my nose is so cold it feels like it's going to fall off, and you think I'm having a good time?'
> (from Melinda Cross, *A Defiant Dream* (1989) – romance fiction)

> Any allegation that she might have been acquainted with a murder victim might have been expected to evoke fulsome excuses from a woman of Miss Mowler's temperament.
> (from Ruth Rendell, *Some Lie and Some Die* (1973) – detective fiction)

> 'Stay right where you're at, you sonvabitch,' roared the lady, 'I got you dead to rights.'
> (from Matt Chisholm, *The Indian Incident* (1978) – western fiction)

The previous writing exercises should have helped consolidate your appreciation of how the genre in which you are writing will determine the style and content of your work. They were also designed to help make you more critically aware of different genres and the ideological implications of some of their conventions. The next chapter is concerned to develop your understanding in more general terms of how a narrative is organized.

Further Reading

Carr, H. (1989) *From My Guy to Sci-Fi: Genre and Women's Writing in the Postmodern World*. London: Pandora.

A collection of essays deconstructing from feminist perspectives some of the key popular genres such as detective fiction, romantic fiction and science fiction. It also contains an essay on contemporary Asian women's writing. A highly readable book which should help you develop critical insights into the genres in which you choose to work.

Moss, G. (1989) *Un/Popular Fictions*. London: Virago.

A stimulating discussion of how girls use romantic fiction to negotiate complex issues about their own identity. Although written for teachers, it is difficult to imagine students, too, not enjoying this book.

Palmer, J. (1991) *Potboilers: Methods, Concepts and Case Studies in Popular Fiction*. London: Routledge.

An interesting but sophisticated discussion of modern critical approaches to popular fiction which would appeal to tutors and those with a grounding in critical theory.

Chapter Four

Organizing a Narrative

In this chapter, you will find sections on:

1. Genette's theory of narrative and narration

2. Non-chronological arrangement of events in works by a range of writers, including American and African-American authors, with particular reference to Toni Morrison's *Sula* and *Beloved*

3. Analepsis (flashback) and prolepsis (anticipation)

4. Duration.

Activities

You will be asked to undertake the following activities:

1. Critical activities concerned with:

   - considering various possible rearrangements of events in a short work you have written
   - the non-chronological arrangement of events
   - the use of analepsis
   - the significance of events in a story you will write in the course of the chapter.

2. Writing activities. You will be asked to

   - write up eight key events, each on its own card, and map different possible arrangements of them in a narrative;
   - devise a narrative based on a landscape and from a particular perspective in which you experiment with time;
   - write a short story or part of a novel about the psychological, spiritual, moral and/or sexual development of a young person.

3. A case study based on F. Scott Fitzgerald's *Tender is the Night* and a research

activity on the novel.

4. A research activity based on D.H. Lawrence's *Sons and Lovers.*

Genette's Theory of Narrative and Narration

An important consideration for many writers which we must pursue before going further is the order of the events. We often first think of a story as a linear narrative. The French theorist, Gérard Genette, called this *histoire* (or 'story'). But this linear story may be very different from the narrative we actually write in which the sequence of events may be rearranged. Genette distinguished this from *histoire* by calling it *récit* (or 'narrative'). The narrative content, the *histoire,* will only be available to us as a text, a *récit,* in which some rearrangement has taken place.

In traditional criticism we tend to conflate the story and the arrangement of the story as it is told or narrated. In modern critical theory we emphasize the distinction between these, so that we begin forcefully with the premise that any text involves an arrangement of a story. The story, or *histoire,* becomes a kind of ideal; it is unable to be realized except as a *récit.* For example, you and five of your friends may describe something that happened to you. What had happened to you would be the *histoire* (or the story). But it cannot be realized until one of you articulates it. Each of you would tell the story differently, arranging its events in a particular order, beginning at a different place or introducing a different set of emphases. Each version would be a *récit* (or narrative).

Before reading further, you may like to turn to the biographical notes and familiarize yourself with Gégard Genette's contribution to modern critical theory (pp.174–75).

The *récit* refers to the text in which the *histoire* may be arranged in a particular way, with characters seen in particular relationships to each other. Genette also introduced a third layer, *narration* (or narrating). This refers to the detail of the way in which the *histoire* is realized as a *récit* (a story realized as a narrative). Many of the elements which Genette envisaged as being included here will be discussed in the course of this book; they include the use of point of view, narrative devices such as letters, and dialect.

Today we are accustomed to some very sophisticated, even unusual, arrangements of narrative events. However, many of us are familiar, if only from the cinema, with the most unsophisticated *récit* (or narrative): the basic adventure story separated into short segments that correspond to separate adventures, where what is important is for the hero, and sometimes the heroine, to be able to escape, to catch up with their companions or to outstrip their pursuers. The words 'suddenly' and 'at just that moment' seem to characterize this type of narrative. The course of events is interrupted almost at random and even war can break out without an explanation being offered! While such works offer us escapism, we normally try to achieve more interesting, innovative and complex arrangements of narrative than this in our own writing.

Critical Activity I

Before you read the next section take a short story, a play or a poem you have written and consider how you might rearrange the events. What different rearrangements have you been able to think of? What do you think is likely to have been achieved or lost by your rearrangements?

Discussion

You probably began revising the structure of your particular work by trying to select a part of the narrative which could be repositioned at a point which was earlier or later than its natural or logical position in the sequence of events. The effect of this might be to plunge the reader into the middle of events rather than place the reader at the beginning of something. In other words, your particular piece of work in its rearranged form may make greater demands on the reader. While the reader may have sufficient grasp of what is going on in order to become involved with your writing, he or she will not have the same sense of the whole as if your piece began at the beginning of a linear narrative.

Non-chronological Arrangement of Events

Case Study

One of the most famous examples of a novel that employs a non-chronological sequence is F. Scott Fitzgerald's *Tender is the Night,* first published in New York in 1934 and a book which its author was still rearranging when he died. When Fitzgerald began, towards the end of 1938, to revise the novel, which is divided into two books, the major change that he was considering involved moving the middle section, the first ten chapters of Book Two, to the beginning of the novel. There were other revisions which he wanted to make and Fitzgerald's constant thinking about the structure of the novel provides an example of how important the arrangement of material is to a writer.

Research Activity I

Before reading the next section obtain a copy of *Tender is the Night* and examine how the material is ordered. Compare the first chapter of Book One with the first and eleventh chapters of Book Two.

Tender is the Night opens on the French Riviera in the summer of 1959 where a seventeen-year-old film actress, Rosemary Hoyt, and her mother arrive for a holiday. Rosemary is attracted to a young doctor, Dick Diver, who is the centre of a group of wealthy and fashionable people. Book One takes the reader quickly from a happy, carefree and, as we later discover, careless society to a disturbing climax in which Dick's wife, Nicole Warren, suffers a nervous breakdown after Rosemary discovers in her room the body of a negro with whom one of Dick's friends has had an argument. But this forward movement of the novel is interrupted by the first chapter of Book Two which suddenly takes us back to Zurich in 1913, where Dick Diver arrives as a young psychiatrist to study. We learn how he first becomes involved with Nicole, a patient recovering from schizophrenia, and how he later marries her. Eventually, the novel returns the reader to 1925 to continue the forward movement of the narrative. The middle section provides the connecting or missing links – Nicole's illness and background and Dick Diver's original ambitions. As the centre of attention shifts from Rosemary to Dick, the reader discovers that Nicole's illness and wealth are destroying Dick. The fact that we start the novel in the middle of Dick Diver's story allows the text to strip away his veneer of happiness and respectability, while exposing the superficiality, violence and corruption of American society in the 1920s.

Most writers who rearrange events so that they are no longer in strict chronological order usually have good reasons for doing so. Few works are so structured in order simply to make greater demands on the reader.

Barthes (1990) distinguishes between two kinds of texts which make different demands on the reader:

1. **Readerly** texts, which rely upon conventions which writers and readers might be expected to share and which contain fixed or closed meanings;

2. **Writerly** texts, which violate conventions and force the reader to work to produce a meaning or meanings which are not even then fixed or final.

Before reading further, we would like you to have some experience of experimenting with the organization of the cardinal functions of a narrative.

Writing Activity I

For this activity you will need about eight blank postcards or eight pieces of paper cut into the size of postcards.

Try to remember a narrative you have written or one that you have read. Write the outline of a key event of the plot on each of the cards.

Lay the cards out on a table or on the floor. Test out different arrangements of the cards, experimenting with different beginnings, sequences and endings.

Consider, or debate with friends, the implications, merits and demerits of each of the arrangements.

Critical Activity 2

Before reading further we recommend you pause and, in the light of what you have gleaned from the above writing activity, try to think of reasons why the events in a work should be arranged in a non-chronological way.

Extended Discussion

The events in *Tender is the Night* are usually linked by more than chronology. Fitzgerald's novel focuses on the psychology of Dick Diver, the reasons for his involvement with Nicole, the explanation of his initial attraction to her and how his involvement with her destroys him. As he becomes weaker, eschewing his career ambitions and falling into obscurity, she becomes stronger, eventually achieving the position and status which her background and wealth suggest she should enjoy.

In referring you to F. Scott Fitzgerald's *Tender is the Night*, we are conscious that you have probably encountered a novel which extends or challenges what you might have expected of a narrative. Non-chronological structure, together with silences and gaps within the narrative itself, are features of a number of recent novels by black women writers – for example, Toni Morrison and Alice Walker. As African-American writers, their works have their origins in the tense interface between a number of cultures, forcing us to question the sources of some of our assumptions about the novel as an art form. The kind of preconceptions we bring to their works will be determined by whether our understanding of what constitutes a novel or even a narrative comes from a reading of Euro-American, African-American or African fiction.

Although you may have read Morrison's *Beloved* (1987) or Walker's *The Color Purple* (1982), you do not have to be familiar with their work to understand the section which follows. This considers the ways in which they have structured their novels, emphasizing the techniques employed rather than the content of the works. However, we hope to whet your appetite enough to encourage you to read at least one of these writers' novels.

At one level, *Beloved* is a romance between Sethe and Paul D, two ex-slaves reunited in post-Civil War America. The historical context makes their relationship special, for under slavery black people were not free to contract physical and emotional relationships. However, their reunion is made problematic by the relationship of each of them to Sethe's children, one of whom is an incarnated ghost of the child murdered by Sethe. Both of them are haunted by their pasts and dehumanized by what they have done or what has been done to them.

The main events of *Beloved* constitute Sethe's past, which the reader has to construct piecemeal. Sethe herself tries to suppress it because it is so painful, yet in order to achieve healing herself she cannot go on denying the past. The backbone of the novel is a concealed text buried within the surface narrative, which the reader has to recover to make sense of the whole, just as Sethe has to reclaim it to make sense of her life. These events include the death of her mother; her marriage to Halle; a whipping which almost kills her; her escape and refuge in the home of her mother-in-law; her recapture and the murder of her own child to prevent it being taken into slavery; and her years in an all-female household where the third member is a ghost daughter.

Why should Morrison construct *Beloved* in a way which requires so much effort of the reader? The novel is fragmentary, frequently revisiting the same event from different perspectives, so that at times it lacks clarity. A critic should not speculate as to an author's motives because there is no reliable way of determining them and writers are not always to be trusted when they tell us. However, we can see the reader's task of piecing the story together paralleled by our difficulty in understanding black history, much of which has been omitted from the history books. The novel retells the story of slavery from the perspective of black women, while most accounts have focused upon what slavery did to black men. It also rejects the notion that there were plantations upon which slaves were treated well; all slavery takes away a human being's freedom and dignity. The novel makes clear that emancipation did not, as is sometimes thought, bring an end to the horrors of slavery. Apart from the fact that racism and apartheid continued quite openly in parts of the American South until the 1960s, and even today has not been entirely eradicated, the years following the Civil War resulted in the mass murder of many black people, including young children.

We have included reference to works by black women writers in this book because they offer a contrast to literature written in the Euro-American tradition. They provide us with examples of new literary possibilities. To study only works by white British or white American writers would be the equivalent of just studying English chemistry!

Many African-American writers were educated in the Euro-American traditions. Although they may on occasion draw upon African creative conventions deliberately to undermine a Euro-American literary custom, it would be misleading to see their work only in relation to British or American literature. Their apparently radical narrative structures are rooted in African or African-American ways of seeing the world and in African forms of narration, particularly the oral tradition. Concepts sometimes associated with Euro-American narratives – such as linearity, progress and chronology – are not always evident in the works of many African-American writers. They are certainly not obvious in Morrison's novels which are evolutionary, circular, repetitive, contradictory and ambiguous, with characters whose histories are generally revealed in fragments from a variety of sources.

A brief summary of the structure of Morrison's second novel, *Sula* (1973), will further illustrate some features of her work which might appear unusual to a reader familiar only with Euro-American literature. The novel, which focuses on the friendship between two black women, is divided into two parts. In the first part, Sula and Nel become childhood friends in a black community and together become involved in the death of a young boy; in the second part, Sula returns to the community as an adult after a ten-year absence which is never satisfactorily explained. Each part in a number of ways is an inverse mirror image of the other. Characters introduced and developed in part one are reintroduced in reverse order in the second part, and the novel opens and closes with an act of memory. There are ten chapters, each located in a specific year, 1919, 1920, 1921, 1922, 1927, 1937, 1939, 1940, 1941, 1965 and, from even a cursory glance at this span of years, it is quite clear that the novel is fragmentary and elliptical. Indeed, the centre of the novel is a blank, a missing decade when the reader knows very little of what happened to Sula. There are other examples of lacunae in the novel, too, such as the sudden departure of Eva, Sula's grandmother, in 1921. Ostensibly leaving all her children with a friend for a day, she returned eighteen months later with no plausible explanation for her amputated leg.

Before pursuing our commentary on the organization of events and time in narrative, we would like you to undertake a preparatory writing activity.

Writing Activity 2

At this stage, we would like you to have experience of experimenting with time in your writing.

Obtain a picture of a landscape. Think about it in the past and the future. What aspect of it would have changed? Write an account in any form you wish of the impact of some of those changes from the point of view of a person living in the landscape, an animal or even an inanimate object. In your account try to experiment with time by moving between the past, present and future.

Flashback and Anticipation

The discrepancies in the relating of time between the *histoire* and the *récit*, between the story and the narrative, Genette called *anachronies*. The two main types of discrepancy, or *anachronies*, you will already be familiar with from the cinema:

1. 'flashback' or 'retrospection'

2. 'foreshadowing' or 'anticipation'.

In order to make a distinction between these techniques as they are employed in verbal as opposed to visual narratives, Genette called them 'analepsis' and 'prolepsis' respectively.

An analepsis is a narration of a story event at a point in the narrative after later events have been narrated. The narrative literally returns to an earlier event. An analepsis may provide additional information about an event occurring or a character involved at the point of the narrative when the analepsis is introduced. However, more unusually, it may provide information about events and characters from another part of the narrative.

A prolepsis is the narration of an event at a point in the narrative before earlier events have been narrated. However, the process of foreshadowing can be subtler than this. An example of a prolepsis occurs, for example, at the beginning of Nathaniel Hawthorne's *The Blithedale Romance*, a nineteenth-century American novel in which Zenobia's death, which ends the promise of her young life is anticipated by the way a cold wind kills the spring buds. The cold wind, then, is an example of prolepsis. Foreshadowing is a more common form of prolepsis than the actual narration of an event 'from the future'.

We normally read a narrative in order to discover what will happen next. A prolepsis changes our motivation in reading to 'how did it happen?' In the film *Woman in Red* we know that the main character is going to end up on a window ledge. The whole film is about how he got there. In a sense the prolepsis turns most of the film into an analepsis. The prolepsis narrates a future for the viewer which is a past for the main character. In literature, narratives which involve prolepsis are normally first person narratives. From the outset, they project us into what is the future to us as readers.

Critical Activity 3
Before reading further, we would like you to brainstorm the different techniques by which an analepsis, or flashback, may be introduced or stimulated.

Discussion

There are many techniques which may be used, and your own list may have included: direct reporting by the narrator or a memory stimulated by a conversation, by monologue, by dialogue between characters, by the discovery of letters or an old newspaper, through old photographs, through revisiting a location, through an old familiar smell such as perfume, through discovering an old object, by the introduction of characters from the past, and so on.

Duration

In addition to determining the order of events, a writer has to decide how much time to spend on each of them. This is a difficult issue because the only norm at which we can arrive is one where the time that the events might take in hours and minutes equals the time it takes to read the narration. But this is an impossible equivalence to measure because every reader reads at a different speed.

Changing the emphasis which is placed upon particular events invariably alters the pace of the narrative. There are also times when it may be desirable for effect to try and equate the actual time it would take to do something with the time it takes to narrate it and for most readers to read about it. In Toni Morrison's novel *Tar Baby* (1981), for example, one of the leading characters, Jadine, stands naked while an older woman from the village where she is staying runs her eyes down her. The time it takes for the narrative to relate this event is roughly equal to the time it would take to happen. In this way the text emphasizes Jadine's embarrassment and we can probably think of a number of narrative situations where this would be a desirable technique to employ. However, there are often occasions when we wish to summarize in the narrative something that would take much longer to occur in practice. For example, we might want to summarize a whole year of someone's life in a few sentences.

Genette called the two extremes of duration which we have described 'scene' and 'summary'. In 'scene', story-duration and text-duration are as nearly as possible identical. In fact, Genette points out that the closest correlation between story-duration and text-duration is in dialogue. In 'summary', a given story-period is condensed into a relatively, or sometimes very, short statement of its main features. In summary narrative, the pace of the narrative is accelerated, while in scene narrative it is slowed down.

Genette's model of time and duration in narrative is important, also, for its identification of 'ellipsis'. As we said in our discussion of Toni Morrison's *Sula,* where the centre of the book is a lacuna – the ten years during which Sula is away and about which we learn little – the gaps and omissions are as important as what is included. In Morrison's novels, the omissions often undermine the different versions of events which we are offered, suggesting that so-called 'truths' – accepted narratives and conventional histories – are not necessarily to be trusted.

The next writing exercise is designed to provide you with an opportunity to undertake a fairly substantial piece of writing which requires careful handling of the organization of cardinal functions and of time and duration.

Writing Activity 3

Before reading the next section, try to write part of a short story or of a chapter of a novel concerned with the psychological, spiritual, moral and/or sexual development of a young person.

If you find difficulty in starting, try to focus on a month or a year in a character's life. Think of possible key events that might have happened in that month or year.

The following critical and research activities are designed to introduce a further discussion of the organization of cardinal functions and of time and duration in narratives concerned with the psychological development of a central character.

Critical Activity 4

Before you read further we recommend that you take a few moments to reflect on the way you have structured your piece in Writing Activity 3. How many hinge-events have you included? Why did you select these? What is the ratio of hinge-events to more generalized comment? Is your extract confined to a single phase in your subject's life, a day, a week, a year? Or have you spanned several years? If you tried to cover a period as long as a year or more, did you have any reservations about the amount of time you were omitting from your subject's life?

Research Activity 2
Obtain a copy of D.H. Lawrence's *Sons and Lovers*, a novel to which we referred in chapter 2, and examine the way in which Lawrence has structured his chapters. In particular, read chapter 4 of the novel and examine how the account of Paul's destruction of Annie's doll is structured.

Discussion

As in your piece of writing, Lawrence is not concerned with events for their own sake but with their emotional significance. The focus of his text, too, is upon the spiritual and psychological development of a character. You probably noticed that he moves freely over a sweeping period of time and from general summary to particular scenes in Paul's life, selected because of their importance to Paul's psychological development. For example, Paul's breaking of Annie's favourite doll and subsequent burning of it as a sacrifice anticipates the way in which he responds later to his lovers. Guilty over destroying the doll, Paul cannot confront his guilt or accept his responsibility for the accident. As later in the novel, his sadism is an indicator of his selfishness and egocentricity.

How does Lawrence manage to move between generalized summary and particular scenes without leaving the reader confused? The account of the destruction of Annie's doll illustrates one of Lawrence's techniques. Imagine that the specific scene in which Lawrence focuses on the destruction of the doll is the centre of a dart board. Each ring which takes us from the outer circumference of the board to its centre contains an increasing amount of specific detail amidst the generalized comment.

The account of the destruction of the doll is preceded by general comments about Paul's relationship with Annie. For example, 'And always Paul flew beside her'; 'But his sister adored him. He always seemed to care for things if she wanted him to'. These are the outer rings which contain very little specific detail. The opening sentence of the paragraph where we find ourselves at a particular moment in time, at the point when the doll is destroyed, is one of the rings near the centre of the board. It introduces the doll as a specific feature: 'She had a big doll of which she was fearfully proud, though not so fond'. It prepares us for the transition to the specific scene, the centre of the board. The scene itself is introduced with a sentence which we may regard as the ring nearest the centre of the dartboard: 'So she laid the doll on the sofa...'.

Moreover, the technique of justifying discussion of a specific incident in the middle of a more generalized piece of writing through emphasizing its lingering effect on Paul is one which Lawrence employs frequently in this chapter. A swollen black eye which Paul's father gives his mother is included in the narrative because it is so indelibly etched on his memory.

After the account of the incident involving the doll, the text describes Paul's attitude towards his father. There does appear to be a rather sharp transition here, but it is commensurate with the selective nature of the chapter as a whole. His attitude is integrated by the association of his hatred of the doll with the hatred of his father: 'All the children, but particularly Paul, were peculiarly *against* their father, along with their mother'. This sort of association is typical of the way in which our memories work and makes the leaps backwards and forwards in time in the writing appropriate.

Another technique which Lawrence uses is to move incrementally from one time scale to another. For example, a paragraph beginning 'They [the Morels] were very poor that autumn' is followed by another that begins 'He [William] was coming at Christmas for five days' and then by one that opens 'Everybody was mad with excitement'.

Lawrence, then, uses a number of techniques to ensure that his experiments with time, duration and organization produce a coherent narrative. Of these, the most important is the way in which the selection of key events appears to mirror the workings of our memories, events which are remembered most vividly being those which made the most profound emotional impact. There is a gradual and carefully structured transition between the use of summary and the use of scenes, especially scenic dialogue; and the narrative point of view directs the reader to parallels between patterns of behaviour in different episodes.

Critical Activity 5

Before reading further we recommend that you review your own piece of writing. Consider the subtlety, or lack of it, of the ways in which you have moved from general comment to specific events. Have you developed the psychological significance of the events which you have selected as far as you might have done? In order to do so, do you need to reduce the number of events which you have selected? Have you put too much weight on some of your events at the expense of others?

In our discussion of Lawrence's *Sons and Lovers*, we touched upon the third of the important areas of decision making for a writer which we listed at the outset of chapter 3: the point of view from which events are narrated. This topic is pursued in the next chapter.

Further Reading

Chatman, S. (1978) *Story and Discourse: Narrative Structure in Fiction and Film*. Ithaca and London: Cornell University Press.

A sophisticated and detailed exposition of the issues involved in narrative, synthesizing the work of a range of European critics such as Genette, Barthes and Todorov. Recommended for tutors.

Tambling, J. (1991) *Narrative and Ideology*. Milton Keynes: Open University Press. Chapters 5 and 7.

A highly accessible account of the ideological implications underlying the structuring of plot and the organization of time in narrative. Particularly useful in the way it is written for the independent reader.

Chapter Five
Point of View/Focalization

In this chapter you will find sections on:

1. Genette's theory of focalization

2. Distinguishing between focalization of the narrator and a character

3. Unreliable narrators

4. Persona poetry.

Activities

You will be asked to undertake the following activities:

1. Critical activities concerned with:

   - focalization in a passage from *Sons and Lovers*
   - Lawrence's use of narrative detail
   - focalization in a piece of your own writing
   - extracts from texts with unreliable narrators
   - the use of persona in poetry.

2. Writing activities. You are asked to:

   - rewrite a passage from *Sons and Lovers* to fulfil specific objectives;
   - narrate a real or fictitious episode in your life from the point of view of an unreliable narrator;
   - in a form of your choice, as an unreliable narrator defend a morally dubious action in which you have been involved;
   - write a poem about a historical or family event from the point of view of the participant;
   - write a poem or dramatic monologue from the point of view and in the voice of a child.

Defining Point of View/Focalization

Apart from the ordering of events, a key issue which a writer has to consider is the point of view from which the events are narrated. Here it is important to understand the distinction between the point of view of a narrative and narrative voice(s). The point of view is the perspective in terms of which an expression is made. It is usually the practical life orientation, the ideological situation or sometimes even the physical place in relation to which narrative events stand. The narrative voice is the speech or other covert means through which events are communicated to the audience.

Many potential writers and students of literature assume that the point of view of the narrator and the point of view of the character in the text from whose perspective the events are seen are synonymous. While this is often the case, it is not necessarily so. Realizing this can help us to become more sophisticated writers and critics. Events may be presented by the narrator and recounted by him or her in the first person. Or the point of view may be assigned to a character who is not the narrator. Or events many be presented in such a way that it is not clear who is presenting them!

A story is presented, then, through a perspective. The French critic, Genette (1972), called this mediation 'focalization'. Unfortunately many of the terms available to describe point of view, such as perspective, focalization and point of view itself have optical-photographic connotations. There is a danger that we might associate point of view with seeing in the purely visual sense, but our point of view, as we have tried to illustrate throughout this book, will be determined by ideological, cognitive and emotional factors.

Rimmon-Kenan (1983) suggests that focalization is a more useful term than point of view because it allows for the fact that characters may be expressing views other than their own. In such a situation, speaking (narrating) and point of view (focalization) are not attributable to the same agent. However, Rimmon-Kenan does not sufficiently allow for the fact that in a case such as this, although the focalization may not be entirely attributable to the character who is speaking, it is mediated by the character's prejudices, preconceptions and bias.

Critical Activity I

Read the following description of Clara from *Sons and Lovers*. What evidence is there that we are seeing Clara from Paul's focalization? If you know the novel well enough, you may like to consider the range of factors and prior experiences that are determining Paul's view of Clara.

> Clara's hat lay on the grass not far off. She was kneeling, bending forward still to smell the flowers. Her neck gave him a sharp pang, such a beautiful thing, yet not proud of itself just now. Her breasts swung slightly in her blouse. The arching curve of her back was beautiful and strong; she wore no stays. Suddenly, without knowing, he was scattering a handful of cowslips over her hair and neck... (Chapter 9)

Discussion

This is a physical, even erotic, description of Clara which provides insight into her character – she is independent and physically aware. We know this from the detail that 'she wore no stays'. But mainly the passage presents Clara from Paul's point of view, in contrast to his view of Miriam, with whom he is also involved. The way in which the chain of associations has been constructed suggests that Paul has been aroused by Clara's body. He sees the individual parts of her – her neck, her breasts, her back – in the way in which people who are so aroused by another do tend to concentrate upon parts of their body. The word 'beautiful' is repeated. It is a strong word which suggests her physical presence; the word 'pretty' would not have the same effect because it suggests a coyness which the independently-minded Clara does not have. The repetition conveys the intensity of Paul's arousal, leading us to Paul's abandonment of all sense of reserve in the last line. But, as a piece of erotic writing, this passage can only be understood in terms of the intellectual and literary traditions to which it conforms and the associations which certain details evoke.

Critical Activity 2
As preparation for the writing activity based on this extract from *Sons and Lovers*, and to help you remember the key points we made in chapter 2 concerning language and meaning, we would like you to undertake the following critical activity.

Either individually or as a member of a group, reread the above extract and examine the associations which are employed to create the eroticism of the passage. What connotations are relied upon to enhance the sensuous quality of the language?

Discussion

Your suggestions probably included the flowers. Their smell and the specifically mentioned cowslips are a metonym of summer, in other words a feature of summer which stands for summer itself. In English literature, summer is a season which we associate with sexual fulfilment or the young love of spring coming to maturity, while autumn and winter are associated with death. In English poetry, and Lawrence as a poet and novelist wrote rather poetic prose, there is a strong traditional correlation between human emotion and nature. Although there is not a specific example in this extract, the European tradition of 'pathetic fallacy', a term invented by the nineteenth-century writer, John Ruskin, to describe the way writers attribute human feelings to natural objects, undoubtedly informs the use of landscape to create the mood of the passage.

There is also evidence of a further European intellectual and literary tradition: nature signifies freedom and release in opposition to the city and the town which are associated with civilization but also with restraint, confinement and inhibition. Clara, leaning forward to smell the flowers, is identified with nature and with freedom, her breasts are swinging inside her blouse and she wears no stays. Paul's scattering of flowers is no ideologically innocent gesture for flowers are traditional images of women's genitalia.

The passage also conforms to a culturally specific Western view of gender relations; Clara as the female is observed by the male, turned by his gaze into an aestheticized object. It is Paul who moves to initiate the passion between them while Clara, as female, is the passive recipient of his advances. In Western art, the female is representative of an idealist aesthetic of wholeness, yet at the same time is often depicted fragmentarily as here. While Paul's attention to the fragmented parts of Clara's body – her neck, breasts and back – may conform to the behaviour of someone who is sexually aroused, it also evokes a particular cultural tradition of representing women in which the power of each part lies in its signification of the whole body. In this tradition of representation, for example in European erotic art, the spectator is placed in the position of wanting to complete the idealized form which each fragmented part of the body signifies.

Writing Activity I

Rewrite the above passage from *Sons and Lovers* in response to the following exercises.

If you are working as a member of a group, share the different versions which you have written. Try to account for the changes which each of you have made.

1. Retaining Paul's point of view, rewrite the passage to connote either his fear of Clara or his inability to interest her in him.

2. Reverse the gender of the narrative point of view. Write a passage which describes Clara's observation of Paul, retaining the sexualized/erotic tone of the passage.

3. Imagine that this passage was an account of a relationship between two people in Africa. Make the changes which would be necessary for it to be convincing.

Discussion

You probably found that the exercises became more demanding. We are all familiar with being afraid of someone whom we desire in case they reject us or we make a fool of ourselves. We have all desired people who do not show the same interest in us. However, we do not all try to think about situations from our own gendered or racial perspectives.

In response to exercise 2, you probably found it was insufficient simply to change the names and that there were further anomalies such as the sexualized anatomical features. You may have tried substituting 'chests' for breasts', but did you find that the passage then retained the same degree of eroticism? What did your adaptations tell you about our cultural views of gender and sexuality?

Merely changing the names was equally inadequate in response to exercise 3. The environmental imagery would be totally inappropriate for a story set in Africa.

You probably found this the hardest of the exercises because you needed to have some knowledge of an African landscape and of the associations which its flora and fauna carry. You probably realized, too, that you needed to know more about the gendered nature of relationships in the various countries of Africa. Are the intellectual and cultural traditions which we identified above pertinent to relationships between, say, Nigerian men and women or are there other traditions of which we need to have knowledge?

The purpose of the above exercises was to provide you with practice in relating narratives from particular points of view. We also hoped to make you aware of how much is involved in pursuing particular perspectives, how point of view is culturally determined and how much thought, care and research are required. The choice of a narrative point of view is not to be made lightly and we need to think through what will be required to sustain it. We should also be aware of how points of view emanating from our own gendered, racialized and class perspectives, however self-critical we may be, are the products of culturally specific intellectual and creative traditions.

Point of View and the Narrator

As we said above, there are many novels in which the point of view of the narrator is not the same as that of the character from whose perspective the events are seen. In *Sons and Lovers*, the events are clearly seen from the perspective of Paul Morel; indeed, his name was to have been the original title of the novel. One consequence of this is that the other characters are marginal to Paul and only seen through his eyes. This is especially true of his first girlfriend, Miriam, but it is true of the others as well. If you already know the novel or have had time to read some of it, you might think about how the depicted events, especially those involving Miriam, might be recounted differently from her perspective. If you have not read the entire book, read chapter 9, 'Defeat of Miriam'.

In first-person retrospective narratives, focalization and narration are separated. Thus, the difference between the perspectives of the narrator and the character in the text from whose point of view the events are told is especially pronounced in *Great Expectations*. The story is narrated by Pip as an adult who is looking back on himself as a child. He is sometimes overtly critical of his younger self. When Pip discovers after his encounter with the convict in the churchyard that he has an anonymous benefactor and is to go to London, his attitudes towards his home, his brother-in-law and good friend, Joe, and towards his girlfriend, Biddy, change. He becomes snobbish and patronizing, as the older Pip with hindsight realizes: 'After that we went in to supper, the place and the meal would have a more homely look than ever, and I would feel more ashamed of home than ever, in my own ungracious breast' (chapter 14).

Such criticism by an older narrator of his or her younger self is not unusual. You may have employed such a device in your own narrative charting a young person's development. If you did not, you may like to think of how you could have done so. It is an approach which has a number of difficulties that in turn reflect the complex nature of the relationship between the perspectives of the narrator and the key character from whose point of view events are narrated. If the younger self is someone of whom the adult narrator is over-critical then he or she may not attract sufficient sympathy or interest from the reader. In a character like the younger Pip, Dickens risked creating a figure so snobbish and pretentious that no reader would be interested in what happens to him. If the adult narrator is over-critical of his younger self then the reader may wonder how the one eventually grew into the other and the whole narrative might become unbelievable.

Before reading further, you may like to pause for a moment and consider how you might resist these problems.

Dickens avoided them in *Great Expectations* by including evidence that the young Pip was capable of more sympathetic behaviour than his snobbishness suggests. For example, his decision to help the convict, Magwitch, despite his moral and social revulsion; his refusal to blame Miss Havisham when he finds out that she is not his benefactor; his early secret determination to help Herbert with his career; and, of course, his appreciation of Herbert's innate goodness. Thus it becomes plausible that the young Pip grows up into the self-critical and generous adult who narrates the story. Pip is also seen as only partly responsible for what happens to him. While the older Pip does not make excuses for his younger self (a further feature which endears him to the reader) it is also clear from the text that in some respects he is a victim. Many of the events in which he becomes involved are initiated by others – for example, by Magwitch, Miss Havisham and Jaggers – and accelerate the destruction of his relationship with others such as Biddy and Joe. In some respects Pip is an unwitting victim.

When we read third person narratives, we tend to draw conclusions about the point of view of the narrative which we then assign to the author. As we intimated earlier, it is still quite common for students to write not about what is in *Great Expectations*, for example, but about what 'Dickens believes' or what 'Dickens says'. In fact, what we construct from a text is not the presence of the author but of an implied author. Even though an author chooses not to narrate his or her story through a narrator such as the adult Pip, it does not mean that in writing he or she has not invented a kind of persona. The force which structures, controls and organizes a narrative and establishes its norms is not necessarily the author but the author's second self.

Unreliable Narrators

Where there is a striking divergence between the views and values of the narrative and those of a narrator we encounter what the scholar Wayne Booth (1961) has called 'an unreliable narrator'. In such a situation, the norms of the work conflict with the narrator's presentation of events. We come to mistrust what the narrator says and doubt his or her competence to relate the story.

David Lodge (1981) has suggested that there is no such thing as an objective, reliable narrator since any presentation of any event will always imply an attitude towards it. Perhaps we should talk not in terms of reliability but degrees of unreliability!

Often it is something that the narrator says that initially causes us to doubt his or her capacity to give us a true version of events. In Toni Morrison's *Jazz* (1992), concerned with Harlem in the 1920s, the narrator admits:

> I lived a long time, maybe too much, in my own mind. People say I should come out more. Mix. I agree that I close off in places, but if you have been left standing, as I have, while your partner overstays at another appointment, or promises to give you exclusive attention after supper, but is falling asleep just as you have begun to speak – well, it can make you inhospitable if you aren't careful, the last thing I want to be.

A number of things she says may alarm us in a narrator: she has lived too long in her own mind and tends to 'close off in places'. In the course of the novel the narrator, who regularly intrudes into the story, undergoes a certain amount of change. Her perspective on events similarly changes. This adds a further and complicating dimension to the book which we may not fully grasp on a first reading.

The unreliability of the narrator of F. Scott Fitzgerald's *The Great Gatsby*, published in America in 1926, is equally important. The novel is concerned with an almost legendary socialite, Jay Gatsby, known as the Great Gatsby. He is a mysterious figure who lives life on such a grand scale that he seems to embody the very nature of the American Dream. He appears to be a person with no background and with no family history although rumours abound whereby he is related to one of the royal families of Europe and has been a German spy. His parties, at which few people are able to recognize him because of his reclusive lifestyle, are lavish affairs but there is also something seedy, tragic and even pathetic about him. Eventually, the text suggests that his wealth probably comes from bootlegging. The lives of his friends appear increasingly shallow and superficial. He himself is in love with one woman whom he has dreamed about for four years and to impressing whom he has dedicated much of this time.

The novel depends upon a narrator who can see through Gatsby, up to a point, but can still be seduced by him. Nick Carraway is able to keep alive the appeal, myth and enigma of Gatsby even though the narrative point of view makes us increasingly sceptical about him. As preparation for this role, Nick is established in the opening pages of the novel as a person who is 'inclined to reserve all judgements'. Indeed, we are soon presented with an example of this in his account of his grandfather who sent a substitute to fight for him in the American Civil War while he developed a wholesale hardware business, presumably when there was much demand but little competition. On the morality of this, Nick, proud of his ancestral line, is noticeably mute.

Writing Activity 2

Choose an event with which you are familiar, perhaps from your own life. You could choose one of the events you included in your account of a young person's development. Narrate it in about 1000 words from the point of view of an unreliable narrator.

Critical Activity 3

If you are working through this section on your own, read the account by the unreliable narrator which you have written and make a list of the ways in which the reader may be led to suspect that the narrator is not to be trusted.

Should you be working with others, exchange stories and make a list, from the story you have been given, of the ways in which you have been led to suspect that the narrator is unreliable.

Discussion

As Rimmon-Kenan (1983) has observed, we may, generally speaking, suspect a narrator's rendering of a story on three counts.

Firstly, the narrator may have an obviously limited knowledge of what she or he is describing. We might suspect a very young narrator or a narrator who is an idiot, as in *The Sound and the Fury* by the American novelist, William Faulkner. Narrators whose perceptions are affected by drugs, illness or even undergoing torture are more extreme examples of unreliability.

Secondly, the narrator may be too involved in what is being described to provide a reliable account. We would mistrust a version of someone by their jilted lover or even an account of someone by a person head-over-heels in love with them.

Thirdly, as in the case of Nick Carraway, we may suspect what a narrator tells us because of his or her sense of values. These might be indicated by contradictions between the narrator's views and the implied author's views, between the outcome of events and what the narrator purports, and between the narrator's views and those held by many of the characters.

Critical Activity 4

Read the following extracts from works employing an unreliable narrator. Either individually or in discussion with others, identify the source of the unreliability in each case and make a list of the ways in which the unreliability of the narrator has been exploited in terms of language, content and style.

Extract A

She ran and bought her ticket and got back on the goddam carousel just in time. Then she walked all the way around it till she got her own horse back. Then she got on it. She waved to me and I waved back.

Boy, it began to rain like a bastard. In *buckets,* I swear to God. All the parents and mothers and everybody went over and stood right under the roof of the carousel, so they wouldn't get soaked to the skin or anything, but I stuck around on the bench for quite a while. I got pretty soaking wet, especially my neck and my pants. My hunting hat really gave me quite a lot of protection, in a way, but I got soaked anyway. I didn't care, though. I felt so damn happy all of a sudden, the way old Phoebe kept going round and round. I was damn near bawling, I felt so damn happy, if you want to know the truth. I don't know why. It was just that she looked so damn *nice,* the way she kept going round and round, in her blue coat and all. God, I wish you could've been there.

Extract B

'Say hey!' he said with his dopey smile, which smile I tried to overlook the whole time I dated him. It was a smile in excess of any possible stimulus. In fact, now that I think about it, Joe Bob's smile was usually unrelated to external stimuli and generally appeared at the most unlikely or inappropriate times. This smile (I dwell on it so obsessively because, like Mona Lisa's, it embodied his very essence) contorted his entire face. Most people smile from their noses downward. But not Joe Bob. His smile narrowed his eyes to slits, raised his cheekbones to temple level, wrinkled his forehead, and lifted his crew cut. And in spite of the exaggerated width of the smile, his lips never parted, probably because of his omnipresent wad of Juicy Fruit gum, which he minced daintily with his front teeth. In short, Joe Bob's smile was demented. But I managed to overlook this fact almost until the day I left him because I wasn't remotely interested in the state of his mind.

Extract C

[This extract is taken from the author's preface to a novel.]
The author is here supposed to be writing her own history, and in the very beginning of her account she gives the reasons why she thinks fit to conceal her true name...It is true that the original story is put into new words, and the style of the famous lady we here speak of is a little altered; particularly she is made to tell her own tale in modester words than she told it at first, the copy which came first to hand having been written in language more like one still in Newgate than one grown penitent and humble, as she afterwards pretends to be...

The pen employed in finishing her story, and making it what you now see it to be, has had no little difficulty to put it into a dress fit to be seen, and to make it speak language fit to be read. When a woman debauched from her youth, nay, even being the offspring of debauchery and vice comes to give an account of all her vicious practices, and even to descend to the particular occasions and circumstances by which she first became wicked, and of all the progressions of crime...an author must be hard put to wrap it up so clean as not to give room, especially for vicious readers, to turn it to his disadvantage.

...It is suggested that there cannot be the same life, the same brightness and beauty, in relating the penitent part as in the criminal part. If there is any truth in that suggestion, I must be allowed to say, 'tis because there is not the same taste and relish in the reading; and indeed it is too true to say that the difference lies not in the real worth of the subject so much as in the gust and palate of the reader.

...There is in this story abundance of delightful incidents, and all of them usefully applied. There is an agreeable turn artfully given them in the relating, that naturally instructs the reader, either one way or another.

Discussion

Each of these extracts provides a different type of, and a different means of indicating, unreliability. With reference to the first extract, your deliberations probably included a discussion of the difference between the narrator's reaction to the rain and that of those around him. On his own admission, the rain storm is particularly heavy but, at another level, he seems oblivious to it. His inactivity is emphasized by the contrast between his over-excited description of the rain and his understated account of his own behaviour, 'I stuck around on the bench for quite a while'. The behaviour of the others is described as if they occupy a different universe from him. His preoccupation, even fixation, with Phoebe emphasizes the dislocation between his inner self and the world outside. Phoebe going round and round on the carousel provokes an extreme response from him which perpetuates his alienation from the rain and also serves, through the continuous circular movement, to underscore his solipsism, his self-absorption.

You may not be surprised to discover that in the next and final chapter of the book the narrator describes how he became ill and underwent psychoanalysis. The extract is from J.D. Salinger's *The Catcher in the Rye* (1951), chapter 25, an American novel in which the narrator is unreliable on account of his youth and, as we discover at the end of the novel, because of his developing illness.

In considering the second extract your discussions probably focused upon the language, particularly the hyperbolic, acerbic wit. The attention given to Joe Bob's smile is somewhat excessive and tells us more about the narrator's loathing of him than about Joe himself. We doubt her reliability because of the contradiction between her self-awareness on the one hand and her failure to check her obsession. The extract provides us with a clue as to the nature of the narrator's unreliability. Joe's smile is said not to be related to any external stimuli: ultimately her account of him, too, becomes detached from its external referent. You probably picked out the particularly devastating comments, 'raised his cheekbones to temple level', 'his omnipresent wad of Juicy Fruit gum', 'minced daintily' and 'demented'.

The second extract is from another American novel, Lisa Alther's *Kinflicks* (1975), chapter 3. The narrator, Ginny Babcock, as you probably suspected, is transferring her guilt over her behaviour as a young woman to Joe Bob – instead of admitting that she behaved foolishly as well – so that Joe becomes even more obnoxious in her account of him than he actually was.

The third extract presents us with an even more challenging example of unreliability. You probably realized that this extract is not from a twentieth-century novel. It is from the Author's Preface to an eighteenth-century text, Daniel Defoe's *Moll Flanders* (1772). Here the author has invented a second author who addresses the reader in the preface and who has supposedly ghost-written, to use a modern expression, a narrative provided by a woman, Moll Flanders. As you no doubt deduced from the above extract, she has lived a rather colourful life. Since the second author has reworked the narrative to his own ends, any evidence of unreliability which we find in the preface will affect our reading of the entire book.

In the first extract, we found ourselves questioning the behaviour of the narrator; in the second extract, the obsessive interest in a single physical feature and the hyperbolic language caused us to question the narrator and her involvement with what she was describing; in the third extract, our suspicions must be aroused by the self-contradictions and the elisions in the evasive way these are negotiated. You probably noticed that in the first paragraph the author says the text is 'a little altered' but in the second paragraph implies that he has had to work extremely hard at altering it. While, at one point, the lascivious events in Moll's life are said to be such that they cannot be presented, at another point it is admitted that 'there cannot be the same life, the same brightness and beauty' in describing the penitent part of her life as in describing these. It is difficult to determine to what extent the story has been cleaned up. Moreover, the supposed author is contradictory about his own attitude, apparently wishing to sanitize Moll's story but, in virtually the next breath, recommending that 'there is in this story abundance of delightful incidents'.

The following exercises are designed to enable you to explore ways of using unreliable narrators in your own writing.

Writing Activity 3

Either individually or as a member of a group, think of a contemporary narrator who has to defend his or her actions. Write a short defence of these actions in the voice of the persona so as to suggest evidence of unreliability and the difficulty the character has in negotiating the moral implications of what he or she has done.

Think carefully about your choice of form and medium. You might, for example, choose a letter published in a newspaper, a preface to an autobiography, an extract from an address or a speech.

If you worked in a group, exchange and discuss your work with the other members. Notice the different ways in which each of you suggested unreliability and tried to elide the moral issues involved.

Writing Activity 4

At this point, we would like you to write a short account of an historical or family event from the perspective of an imagined participant, in the form of a poem.

Persona Poetry

You may have been surprised that we asked you to write a poem in the voice of an invented character or persona. We tend to think of the writer, and especially the poet, as the articulator of the writer's worldview. But many poets produce persona poems.

Critical Activity 5
We would like you to pause now and try to make a list of the creative advantages of looking at an event in a poem from a persona other than your own.

Discussion

A writer who habitually works in other personae risks being accused of writing about experiences with which he/she is not sufficiently familiar. Projecting oneself into the place of others is very difficult. But without the capacity at least to try to extend our sympathies imaginatively, we are morally the poorer. It is something we need to do quite frequently in our lives. For example, we try to imagine how a friend, a partner or a colleague is experiencing events in which we may not be directly involved.

Writing in a persona involves more than simply an extension of our sympathies. It also provides an opportunity for ironic detachment, as in the following poem, 'Dedicating the House of Art' (1993a), by Tony Curtis, an acclaimed poet from South Wales. Curtis's poem is written from the perspective of ordinary people in Munich in the 1930s. It is not intended as a crude device to beat the Germans but is an attempt to explore the nature of evil as an everyday event in ordinary people's lives. We can never really anticipate where a course of events will lead, so the poem disarmingly encompasses all of us. If, at this time, we were young and living in Germany, where only a few years previously unemployment had been high and inflation crippling, we might have welcomed a government that could get people back to work and restore national pride. With hindsight, much in the poem is deeply ironic; the faith in the future hopelessly misplaced.

Critical Activity 6
We would like you to read Curtis's poem in the light of this discussion. Try to notice as many features as you can which appear to be ironic with hindsight. Notice the subtlety with which Curtis negotiates the gap between enthusiasm for the present and the wisdom of hindsight. The latter is never allowed to swamp the poem; we are drawn into the sense of excitement and celebration, at times against our better judgement.

Dedicating the House of Art

For weeks we cleaned and dressed the town.
This was our festival, our moment.

A million hours of planning, sewing, embroidery.
We hammered nails into the night.

And all the important people came,
the trains were packed, there were
aeroplanes stitching the sky.

Our mayor and officials were lined in welcome.
This was a people saluting itself,
a new world of hope and possibility –
our Leader himself began as an artist,
a chicken farmer became chief of police.

The parade was hours long, following
the route of our great historical buildings
from the boulevard of the old Emperor
to the new House of Art.

Only the best were chosen –
the tallest with fair hair and features.
This was a Folk celebrating itself
as we wished to be. Knights on horseback,
foot soldiers with pikes and banners.
The tableaux of our women,
the warmth of our mothers, sisters and wives,
scenes of pastoral beauty in our land
pulled by oxen, great horses steaming in the sunshine.

Lifted on the shoulders of my father
I swayed to the music and the drum.
And our shouts, and our cheers.

The polished bronze of the sculptures,
the glistening paint of the canvases.
He proclaimed: We have cleansed
our art of the decadent, the modern,
the distortion of truth.

And each of those days, it seemed, was fine
without exception – blue skies, marshmallow clouds.
Such times, such fortune,
we would nod to each other and say,
Hitler days.

Discussion

The voice in this poem, like that in Dickens' *Great Expectations,* which we
discussed earlier, is of an adult looking back on childhood. The female narrator is

not primarily concerned with what she and her friends failed to see, though the worry is certainly there, but with the fun and exuberance of those years. Disturbingly, the poem asks why did we, the imaginary participants, not see what was really happening? Could we, the readers, make, indeed be making, a similar mistake?

There is a further disturbing dimension to this poem which the use of persona enables Curtis to explore. In later life, most of us look back to at least some aspects of our childhood and adolescence with affection. That period is often ingrained nostalgically in our memories, embarrassingly sometimes. How does one retain happy memories of being young in a period which, with hindsight, was the breeding ground for such terrible evil? As Curtis (1993b), *in persona*, says in an essay about this and some of his other persona poems:

> Yes, this was my youth, my formative years; we picnicked with mother and father in the woods towards Dachau. A military guard waved to us in a friendly way and his bike wobbled dangerously. We laughed and the sun always seemed to be shining. (p.31)

Curtis acquired the material for 'Dedicating the House of Art' from a television documentary where women who were girls in the 1930s talked enthusiastically about their early adolescent experiences.

The following exercise enables you to attempt a piece of writing of your own in the voice of a persona which requires a great deal of imagination and considerable skill in achieving an appropriate language. It also provides scope, should you wish, for irony. The exercise is intended, too, as a preparatory activity for the next chapter which takes up an issue which we touched on earlier, multiple voices in literature.

Writing Activity 5

Write a poem or dramatic monologue from the perspective of a child about his or her secret pleasures in life, about which the adults in the family know nothing. Try to achieve a voice appropriate to the age, education and background of the child you imagine.

Further Reading

Rimmon-Kenan, S. (1983) *Narrative Fiction: Contemporary Poetics*. London: Methuen. Chapter 6.

An accessible introduction to focalization as a textual factor relating to both story and narration. At the end of the chapter there is a hint of an argument to come in a future work which challenges Genettian theory, which advanced students may like to ponder.

Webster, R. (1990) *Studying Literary Theory: An Introduction*. London: Routledge. Chapter 3.

A very accessible account of the implications of Genette's work on focalization for modern criticism, but more schematic than Rimmon-Kenan (1983).

Chapter Six
Multiple Voices

In this chapter you will find sections on:

1. Conflict and differing opinions within groups

2. The concept of multiple voices within the novel as a literary form

3. Characters and multiple voices in the novel

4. Responding to conflict within communities, cultures and societies

5. Employing plausible voices and convincing dialogue

6. Dialogue in prose fiction and drama

7. Writing dialogue for radio

8. Accents and dialects.

Activities

You will be asked to undertake the following activities:

1. Critical activities concerned with:

   - differences within your community, family and society
   - differences in language and culture in Hardy's *Tess of the D'Urbervilles*
   - the use which novelists make of other modes of writing within their novels
   - conflict between individuals in communities
   - the story you wrote about the psychological, spiritual and moral development of a young person in chapter 4
   - the employment of different voices in Jackie Kay's *The Adoption Papers*
   - the functions of dialogue in prose fiction
   - the use of dialect in *Sons and Lovers* and in David Dabydeen's poem 'Nightmare'.

2. Writing activities. You are asked to:

- undertake a piece of writing based on your own research and fulfilling specific objectives designed to help you develop your handling of different voices;
- write brief but detailed biographies of three fictitious characters and invent a plausible conversation which takes place between them;
- write a narrative based on the many possible interpretations of a person's single statement;
- write the dialogue of a dramatic, anonymous and convincing telephone conversation;
- write a conversation in dialect.

3. Group activities:

- based on your research for the first writing activity in 2 above
- brainstorming the potential of radio as a medium.

Conflict and Differing Opinions within Groups

Like many writers, including probably yourself, Thomas Hardy recognized that we are primarily social beings. The self exists not in isolation but in society. In a few moments, we would like you to pause and consider the interaction between yourself and the society in which you live and work from a particular perspective. We would like you to think about your immediate home environment, your neighbourhood, the people with whom you come into regular contact, your town, city or village, your school and college environment. Although there may appear to be a consensus which holds your family together or bonds you with your group of friends, you will probably find there is also debate, contradiction and conflict.

Critical Activity I
Consider, possibly with others if you are working in a group, the different views, attitudes and conflicts which you have to negotiate in your family, your college or school, your place of work or with your friends as you go about your daily business.

Discussion

As you reflected on the above, you probably realized how critical you are of much that constitutes your daily life, without being estranged from it. Of course, there are people who constitute our immediate society with whom we are in conflict and from whom we do feel alienated. Yet it is also possible for us to have disagreements and to be in conflict with others without being alienated from them. You may be critical of some of the opinions of your friends or those with whom you work, or you may be in opposition at some level to members of your family.

You have been influenced and shaped by the various environments in which you exist. Some of these influences you may be aware of, while others may have affected you subconsciously. Some you may have consciously and willingly accepted, while others you may have resisted.

Bakhtin tried to find a single phrase to encompass the complex relationship we all have with the society in which we live. He sought to avoid the simplistic assumption that we are all solely the products of our environments and to allow for the fact that many of us are also critical of and resistant to the environments which have made us. He argued that the self and society exist in what he called a 'dialogic process'. In other words, the self exists in a complex social territory where much is always changing and where there is heterogeneity – diversity in class, ethnicity and social background – rather than homogeneity or social uniformity.

Novels invariably present their heroine or hero at odds with the world. They either suggest that society as a whole is generally acceptable and focus on the need for the heroine or hero to mature and adjust to it, or they admire the rebel for refusing to compromise. At this point, let us pause and consider the nature of the environment in which Tess lives at the opening of *Tess of the d'Urbervilles*.

Critical Activity 2

Read the following extract from the second chapter of Thomas Hardy's *Tess of the d'Urbervilles* (1891). The novel is about the daughter of a Blackmoor Vale villager, John Durbeyfield, who discovers from a parson that he is a descendant of an ancient and knightly family, the d'Urbervilles. Thinking of himself as Sir John d'Urberville, he immediately begins to assume airs and graces, eventually over-celebrating his new-found social status at the inn. What do you notice about the use of different voices and different types of language?

The forests have departed, but some old customs of their shades remain. Many, however, linger only in a metamorphosed or disguised form. The May-Day dance, for instance, was to be discerned on the afternoon under notice, in the guise of the club revel, or 'club-walking', as it was there called.

...They came round by The Pure Drop Inn, and were turning out of the high road to pass through a wicket-gate into the meadows, when one of the women said –

'The Lord-a-Lord! Why, Tess Durbeyfield, if there isn't thy father riding home in a carriage!'

A young member of the band turned her head at the exclamation. She was a fine and handsome girl – not handsomer than some others, possibly – but her mobile peony mouth and large innocent eyes added eloquence to colour and shape. She wore a red ribbon in her hair, and was the only one of the white company who could boast of such a pronounced adornment...Durbeyfield, leaning back, and with his eyes closed luxuriously, was waving his hand above his head, and singing in a slow recitative –

'I've-got-a-gr't-family-vault-at-Kingsbere – and knighted-forefathers-in-lead-coffins-there!'

> The clubbists tittered, except the girl called Tess – in whom a slow heat seemed to rise at the sense that her father was making himself foolish in their eyes.
>
> 'He's tired, that's all,' she said hastily, 'and he has got a lift home, because our own horse has to rest today.'

Discussion

It is impossible not to notice the variety of language in this extract. The divisions between characters are emphasized by the differences in the language they use, what Bakhtin called 'other tongueness'. The language registers used by the third person narrator, by Tess, by the villagers and by John Durbeyfield are different.

All of us have a working vocabulary which depends upon our age, education and linguistic sensitivity. Most of us are able to understand many more words than we commonly use. Moreover, we all have access to pockets of language, which we draw upon to a greater or lesser extent, which might consist of specialized/technical vocabulary, slang, dialect, or archaic vocabulary. Earlier, we said that the words of a language form what is called a 'paradigm' in the way in which clothes determined by the dictates of fashion form a wardrobe. There are paradigms of words appropriate to certain situations – for example, to a legal document, a love letter, a conversation with friends, visiting a relative in hospital. In the extract which you have just read, you will see that Hardy is drawing upon a number of pockets of language.

Many commentators on Hardy's work have drawn attention to his use of dialect to create convincing rustic characters. They have also drawn attention to his self-conscious preference for Latinate language rather than Anglo-Saxon vocabulary. For example, he has written 'diurnal' where 'daily' would have done, called a fork in the road 'bifurcation' and a sleepwalker a 'noctambulist'. In the extract above you may have felt that the use of 'metamorphosed' or 'discerned' was rather cumbersome. But there is more to Hardy's linguistic divisions than these observations suggest.

We have discussed in the previous chapter how all forms of writing involving a narrator free the author from a unitary and singular language. In writing *Great Expectations,* Dickens had to write with the language which Pip would use, bearing in mind, for example, his education (an anomaly in the novel, however, is that the narrator's command of English is better than his origins would suggest!), his experiences, and what he has learned, or not learned, from those experiences. The character of the adult Pip enables Dickens to develop a different voice from the one which he would have employed if the novel had been narrated in the third person.

Even when an author works in the third person, as is the case in *Tess of the d'Urbervilles,* where the author's voice seems at first glance to be singular, consistent and directed at an intention which a reader might discern, much of the language, as Bakhtin argued, is drawn into battle between different points of view and value judgements. These multi-registers are one of the characteristic features of the novel as a literary form which Bakhtin labelled 'heteroglossia'. Again, do not be put off by the term, the concept is a particularly exciting one for writers.

How is heteroglossia incorporated into a novel? Bakhtin identified a number of strategies in this respect, two of which are particularly important and easily appropriated, even by new writers. Firstly, as we observed earlier in our discussion of realism in chapter 1 and as you would have confirmed by looking at one of David Lodge's works, the novel is capable of incorporating a variety of modes of writing – for example, letters, diaries, inserted short stories, poems, lyrics, and dramatic scenes. Indeed, as we said, it is one of the ways in which the novel as a literary form establishes its realism.

Tess of the d'Urbervilles contains examples of a number of modes of writing including the texts of a number of letters written by characters in the novel – for example, the letter to Tess from her mother in chapter 31, Angel Clare's note from his father in chapter 34, and Tess's letter to her husband in chapter 48; quotations from Classical poets and from the Bible; and stories inserted into the text such as Dairyman Crick's anecdotes of unfortunate lovers.

Each of the modes of writing which it is possible for a writer to incorporate in the novel possesses its own verbal and semantic forms for assimilating various aspects of 'reality'. Including them in a novel allows the author to set up an interplay between conflicting opinions, different ways of using language and various ways of looking at the world. This has to be done with considerable tact and care. If you examine how Hardy incorporates quotations from a range of sources into *Tess of the D'Urbervilles* you may feel that he is not always successful. Critics are divided, for example, in their opinion of the stories which Dairyman Crick tells about love. As a commentary on Tess's own situation, they are so closely linked to what has happened in her life that they seem contrived. However, it could be argued in their defence that they are the kind of anecdotes which a countryman might relate in his daily work.

There are examples of narratives which consist of different voices without much or any reliance upon a third person narrator. William Faulkner's novel, *As I Lay Dying* (1930), recounts successive episodes in the death and burial of Addie Bundren, recounted by members of her family. Each chapter is headed by the name of the character who is relating the story at that particular moment. The reader tries to make judgements about each character from what they say, compared with other characters, and how they say it. This is a very difficult, but exciting, format in which to work. Not only has each voice to be distinct from the others, but, at any given moment, all the voices must be internally consistent with earlier and subsequent utterances.

You will also discover novels and short stories wholly based on modes of writing normally included in traditional novels as inserts. For example, Michael Carson's short story, 'Peter's Buddies', details, in letter form, an account of an enquiry into the whereabouts of the main character, Peter. The enquiry takes place as a series of chain letters which ends with a letter from Peter who has subsequently died of AIDS. The transmission of the letters mimics the transmission of the virus. Each letter passes on the same information, but is written by a different character who has had some acquaintance with Peter, albeit in a variety of different capacities and contexts. The teleological effect of the final letter – that is, the way in which we adjust our reading of the narrative with the hindsight of its conclusion – is to implicate all the people whom Peter has contacted with the continued transmission of the virus. The consequence of the different people and contexts through which the message passes is delayed in relaying the information that Peter has been diagnosed as having AIDS, a crucial factor which puts all his 'buddies' at risk.

Critical Activity 3

Employing a range of modes of writing in order to introduce a variety of voices into your work requires careful thought as to what the reader would be able to deduce from each mode of writing you incorporate.

Read the following letter from Hardy's *Tess of the D'Urbervilles*, chapter 31. In it Tess's mother, Joan, writes to her about Tess's impending marriage and illegitimate child and makes a passing reference to Tess's father's discovery that the family is descended from a noble ancestral line.

What does the letter tell us about Tess's mother?

> Dear Tess, – J [sic] write these few lines. Hoping they will find you well, as they leave me at Present, thank God for it. Dear Tess, we are all glad to Hear that you are going really to be married soon. But with respect to your question, Tess, J say between ourselves, quite private but very strong, that on no account do you say a word of your Bygone Trouble to him. J did not tell everything to your Father, he being so Proud on account of his Respectability, which, perhaps, your Intended is the same. Many a woman – some of the Highest in the Land – have had a Trouble in their time; and why should you Trumpet yours when others don't Trumpet theirs? No girl would be such a Fool, specially as it is so long ago ... Besides, you must bear in mind that, knowing it to be your Childish Nature to tell all that's in your heart – so simple! – J made you promise me never to let it out by Word or Deed, having your Welfare in my Mind; and you most solemnly did promise it going from this Door. J have not named either that Question or your coming marriage to your Father, as he would blab it everywhere, poor simple Man.
>
> Dear Tess, keep up your Spirits, and we mean to send you a Hogshead of Cyder for your Wedding, knowing there is not much in your parts, and thin Sour Stuff what there is. So no more at present, and with kind love to your Young man. – From your affectte. Mother,
>
> J. Durbeyfield

Discussion

Throughout the novel there is bleakness, but there are also counterpoints provided by examples of resilience and a variety of voices which give expression to the resourcefulness of people in the face of adversity. From her letter, you would have deduced that Joan Durbeyfield is not as well educated as her daughter. She is resilient but in an insensitive way. The birth of an illegitimate child, with which Tess finds it difficult to come to terms, is a passing accident to her. Notice the way in which it is referred to obliquely as 'a Trouble'. She has a down-to-earth attitude and a pragmatic readiness to try to put things into perspective, possibly derived from her own rather frugal struggles. There is obviously a close bond between her daughter and herself which excludes her husband. She would seem to have little respect for and no delusions about him. She does not mince her words and is candid about Tess's naïvety. The reference to cider betrays the importance of drink in her own life. While earlier in the novel Tess is more embarrassed by her father's drinking than anything else, Joan significantly makes no reference to this particular vice in him.

Characters and Heteroglossia

We tend to think that each person has their own voice and unique way of talking. You may like to pause for a moment and recreate the many different voices you carry around in your head from all the people with whom you associate. Often when we dream about people we know their voices are exaggerated and sometimes they reverberate in our minds after we have woken.

Although each of us has distinctive speech patterns, we have a variety of voices within us. For example, we have an authoritarian voice, a hurt voice, an angry way of speaking, a seductive voice, a calming and gentle voice.

Bakhtin identified the use of characters and their different voices as a means of incorporating and organizing heteroglossia in a novel. Each character's speech expresses its own belief system (or ideology) and constitutes another language for the author. Moreover, each character's way of viewing the world is also reflected in their action. Thus they have a sphere of influence in a novel which is broader than their actual words. This sphere of influence is extended through the way in which each character's individual fate is determined by particular discourses.

Tess, for example, reveals her own belief system through what she says and by the way in which she reacts to circumstances. A reader will form an opinion of Tess based on evidence from these sources. It would take into account how she is changed by experience in the course of the book and may emphasize her fatalism, which she has no doubt inherited from her mother, her courage and her passivity. Tess's own beliefs are brought into conflict with the views of those around her, such as the sign painter at the beginning of the novel. His signs, which condemn adultery, present the last vestiges of an evangelism through which Christianity had become a stern, uncompromising and unforgiving moral creed.

Tess's own fate, determined by further discourses, extends her influence in the novel in other ways. It is impossible to read any novel without reflecting on the fate of characters. It is perhaps less common to consider the discourses determining those fates. The pattern of Tess's life is a sad, if not pessimistic, one. Fluctuating between extremes of joy and despair, Tess never abandons her sense of the misery and transience of life. But it is structured in a way which is at times too ideologically determined. Not only does coincidence play too large a part in her life – the appearance of the painter of signs, Clare's meeting with Alec, the farmer at Flintcomb-Ash turning out to be familiar with Tantridge and hence Tess, and so forth – but her life seems to be predestined through, for example, her likeness to the family portraits in Wellbridge Mansion and her final discovery of happiness at, of all places, Stonehenge. The effect of these strategies is to articulate and drive home for the reader the wider implications of the story. Fulfilment seems only to be possible through suffering, while Tess herself demonstrates the ability of the human spirit to endure at the hands of complicated, indifferent and hostile social forces. Around these premises there are further intersecting discourses about the gendered nature of the plot, the fact that the character who suffers is a beautiful, generally passive, young woman. The titles of the 'phases' (rather than chapters) into which the novel is divided – 'The Maiden', 'Maiden No More' and 'The Woman Pays' – confirms these discourses while, through the suggestion of an analytical study rather than a work of fiction, legitimising it as objective method.

In some recent works, each voice appears to have the same status in the novel as other voices. Such works come from an intellectual milieu in which all ideas are perceived as socially constructed, that is as the products of particular, historically specific cultural contexts, rather than as universal truths. You may like to consider for a moment the ways in which, in Europe alone, so many of our ideas about, for example, gender relationships, religion, or the environment have changed from one social and historical context to another. In such circumstances, texts sometimes reflect their writers' reluctance to elevate any idea to the level of truth. But nineteenth and early twentieth-century novels are often organized in such a way that the reader is directed to give more priority to some voices than to others. For example, Estella is an important voice in *Great Expectations* but we are directed by the text to be critical of her; we see her through Pip's eyes, we encounter her after we have seen the way Biddy treats Pip and we see her in the context of Miss Havisham's influence and bitterness. Novels of the nineteenth and early twentieth centuries appear to be imbued with an unproblematic sense of their moral purpose and conviction which some contemporary writers are reluctant to share, writing far more sceptically and, some might say, cynically.

Preparatory Research Activity

Go out into a number of public environments such as a street, a town centre, a bus station, a pub, a disco, a cinema, a football crowd, and discreetly listen to people's conversations.

Using a notebook or a small cassette recorder to record your findings, collect snippets from at least ten different conversations. You should try to obtain as wide a range of dialects, idioms and idiolects as possible.

As you try to record pieces of the different conversations, observe the people who are talking. What can we learn about them from their clothes, their way of speaking, their mannerisms, and so on? How typical are they of the people who are around them? As you move to different locations, try to notice changes in the people. Are they generally older or younger? Are there more of one gender or of one age group than another? Are they generally of a different class? Are they dressed differently? For example, you will find many differences between people at the refreshments stall of the local market and those in the tea-room in a large department store.

If you find that you only have access to a limited number of public venues, return to the same ones at different times of day. For example, a café may have different types of people in it at mid-morning, compared with late afternoon when schools and colleges finish.

Writing Activity I

Choose one piece of information from your collection and write up the same incident, or statement, in a variety of different contexts. You could use some of the settings in which you gathered the conversational material.

Throughout this exercise, aim to develop a narrative which:

1. uses as many voices, and/or different registers as possible, drawing on the bank of examples you have collected;

2. is based on a misunderstanding that has arisen because a statement has been recontextualized, in other words removed from the context in which it originated to one that changes its meaning, or has been misunderstood.

You will need to think of different contexts in which the piece of information you have selected might occur and to consider carefully, perhaps in a discussion with your friends, how these different situations and environments might transform the original meaning. Or you may like to imagine your piece of information being passed on from different people in different contexts and becoming distorted. There is a well known, probably apocryphal, anecdote from the First World War of a message being sent down the trenches: 'Send reinforcements we are going to advance'. But by the time the message is received it has become: 'Send three [shillings] and fourpence we are going to a dance'. The changes to your piece of information might have consequences for the lives of some of the people involved in its transmission.

Discussion

Many writers, and not only novelists, glean valuable information from the people around them. The Welsh poet, Gillian Clarke, whose poem 'Swinging' we discussed in chapter 2, admitted in an interview with Susan Butler (1985):

> As I began to read Welsh poetry in translation, and then in the original language with the help of translations, and as I heard conversations mainly in Cardiganshire between Welsh people around me, between the farmers in the landscape which I regard very much as my landscape now – how else, what else would one be but influenced? The stories I heard the farmers tell were in Welsh, and they come into my poems in English. (p.196)

The form or style of speech is a common means of characterization and distinguishes a characters' language from that of the narrator. As you listened to the various conversations you probably noticed how speech may be indicative of age, gender, ethnic origin, social class, educational background, regional identity, or profession. Sometimes the speech of people who grew up in a particular milieu is characterized by its speech patterns or idiosyncrasies. For example, people who grew up in the 1960s may still use expressions fashionable at that time, such as calling each other 'man' as a gesture of camaraderie. In particular milieux, new words often enter a language – for example 'rave', which became part of English vocabulary in the 1960s meaning 'party' (rave-up) and was revived with a slightly different connotation in the 1980s, signifying a party held in a club or disused warehouse. The latter became known by the term 'acid house'. 'Reggae' entered the language in the late 1960s signifying a particular type of West Indian music. Other words have acquired new connotations, such as 'brilliant', 'evil', 'wicked' or 'wild', each of which in slightly different ways has become a complimentary expression in youth subculture. You may like to pause for a moment and consider how some of the differently aged people in your family, your college or your place of work use different expressions.

Group Activity I

Each of you select four snippets of conversation from those which you have collected and where you were able to observe the speakers; no more than a few sentences in each case.

Record each piece of conversation on to a cassette. Listen to each other's examples and try to draw conclusions about the age, background, ethnic origins and so on of the speaker.

Discuss among yourselves what made you come to your conclusions. How might this knowledge help you to write convincing dialogue and create convincing characters in the future?

This exercise should provide you with some valuable information for your notebooks.

Critical Activity 4

Reread the extract from *Tess of The d'Urbervilles* above (pp.109–10) in the light of what we have said about the heterogeneous nature of society. You have already noticed the way in which Hardy employs different voices. What evidence is there of conflict or potential conflict between individual 'belief systems' in this community?

Discussion

At one level, Tess and her fellow villagers are in conflict. As is clear from the way in which she speaks, Tess is different from them. But the linguistic difference emphasizes not only educational difference but Tess's disposition. Her advanced sexual maturity is revealed in the red ribbon that she wears as red is the colour of passion. Tess is set apart from the innocence of the others in the procession and from the introverted, secluded nature of the Vale of Blackmoor. Yet she is also part of that community.

We have a tendency to see community in idealized and holistic terms. Community in Hardy's work is often divided and contains considerable tensions. Even though the Vale of Blackmoor is a rather idyllic place, there is still more than a hint of tension here; possibly the villagers delight in using Tess's father's drunkenness to embarrass her because she is better educated than them, with different aspirations. The linguistic division underlines the social divisions. The conflict within Tess's family is betrayed in the way Durbeyfield's inflated dialect – inflated because of his new status – jars with Tess's own controlled and polished speech. Not only is her way of speaking different from his but her embarrassment is evident in the speed with which she makes an excuse, and an unconvincing one, for his behaviour.

Critical Activity 5

Read again the extract of a short story concerned with the psychological, moral, emotional and/or sexual development of a young person which we asked you to write in chapter 4. How far have you employed a variety of voices, each linguistically distinct and also different from each other in content? How far does the self which is at the heart of your story interact with others critically and in terms of conflict? What sense is there of people's identities being constructed in a territory and culture that is divided, changing and open to conflict?

Discussion

Now that you have re-read your story, you may feel that with the benefit of hindsight you have over-stressed the 'heteroglossia', the multiple and contradictory voices, of the milieu in which your narrative is set. Or, with hindsight, you might think that you could have made more of this. Whatever the case, you may now like to consider how far the different voices which populate the epoch in which you set your narrative – whether the present, the immediate past, some distant past, or the future – were influenced by your view of the society and time in which you live.

Whatever the period in which you placed your writing, you will no doubt have realized now, even if you were not aware of it at the time, that the different voices which you created are based on some of the different voices of your own environment. In other words, you have used the different voices in your story as filters for some of the voices around you. In that process of filtering, the heteroglossia – the multiple and contradictory voices – of *your* present has been organized by you in a particular way. On another occasion, at another period in your life, you may make a different selection, write with a different set of concerns and prejudices. Another writer might have organized the different voices of your own epoch differently.

A writer not only employs a range of voices but organizes them in particular ways in order to make particular points. Whether you were fully aware of it or not, you organized the different voices in your writing in a particular way. You may have done so to convey a particular argument or to explore a complex subject. The more aware you are of this process, the more effective you are likely to be as a communicator.

At this point, let us consider an extract from a poem in which the organization of the different voices employed is especially effective and dramatic.

Critical Activity 6

Read the following extract from Jackie Kay's *The Adoption Papers* (1991) which tells the story of a black girl's adoption by a white Scottish couple from three different viewpoints: the mother, the birth-mother and the daughter. Consider how the organization of the different voices raises quite complex issues:

Maybe that's why I don't like
all this talk about her being black,
I brought her up as my own
as I would any other child
colour matters to the nutters;
but she says my daughter says
it matters to her

...

I chase his *Sambo Sambo* all the way from the school gate.
A fistful of anorak – What did you call me? Say that again.
Sam-bo. He plays the word like a bouncing ball
but his eyes move fast as ping pong.
I shove him up against the wall,
say that again you wee shite. *Sambo, sambo,* he's crying now

I knee him in the balls. What was that?
My fist is steel; I punch and punch his gut.
Sorry I didn't hear you? His tears drip like wax.
Nothing he heaves I *didn't say nothing.*
I let him go. He is a rat running. He turns
and shouts *Dirty Darkie* I chase him again.
Blonde hairs in my hand. Excuse me!
This teacher from primary 7 stops us.
Names? I'll report you to the headmaster tomorrow.
But Miss. Save it for Mr Thompson she says.

My teacher's face cracks into a thin smile
Her long nails scratch the note well well
I see you were fighting yesterday, again.
In a few years time you'll be a juvenile delinquent.
Do you know what that is? Look it up in the dictionary.
She spells each letter with slow pleasure.
Read it out to the class.
Thug. Vandal. Hooligan. Speak up. Have you lost your tongue?

Discussion

The definitions which the black girl is made to read out from the dictionary remind us of the cultural connotations which language acquires over the centuries as words are redefined in different socio-cultural milieux. But they also remind us of how particular peoples and cultures can be scapegoated and stereotyped. Hence the word 'vandal' refers to a people historically labelled barbarians: destroyers of the cultures of others without any culture of their own.

This piece of writing is dependent for its dramatic effect upon four voices that intersect each other. Initially, there is the voice of the foster parents who, though well-meaning, have no real awareness of what it means to be black in a white society. Their naïvety is exposed by their adopted daughter's experiences at school. The voice of the small boy who taunts the girl is complex: expressing cruel, learned racism at one point, and grovelling fear at another. He moves from bully to victim while the girl moves from victim to bully. Her initial reaction probably wins our support – she is fighting back against institutionalized white racism – but when she continues to punch him in the stomach, her actions may start to repel us. No sooner does she let him go than he demonstrates he has learned nothing. Whatever sympathies we may have had towards him as victim are dissipated. Yet he is a victim, of attitudes perhaps learned from his family, from his peers, from some of the adults at school and from the media.

The final voices in the extract are those of the teachers – the one unable to appreciate what she is witnessing and the other demonstrating a more calculating, sadistic cruelty. The way the latter speaks emphasizes a learned discourse as well as learned methods of discipline, and no doubt she has humiliated other children in this way. It betrays a public discourse about 'blackness', black people being associated with crime and juvenile delinquency. The small boy employs a learned discourse, too, using words that betray historically determined meanings. The small boy and the class teacher provide a thought-provoking juxtaposition, because, whereas the boy acts out of ignorance, the teacher knows full well what she is doing.

Writing Activity 2

Write brief but detailed biographies of three fictitious characters including their background, education, appearance and personal idiosyncrasies.

Write a conversation which takes place between them. Establish a voice suitable for each character. Imagine the kinds of thing each would say; the views they would be likely to hold; how they would interact with each other; how they would behave within the conversation.

Writing Activity 3

Write down the sentence: '"Oh, I do like your hair" said Alison.'

Either individually or with friends, brainstorm the different messages this statement may be sending in different contexts.

In each case, write down an appropriate action to follow the statement which would confirm the intended message, such as reaching out and touching the person being addressed. Bear in mind, though, that actions can also send ambiguous signals!

Select one of the examples each and continue the dialogue taking care to enhance the latent meanings in the conversation.

Discussion

Your list of possible messages may have included the following: that Alison does not like the hair of the person she is addressing; that she is shy and does not know what else to say to the person; that she is telling the other person that she likes him or her; that she is asking the other person to like her; that she is drawing attention to her own hairstyle and wants the compliment to be reciprocated. In order to make your meaning clearer you may have added an adverb such as 'said Alison bitterly' or 'said Alison coyly'.

You probably gave a great deal of thought to whom it is that Alison is addressing; to the relationship between them; to the age, gender and ethnicity of the other person. Alison might be addressing a tutor of hers, or her mother, a person to whom she is attracted, an ex-lover, or somebody she either dislikes or envies. The point at which the statement occurs in the conversation is also important. Is Alison initiating the conversation or is she responding, maybe to a compliment or veiled attack from another person? The context is obviously crucial. Has Alison decided to take advantage of an occasion to approach the other person or has she been taken by surprise? Are the surroundings such that she feels comfortable, relaxed, inhibited, embarrassed, stressed, angry, etc?

Writing Convincing Dialogue

Writing convincing dialogue is more difficult than we might think. We often do not appreciate the skill and sensitivity behind many examples of dialogue that we read in novels or listen to in films, in plays or in radio drama. When you went out into some public places and listened to people's conversations, you probably noticed that they tended not to follow logical sequences. Conversations are organic; people often talk in parallels, hop from one subject to another, and return in cycles to the same topics. Silences and breaks in the conversation are also important. The rhythm of a conversation is never constant; it will flow quickly for a while and at other times become slow, even stilted. People often do not answer each other or even listen to each other.

Dramatic dialogue is not the same as everyday speech and conversation. Rosemary Horstmann (1988) defines dramatic dialogue as:

> everyday speech boiled-down into a concentrated essence, in which every word has a reason for being there, whether to illustrate character, to carry the plot forward, or to build atmosphere and a sense of location. (p.28)

As Horstmann suggests here, dialogue can be an important part of your imaginative writing.

Critical Activity 7

Before reading further, we would like you to take twenty minutes or so and brainstorm the functions which dialogue might serve in a work of prose fiction.

Discussion

The list of functions which you produced could probably be grouped under three headings:

1. **Plot:** dialogue can enable us to reveal new plot information without having to rely on the narrator;

2. **Character:** dialogue can reveal a great deal about a character without the narrator having to tell the reader what to think of someone. This method means that the reader has to employ his/her own deductive powers to glean information about a character's background (educational, occupational, familial, racial, etc.), social behaviour, relationships with others and personality;

3. **Theme:** various attitudes and ideas can be put forward through characters acting as mouthpieces, as we discussed above.

Writing Dialogue for Radio

The dramatic medium in which dialogue has the most important role is the radio play. Before we explore some of the implications of Horstmann's definition of dramatic dialogue we would like you to listen with your friends to a radio play which you have recorded.

Group Activity 2

While listening to the radio play, list some of the functions which the dialogue has to perform in this particular genre. What do you notice about the way in which each scene is written that makes it easier for the listener to follow the story-line? Brainstorm some of the possibilities which radio as a medium offers the writer.

Discussion

Of course, a radio play has to have some of the features of a play in any medium: plot, character, theme, mounting tension, climax and resolution. But the dialogue in a radio play does more than in any other dramatic medium because the writer is unable to call upon costume, scenery and lighting. There are particular skills and techniques that need to be acquired in writing radio drama; take away the stage directions and the camera directions of a television play script and you are not left with a radio play! The list of functions performed by dialogue in a radio drama probably includes the following:

- the portrayal of characters
- the creation of time and space
- the creation of context
- moving the plot forward
- conveying a range of human emotions.

Of course, dramatic dialogue can be supported by music and sound effects, but they cannot, as Horstmann says, relieve dialogue of its responsibilities.

As you listened to the radio play, you probably noticed several ways in which the script helped the listener follow the plot, such as:

- each character had an aurally recognizable personality;
- each character talked consistently throughout and there were no lines out of character;
- each scene consisted of a limited number of characters so as to minimize the risk of the listener becoming confused;
- the play was not divided by the dialogue into conventional acts and scenes;
- the lengths of the sequences were varied and short sequences were used to create tension;
- a variety of methods may have been used to move from one sequence to another, such as slow fade-outs of scenes or sudden cuts on a sound effect or at the end of a sentence;
- only necessary information was given through the dialogue and that was provided in as natural a way as possible, avoiding obvious signposting;
- sound effects and music were used judiciously without becoming characters in themselves;
- sounds of pedestrian actions such as people walking, opening doors, climbing stairs, stirring coffee were avoided.

As you and your friends brainstormed the potential of radio as a medium, you probably discovered that it offers a number of distinct advantages. Characters may be moved instantly across time and space. Radio lends itself to science fiction and fantasy where even animals, plants and inanimate objects may acquire human speech with consummate ease.

Writing Activity 4

The aims of this exercise are to provide you with experience in finding characters' voices and in writing convincing and lively dialogue.

Imagine that you have tried to telephone a friend, but that you have obtained a crossed line. For a few minutes, you listen to a dramatic conversation.

Write down the several minutes of the conversation to which you listened. Remember that it has no beginning and no end.

Everything must be written in direct speech; you are not allowed to use any 'he-saids', 'she-saids' or directions. For example, you cannot say, 'She enthused' or 'He sounded depressed'.

Accents and Dialects

It is difficult to go very far in writing dialogue without regard to accent and dialect. These two words are often confused. An accent is the way in which we pronounce or lay stress on particular words. When we say that someone has a particular accent, we are often referring to dialect. Dialect is a form of language which is used in a particular region or district. The way in which we speak frequently reflects the area in which we were brought up.

In *Sons and Lovers*, you probably noticed that Paul Morel speaks mainly in middle-class English despite his working-class origins in Nottinghamshire. In this respect, he has taken after his mother and his teachers rather than his father and their neighbours. There are occasions, however, when he lapses into dialect – for example, after he has made love. They are occasions when he seems to display a new-found warmth and appears to show some of the physical and emotional qualities of his father:

> She looked at him heavily as she put back her hair. Suddenly he put his finger-tips on her cheek.
> 'Why dost look so heavy?' he reproached her.
> She smiled sadly, as if she felt alone in herself. He caressed her cheek with his fingers, and kissed her.
> 'Nay!' he said. 'Never thee bother!'
> She gripped his fingers tight, and laughed shakily. Then she dropped her hand. He put the hair back from her brows, stroking her temples, kissing them lightly.
> 'But tha shouldna worit!' he said softly, pleading.
> 'No, I don't worry!' she laughed tenderly and resigned.
> 'Yea, tha does! Dunna thee worrit,' he implored, caressing.
>
> (chapter 12)

In this extract, Paul's lapse into dialect is contrasted with Clara's received pronunciation. The relationship between them at this point is close but tense. Although there is considerable intimacy, there is also distance. Paul is worried by her behaviour, does not understand it, feels concern for her and also reproaches her, maybe out of frustration.

Critical Activity 8

Analyse the dialect in which Paul speaks in the above extract and the dialect which is used in the poem below, written by David Dabydeen who was born in Guyana. List the key features of each.

Nightmare

Bruk dung de door!
Waan gang sweat-stink nigga
Drag she aff she bed
Wuk pun she
Crack she head
Gi she jigga
Tween she leg!

Dem chase she backdam:
Waan gang cane-stiff cack
Buss she tail till she blue and black
Till she crawl tru de mud an she bawl an she beg.

Dem haul she canal-bank like bush-haag
Cut she troat over de dark surging wata
When dem dun suck dem raise dem red mout to de moon
An mek saang,

Deep in de night when crappau call an cush-cush
Crawl dung hole, lay dem egg in de earth
When camoudie curl rung calf dat just drap
An black bat flap-flap-flap tru de bush...

Wet she awake, cuss de daybreak!

Writing Activity 5

Write a short dialect conversation between two people who come from a region or district other than your own.

You may have to base your conversation on library research, drawing on the work of authors who have already written in a particular dialect or a book on a particular dialect, or experiential research, based upon your own street research.

In order to help you, we have suggested some of the types of people you might include: market stall holders, elderly people who have lived a long time in a particular district, football supporters, railway staff, cleaners, school children, factory workers and so on.

Through the above writing exercises, you will have realized how important convincing dialogue can be to the creation of character. Character and characterization are the subjects of the next chapter.

Further Reading

Bakhtin, M.M. (1981) *The Dialogic Imagination: Four Essays*. translated by Emerson, C. and Holquist, M. Austin: University of Texas Press.

An accessible book for tutors who want to pursue the concept of different voices as a characteristic of the novel form.

Horstmann, R. (1988, revised 1991) *Writing For Radio*. London: Black.

A short, highly readable introduction to radio as a medium and a good, practical beginner's guide to writing radio scripts.

Sellers, S. (1991) *Taking Reality by Surprise*. London: Women's Press. Final Section.

A number of creative writing tutors and practitioners offer practical advice in preparing and submitting manuscripts for a range of media including radio drama, television drama and the theatre.

Chapter Seven

Character and Characterization

In this chapter you will find sections on:

1. Character study and analysis

2. Defining character

3. The 'common-sense' view of character

4. The realist approach to character

5. Free indirect style

6. Characters' names

7. The structuralist approach to character

8. Adapting narratives

9. Barthes' five codes

10. Post-structuralism and character

11. Alternative models of character

Activities

You will be asked to undertake the following activities:

1. A preparatory activity.

2. Research activities concerned with:

   - researching definitions of 'character'
   - conducting a survey of the use of characters' names in the works of two nineteenth-century writers.

3. Critical activities concerned with:

   - the problem of writing about characters in environments or situations of which you have had no direct experience

- listing 'type' character roles in relation to a specific genre of writing
- examining a contemporary narrative to discover the archetypal narrative structures, involving relationships between characters, that underpin it
- your observations following a specific writing activity
- listing some of the ways in which you may be labelled by 'official' versions of identity
- listing your different social roles.

4. Nine writing activities in which you are asked to:
   - draft a realist characterization;
   - redraft an earlier piece of characterization using a variety of techniques for incorporating character speech;
   - **either:** write a short story paying specific attention to characters' names; **or:** rewrite an earlier piece of prose, giving two different versions of a 'real' setting and experience;
   - adapt a narrative;
   - **either:** write a 'twist-in-the-tail' short story involving character action; **or:** write a short story in which a central enigma is never resolved and is used strategically in character construction;
   - write two pieces of characterization, the first based on informants, the second on indices;
   - **either:** adapt a piece of renaissance drama by giving it a present-day context; **or:** hold a workshop in which you listen to and discuss audio-recordings of a variety of characters' voices and write a piece of characterization based on the session;
   - describe the same character in a number of different formats;
   - **either**: Use any of the five methods of characterization described as the basis for a short story; **or:** compose a piece of futuristic writing in which an extract of contemporary text or a current word is employed in a new context.

5. A reading activity involving different ways of constructing character.

Preparatory Activity

If you have studied English Literature previously, you will probably have been asked to undertake a character study. We would now like you to consider the features of a character study, since they indicate some of the key methods of character construction. List as many key features of the ways in which we might construct, or analyse, characters as you can think of. Re-read a section from a novel or short story you are familiar with, or read a piece of characterization you have written, to help you in your thinking.

Discussion

In character studies you are required to analyse a character through a detailed focus on the following features:

- *Description* – how and in what ways a character is described in terms of appearance, actions, speech and mannerisms;
- *Dialogue* – what does the character say, to whom, and in what ways? Is the speech given to characters consistent or does it vary, in its form or content?
- *Action* – what does the character do? To whom, when, where and in what ways?

Further ways of studying character involve examining *relations between characters,* by contrasting your analysis of the character in question with other characters in the text. This second layer of analysis often reveals how minor characters serve as foils to the central characters, illuminating their chief characteristics or even casting doubt on their representation. An important method of contrasting the representation of characters is to focus on the *language* they use, examining the linguistic devices employed. In particular, try to notice whether the author changes register at any point and, if so, ask yourself why? Before we begin to look at character we would like you to attempt the following exercise to try to discover what is meant by the word 'character'.

Research Activity I

First, think of how many ways we might interpret the word 'character'. What do you think it means? How many different meanings can you think of? Do these meanings overlap in any way? Next, look up the word 'character' in a good dictionary such as the *Oxford English Dictionary* or equivalent. Make a list of the meanings. Consider how some of the meanings of the word have changed. What are the origins of the word? Did all the meanings seem distinct from one another to you?

Discussion

Most dictionaries provide a variety of definitions of the word 'character'. In its concise edition, the *Oxford English Dictionary*, for example, lists seven possible meanings. We can summarize these as follows:

1. distinctive marks; inscribed letters, figures and graphic symbols, particularly denoting sounds or ideas;

2. characteristics, of a biological species; collective peculiarities, idiosyncrasies and style of a group, race or person; distinction and individuality;

3. developed moral strength or a good reputation;

4. personage, personality; person portrayed in a novel or drama; person acted out in drama; in, or out of character – appropriate to these or not (in terms

of actions), in accord or not with a person's character;

5. eccentric or noticeable person;

6. in relation to the above meanings the word 'characterless' also becomes relationally linked to that of 'character';

7. inscribe or describe.

You may have noticed that some of the meanings which you discovered overlapped. For example, the particularities, idiosyncrasies and details of personality – or in sum the idea of character traits – can be applied both to real people *and* to fictional characters in novels or drama. So we might be forgiven for commonly forgetting to differentiate between characters and real people when we read fiction.

In some cases the word 'character' seems synonymous with the ideas of personality and personal identity, of both fictional characters and real people, through their links with behaviour and actions. We might conclude from a person's behaviour that he is a 'bad character'. We also tend to conflate character and personal integrity or moral worth, as in the statement 'she is of upstanding character'. The phrases 'in character' and 'out of character' seem to imply that both fictional characters and real people have some kind of central static core or a coherence and consistency of character. In other words, they have a stable personality or fixed identity, by which we come to know them, and against which they can be measured as acting 'out of character'.

The word 'character' has also been used to establish *taxonomies,* or different classifications, of people, which have in turn been related to biological or racial groupings. Finally, the word also relates to signs, symbols, and particularly to language because it can mean a sign, a 'distinctive mark' or a set of signs together, forming 'description' and 'inscription'.

The 'Common-Sense' View of Character

Modern literary studies take issue with the traditional way of looking at character – what we might call the 'common-sense' view of character. How might we describe this? Basically, it refers to our tendency to respond to characters as though they were real people. Despite our knowing, at one level, that literary characters are fictional, at another level we are seduced into believing that at times they are as real as ourselves. Why should this be the case?

One explanation is that we often come to know of real people we have never met through texts. We are accustomed to reading reported descriptions of people we do not know, and places we have never been to, through newspapers, magazines, reports, letters, biographies and travelogues, in order to map 'real' life. Effectively, the one medium of language describes to us those things which have some correlative object in the real world – such as real people – as well as those which don't – for example, fictitious people. There is nothing in the system of language itself to register any distinction between the real and the fictive. Realist literature uses the same techniques of communication within fiction as we use in our everyday lives, outside fiction. As we saw in the definitions 2 to 5, many aspects of the word 'character' can be applied to both real and fictive 'people'. This correspondence between the way language is used within the novel and outside it, as we said in chapter 1, is one of the ways in which realist literature achieves its effect of being a transparent medium.

We have also seen that modern critical approaches challenge this view by exposing that realist literature is contrived as any form of aesthetic communication.

A second explanation for the naturalization of the idea that characters are the close equivalents of real people lies in the pedagogical methods employed in teaching creative writing, particularly exercises based on character study. Often such exercises ask students to imagine a character in other situations or from the perspective of a minor character. You are often asked to imagine yourself as the character, to put yourself in the 'I' position of a figure and to write down your feelings about or responses to the situation the character is faced with. We have asked you to undertake such exercises in the course of this book to help you understand the strategies by which particular focalizations are achieved. Such exercises create an elision between you, as the author and real person, and the character. The technique of using personal testimony within the process of constructing character seduces us into thinking of characters as if they were real people, that they are a part of our 'real self'.

Although modern criticism has subjected it to scrutiny, many novels are still written in the realist tradition. As we shall see, there is nothing wrong with writing from a common-sense view of character, providing we recognize that it is only one of a number of modes of writing.

The Realist Approach to Character

As we have suggested, although most readers realize that a literary character is fictitious, there remains an almost irresistible tendency for a reader to become emotionally involved with a character, as though the representation were a transparent mediation or clear unproblematic reflection of a real person. The illusion of language as a transparent medium, and thus of character representation as similarly transparent, results from two major writing strategies. Firstly, importance is attached to detailed descriptions of physical appearance, personal identity (including a personal name, a role name, in the sense of a kinship term, and some sense of an inner state of emotion and thought), clothing, social habits and customs (linked to occupation and lifestyle), and speech (for example, consistent notations of idiom, dialect and register). Secondly, there is correspondence between most of the details described and their external referents to be found in the world of objects surrounding the reader.

Writing Activity I

1. Using the above criteria, make a realist character sketch. Draw details for your characterization by describing aspects you associate with a real person who has caught your attention for some reason or whom you know fairly well.

2. Describe the character in relation to one or more of the following: their first day at school, work or university; an adventure holiday; moving house; winning something; being burgled; being ill; going to a party; an argument; a hobby; a phobia.

If you are able to create more than one character sketch or if you have others in your journal, describe different characters in relation to the same event.

Reading Activity

Compare the following character descriptions. The first is from *Nice Work* by David Lodge, a British novelist, the second and third extracts are from *Myal* by Erna Brodber, a Caribbean woman novelist. Identify and make notes on what writing techniques are being used. Decide which extract you find the most realistic. Consider what is being described and make a list of the familiar signs and symbols. Consider how much detail there is and the form in which it is provided.

Extract A

He steps on to the bathroom scales. Ten stone, two ounces. Quite enough for a man only five feet, five and a half inches tall. Some say – Vic has overheard them – that he tries to compensate for his short stature by his aggressive manner. Well, let them. If it wasn't for a bit of aggression, he wouldn't be where he is now. Though how long he will stay there is far from certain. Vic frowns in the mirror above the handbasin, thinking again of last month's annual accounts, the quarterly forecast, the annual review...He runs hot water into the dark purple bowl, lathers his face with shaving foam from an aerosol can, and begins to scrape his jaw with a safety razor, using a Wilkinson's Sword blade. Vic believes fervently in buying British, and has frequent rows with his eldest son, Raymond, who favours a disposable plastic razor manufactured in France.

(Chapter 1)

Extract B

Ole African had made himself a house on the outskirts of Grove Town. He had found himself two parallel rows of four cane-roots on the nearby property and had twisted them into a shelter. He was resting when the tap, tap, tap of Dan's code came through to him. It was dusk and Reverend Simpson had returned tired from a day of visiting. He settled himself in the old rocking-chair and let his mind move where it would to deal with what issue it would. It went to the cane-piece on the outskirts of Grove Town, to the man with the dirty tattered skirt and the leather strips for hair, to talk of things ancient and modern.

– Willie, I've got your message, – Dan said.
– Yeah – said Willie.

(Chapter 10)

Extract C

...Cook say it was like twenty thousand dead bull frog, the scent that escape from that chile's body. That had to be the hand of man, Cook say to herself...And she ask herself what that poor little chile could do anybody, fi mek dem do her so. Sorry fi her so til! Couldn't keep it to herself. She had was to turn to Miss Maydene and put the question to her: "What poor Ella coulda do anybody, that them fix her that way?" The lady turn to her and say, "Is not all the time is somebody do something; sometimes is you do you own self something." Only that.

(Chapter 14)

Discussion

Each extract is taken from a text published in 1988. To what extent were you familiar with and able to recognize what was being described in each extract? In the first extract a middle-aged Englishman, Vic Wilcox, is performing his ablutions in a bathroom. In the second extract two Caribbean men, Ole African and Reverend Simpson settle down at dusk in their respective homes and begin a telepathic conversation with one another.

What familiar signs were there in each scene? Did you know what 'a Wilkinson's Sword blade' was? Could you identify and visualize 'a disposable plastic razor manufactured in France' more – or less – easily than 'the man with the dirty tattered skirt and the leather strips for hair'? Are 'cane-roots', a 'cane-piece' and 'twenty thousand dead bull frog' figurative expressions you would instantly or easily include in a piece of prose? Or do you think descriptions such as 'the mirror above the handbasin', 'He runs hot water' or 'shaving foam from the aerosol can' construct a more realistic piece of writing?

Your response to the different settings was probably determined by the extent to which each extract corresponded to your own experience of the real world. The reaction of a Caribbean reader, an English reader, an Anglo-Caribbean reader and an African reader would, of course, be very different, so we can see that realism is a variable and not a fixed concept.

How does the way each piece is written help to construct the illusion that literature is showing us a 'slice of life'? In the first extract we learn Vic's name, that he is employed in the business world in some supervisory or managerial capacity, that he has a son, and about some of the things which preoccupy him. We are also given a fairly precise description of Vic's physical appearance. The second extract also provides some details of physical appearance and occupation. In the full context of Brodber's novel, we would also be aware that Reverend Simpson and Ole African have the corresponding role names of Dan and Willie respectively, in a telepathic network within the community based in Grove Town. Whether these are the kinds of social roles a reader would automatically recognize might depend largely on cultural background. To understand Brodber's references, we would need to have lived in a community structured like the one in

Grove Town or we would need to have had an opportunity to read and learn about one. In each case, our perspectives would be different from those of readers who had no context for making sense of who the characters of Dan and Willie were.

Free Indirect Style

In the first extract we are given a sense of Vic's personality through the use of free indirect style. This is prose written from an omniscient narrator's perspective, but in the style of a character's speech patterns. For example, the combination of syntactical arrangement, collusive address, and the balance between form and content of some of the lines remains very close to the way they would be written as a first person narrative, in the direct speech of the character. This is evident if we substitute first for third person pronouns:

> Some say – *I've* heard them – that *I* try to compensate for *my* short stature by an aggressive manner. Well, let them. If it wasn't for a bit of aggression, *I* wouldn't be where *I am* now.

> (our substitutions in italics)

Free indirect style, as David Lodge has argued elsewhere, is one of the distinctive ways in which realist literature creates 'an effect of intimate access to the character's inner self...without relinquishing the task of narrating to the character entirely, as in the pseudo-autobiography or interior monologue' (Lodge, in Mellor, 1990, p.102).

The technique of free indirect style is also used by Erna Brodber in the third extract. The character of the Cook is being described through the external focalization of an omniscient narrator but *in the style of* Cook's creolized speech patterns and rhythms. Again, some of these lines come very close to the direct speech of the character, as we can see if we change the personal pronouns in this piece:

> *I* say to *myself*...And I ask *myself* what that poor little chile could do anybody, fi mek dem do her so. Sorry fi her so til! Couldn't keep it to *myself*. *I* had was to turn to Miss Maydene and put the question to her: "What poor Ella coulda do anybody, that them fix her that way?" The lady turn to *me* and say, "Is not all the time is somebody do something; sometimes is you do you own self something."

> (our substitutions in italics)

In Brodber's novel, the sense that the speech rhythms are designed to re-create and thus to characterize the Cook is reinforced by the fact that these rhythms are not used consistently throughout the whole novel, and also because they override the characterization of Maydene's speech as it appears elsewhere in the novel.

As we have suggested elsewhere, the advent of classic realism saw a reaction to the over-generalized typology of characterization evident in pre-novelistic works such as John Bunyan's *Pilgrim's Progress* and William Langland's *Piers Plowman*. The shift from generalization to particularity of detail in terms of time, place and setting, which we discussed earlier, also affected characterization, as you probably realized in the writing exercises in chapter 1. For example, to construct characters as representations of individual people whom we might think of as 'realistic' requires a writer to pay careful attention to the detailing of dress (description), social mannerisms (actions and dialogue) and names (both personal and place).

Although, in the examples we have looked at, both novelists use the conventions and techniques of realist literature to construct character, they are each writing about alternative ideas of the 'real'. In Brodber's novel the idea of telepathic or spiritual communication is taken as a cultural norm, whereas there is no mention of such a mode of communication in Lodge's book. Also, their realist descriptions are of two quite different environments, to which various readers might relate and respond differently, depending upon their cultural and familial background.

Although contemporary theory has identified many problems with classic realism as a literary practice, based on a critique of the fundamental ideas which underpinned it, many writers continue to write fiction and construct character, adopting the methods of the realist tradition. However, among those writers using the realist tradition there is a plurality of 'realisms', reflecting the plurality of cultural backgrounds of both writers and readers.

Preparatory Activity

Make a list of the ways in which you might represent the inner self of a character through the character's speech. Using free indirect style is one method.

Writing Activity 2

Having identified some alternatives, try rewriting a short piece of character description, using each of the methods you identified for representing the speech codes of the character. Some of your ideas may require you to introduce more characters into the narrative. You could try this exercise using a character description taken from a published work or one of your own pieces of writing.

When you have used as many methods as you could think of, read through your work and assess each method, commenting on which you find the most and the least interesting. Record your thoughts in your journal. If you are working in a group you may like to share your results and comments.

Discussion

Your list may have included third person description by an omniscient narrator – of character actions, speech and thoughts; or first person description – addressing the reader directly. You may have listed techniques for representing inner thoughts such as monologue, soliloquy, autobiography, statement, or reported speech by the character, other characters or the narrator. Different tenses may be used to distinguish whether a character is engaging directly in an action or is relating a past or present event. Characters' speech may be represented in speech marks, or outside speech marks; it may even be contained within the speech marks indicating other characters' speech – as in the example of Maydene's speech which is framed in the free indirect style 'voice' of Cook.

You may have noticed that it is possible to achieve a greater sense of immediacy with some modes of writing characters' speech than with others. Identifying contrasting ways in which speech can be represented allows us to think about the different levels of immediacy or distance of action and events that can be achieved through the various ways of expressing characters' speech or action. This can radically transform the intensity and dynamism of a piece of writing.

Many writers have agreed that there are two major modes of verbal representation. Socrates distinguished two modes for communicating speech: *diegesis,* when speakers act or speak as themselves, and *mimesis,* when speakers attempt to speak as if in someone else's voice or create an illusion of this. The former means speaking in the 'I' position of yourself, while the latter means adopting the 'I' position of someone else. For example, Agatha Christie speaking *as herself* about her character, Hercule Poirot, would be an example of *diegesis* while an actor speaking *as Hercule Poirot* would be an example of *mimesis.* This two-point model can be applied with a little adaptation to different features of self-expression as well as different modes of representing the speech of characters and narrators within fiction.

In contemporary usage a similar distinction is made between 'telling' (direct speech) and 'showing' (reported speech). David Lodge suggests that another way in which this dichotomy exists in a text is in the contrast between the narrator's and the character's voices. These two voices, according to Lodge, form the warp and weft of all narratives. The former – the equivalent of 'summary' – is most often used for the 'telling' (or describing) of a character's action and speech, while the latter – the equivalent of 'scene' (pp.88–9) – is more often used for the 'showing' (or enactment) of a character's action and speech (Lodge, in Mellor ed., 1990, p.99). If you recall our definition of focalization in chapter 4, Lodge's analysis can be seen as a distinction between interior and exterior focalization (a narratorial perspective located on the inside or outside of a character), while free indirect style can be seen as a combination of the two.

Socrates' distinction was originally used to separate enacted dramatic speech from the spoken word in the 'real' world. However, in contemporary writing the distinction is no longer used to indicate differences between the 'real' and the 'fictive', but to identify contrasting features within the fictive. Usually both *diegetic* (narrator telling) and *mimetic* (character showing) aspects exist within the same narrative form, for example, the novel.

To some extent the use of free indirect style, which weaves together the narrator's perspective with the character's voice, merges these two modes of representation – narratorial perspective and character idiom – to represent the interior life of a character. From our account of two aspects of realist character construction – the use of detailed description from an exterior point of view and the use of free indirect style to represent interiority – we now move on to look at a third dimension commonly associated with character, that of naming.

Characters' Names

As we suggested earlier, prior to the advent of classic realism, representations of character were often two-dimensional stereotypes, relying strongly on the significance of a singular name to evoke an assumed vice or virtue. Names were employed in order to represent a character type rather than to create a representation of a particular individual whom, through the willing suspension of disbelief, we might imagine to be the equivalent of a living person or of someone who had once lived.

In stark contrast to these earlier literary forms, the extensive and often detailed particularity of realist characterization should offer accurate descriptions of social practices such as dress codes, language usage, personal and place names, social mannerisms and codes of behaviour. Thus, the literary conventions for representing character were transformed quite radically at the end of the seventeenth and the beginning of the eighteenth centuries.

However, the demarcation of literary conventions by historical period can only be taken so far. While the rise of classic realism saw the introduction of particular names and terms of address, creating the illusion of realism, the use of names to signify archetypal characteristics continued as a strong literary tradition. Both Thomas Hardy and Charles Dickens used names to connote the moral, ethical, political and personal persuasions of their characters.

Research Activity 2

We would like you to find and read a selection of extracts from the novels of Thomas Hardy or Charles Dickens and consider why and how each writer makes distinctive use of 'type names' in their characterization.

Either look at a range of characters in the novels of Charles Dickens, such as Wackford Squeers and Smike in *Nicholas Nickleby* (1838–9), Mr Gradgrind in *Hard Times* (1854), Scrooge in *A Christmas Carol* (1843), Mrs Gamp in *Martin Chuzzlewit* (1843–4), Mr Tite Barnacle in *Little Dorrit* (1855–7) and Mr Boffin in *Our Mutual Friend* (1864–5), *or* focus on the characterization within a particular novel. For example, what connotations can be derived from Thomas Hardy's choice of the names Angel Clare, Mercy Chant, Tess Durbeyfield and Alec D'Urbeville in his novel *Tess of the D'Urbevilles*?

Discussion

Hardy and Dickens use names to connote both archetypal and personal – for example, occupational – characteristics. Their use of type names is often hyperbolic for the sake of polemical or humorous effect. Each uses type names to parody or criticize particular ideologies. The differences between these writers' use of type names and those of Bunyan or Langland are that the Victorian novelists' characterizations are generally represented with more particularity and in greater depth than the earlier writers' use of stock characters with type names. Where they are not, they are marginal characters who act as foils to the major characters, emphasizing by contrast the complexities of the major characters or advancing the mechanics of the plot. Most importantly, such typological characters form part of a narrative which is generally couched in the voluminously detailed specificity of the classic realist text.

Conversely, Dickens' use of type names can be contrasted with the manner in which they are employed in some contemporary novels, where the literary convention of associating names with character traits is subjected to scrutiny or even inverted in complex reworkings of the convention. In Jamaica Kincaid's *Lucy* (1994), for example, the novel's central character, Lucy, a nineteen-year-old black Antiguan, emigrates to North America to become a nanny to four children in a white middle-class American family. Through emigration, Lucy encounters her distinctiveness from others, in both her new and old environments. Identity is a potent theme in Caribbean literature, since hybrid racial and national identities form a significant part of Caribbean history. Towards the end of the novel this preoccupation with identity is focused on the issue of naming:

> I reached into the top drawer and retrieved a small stack of official documents: my passport, my immigration card, my permission-to-work card, my birth certificate, and a copy of the lease to the apartment. These documents showed everything about me, and yet they showed nothing about me. They showed where I was born. They showed that I was born on the twenty-fifth of May 1949. They showed how tall I was . . . These documents all said that my name was Lucy – Lucy Josephine Potter. I used to hate all three of those names.
>
> (Chapter 5)

Having indicated the instability and unreliability of naming and documenting people, the passage suggests that a word, as Derrida argued in his concept of *différance,* has neither a fixed point of origin nor a stable or permanent relationship to its meaning. When Lucy unravels the possible meanings of her name, its meanings are seen to be in flux, shifting from connoting a relative she was named after to her British ancestry and, finally, to Satan or Lucifer.

Such use of name and character in a novel not only undermines the notion of words having fixed meanings, but casts doubt on the literary convention that there is a direct and uncomplicated correlation between name and character. It markedly differs from Dickens' use of the convention, which assumed fixed relations between names and their meanings. While both Dickens' and Kincaid's fiction encourages us to question the real, Kincaid's text goes further in challenging some of our commonplace assumptions about the relationship between language and meaning. In this respect, her novel may be seen as 'postmodern', a concept which we will discuss in the later sections of this chapter.

Writing Activity 3

Either: Compose a short story in which the significance of naming is an important aspect. Try using some of the ideas we have discussed or write about one of the following themes where naming might be significant: murder, mystery, adoption, inheritance, travel, race, gender, class. *Or:* Rewrite one of the characterization pieces you completed for Writing Activity 1, changing the character's national identity or the geographic location of events suggested in part 2 of that exercise. For example, write two versions of the 'first day at school' setting, describing firstly, a realistic account of an English character's first day at school in England and, secondly, a realistic account of an African or Indian character's first day at school in an African or Indian school. When you have finished, compare some of the stories and discuss the extent to which it is possible to talk in terms of shared experiences and a shared reality.

Critical Activity 1

Discuss, in a group or with your tutor or supervisor, how writers can overcome the problem of writing about something of which they do not have first-hand experience.

Discussion

Many of you will have realized the necessity to undertake some form of research to complete Writing Activity 3, probably through reading fictional and non-fictional accounts of geographic settings, social practices and institutions with which you are unfamiliar. Some of you will have the advantage of oral or written accounts from friends and relatives to provide background information. On the one hand, this activity shows there are different 'real' worlds and different 'real' experiences to be described in realist literature – consider, for example, the potential for a variety of different versions of 'a first day at school' narrative. On the other hand, this exercise casts doubts on all representations of reality because you constructed a realist description of places you had never seen in the *writing style* of personal testimony – as if you *had* seen them. Realist writing is no more than a set of stylistic devices which do not guarantee the authenticity of personal experience and involvement in the eye-witness accounts they describe. Nor do they guarantee a stable or reliable account of the world they seek to represent.

As we said at the outset, one aim of this book is to help you to think critically and analytically about your own creative work. The realist tradition is an important one to approach critically for various reasons. Firstly, many writers world-wide continue to write in the realist tradition, and much popular fiction is still written according to these conventions. Secondly, much of contemporary literary critical theory has been developed reactively against the assumptions of the realist tradition. Thirdly, many contemporary western writers, as we shall see in our final section, write in styles and employ strategies of writing which generically might be identified as 'postmodern'. One of the distinguishing features of postmodern literature is that it often uses the conventions of realism as a foil to highlight its own techniques.

Realism, then, is still an important tradition and an ability to distinguish its techniques remains useful, if not essential. Having looked at traditional conceptions of character and characterization, in the next sections we shall examine the theoretical assumptions and paradigms behind alternative ways of constructing character.

Structuralism and Character

As we suggested in chapter 2, structuralist theories of literature were crucial in exposing the techniques of realist literature as just that, a set of techniques. They also undermined the common-sense view of character as a straightforward reflection or representation of a 'real' person living in the 'real' world. Basically, these theories brought about new ways of writing character incorporating such ideas as:

- the loss of faith in the reliability of language as a medium for representation
- the shifts of focus from author to text to reader
- (perhaps most importantly) shifting notions of what the referents of realist fiction are assumed to be
- shifting notions of the 'real world'
- (where character is concerned) shifting notions of the human being and human identity.

In the next two sections we revisit some of these ideas to see how they might challenge realist conventions of characterization and, by contrast, provide alternative ways of looking at character.

In chapter 2 we saw how structuralist theories were indebted to two areas of European linguistics: the work of Ferdinand de Saussure – particularly his idea that languages work as systems of signs, only generating meanings when they are related to other parts of the same system – and the Russian Formalists, who attempted to identify why some types of language usage are regarded as more 'literary' than others. Structuralist critics, we suggested, analysed literature by looking at how words relate to other words rather than how words relate to the world of things they are commonly assumed to describe. For example, nothing needs to have changed in the world of objects in order for the meaning of the word 'bed' to change according to the other words to which we relate it, as in 'flower-bed' or 'bed-linen'.

Structuralist approaches to literary analysis pose problems for our study of character. To structuralist critics the idea that representation could be seen as a transparent mediation of the world became an illusion. This meant that characters could no longer be thought of as synonymous with 'real' people:

> Narrator and characters, however, at least from our perspective, are essentially "paper beings"; the (material) author of a narrative is in no way to be confused with the narrator of that narrative…Structural analysis is unwilling to accept [the] assumption [that a narrative is the straightforward expression of the consciousness of its author]: *who speaks* (in the narrative) is not *who writes* (in real life) and *who writes* is not *who is.*
>
> (Barthes, 1977, pp.111–12)

As a matter of fact, the theories of structuralists were not suited to analysing character and they gave a low priority to it. In effect, they followed Aristotle's view and placed the 'notion of character [as] secondary, entirely subsidiary to the notion of action' (Barthes, 1977, p.104). They could not ignore character entirely, of course, and, since characters form one of the most significant parts of narrative, structuralists had to devise some method for analysing them. Resistant to the idea of seeing characters as 'real' people, they developed a vocabulary for discussing character primarily in relation to narrative action:

> structural analysis has shown the utmost reluctance to treat the character as an essence…there is not a single narrative in the world without "characters", or at least without agents. Yet, on the other hand, these – extremely numerous – "agents" can be neither described nor classified in terms of "persons"…Structural analysis, much concerned not to define characters in terms of psychological essences, has so far striven, using various hypotheses, to define a character not as a "being" but as a "participant" …
>
> (Barthes, 1977, pp.105–6)

At this point we would like you to take a few minutes to consider the ideas for character study you listed as a Preparatory Activity (pp.127–28).

You may have included in your list the aspect of analysing a character's role in the novel in response to questions such as: are they active or passive? central or marginal? in what senses are they operative or operated upon? how does what they do affect other characters or the development of the plot? Most of these questions lead us to consider a character's role in the plot. To some extent this is analogous with the structuralist's view of character. In structuralist analysis, characters are primarily identified by what they *do* in terms of the development of the narrative's plot.

Critical Activity 2

We would like you to make a list of as many character roles you can think of. By this we mean 'type' roles. It may be helpful if you think of a particular genre of narrative before you make your list, such as the detective narrative, the romance genre, the western, the horror genre, the fairy-tale and so on. You may also find it useful to think of the narrative genres of film, television or stage.

Discussion

How many roles could you think of? Depending on what genre you looked at your list may have included: the hero, the heroine, the sidekick, the victim, the perpetrator, the inquisitor, the magician, the *femme fatale*, the mother-in-law, the wife, the boss, the wise guy, the sneak, and so on. Your list may have comprised a series of oppositions or related pairs such as: good guys/bad guys; hero/villain; husband/wife; parent/child; lover/beloved; detective/murderer; wise man/fool; fairy godmother/wicked witch, and so on.

From the list of roles *you* made see if any can be paired together through the similarity or opposition of their relationship through actions.

Having paired together some of the roles you identified, can you see any ways in which, through the similarity of relationship in some of these pairs, we might reduce our list of types even further? From our list there are at least three pairings which share a similar structure, that of the quest/questor relationship. The lover/beloved relationship can be seen as linked to the structure of a quest narrative, with the lover as subject of a quest (questor/pursuer/desirer of an object) and the beloved as the object of a quest (quested/pursued/desired by the subject). Having identified this 'sphere' (type or sequence) of action as the common base we can see that this relationship of questor/quested is repeated in two other pairings: those of the detective/murderer and the hero/villain.

In each of these pairings we can similarly identify a questor/quested sphere of action relating the two characters together. In a detective narrative the detective pursues the murderer, while in many epic narratives a hero pursues and destroys or defeats a villain. In each of these examples it is the repetition of the sequential action of a quest which makes the relationships seem similar. Thus we can see how actions, for structuralists, helped to classify characters, since identifying character types was specifically determined by actions, their role in narrative action.

As we said in chapter 3 (p.66), Vladimir Propp (1968 [1928]) analysed 200 Russian folk-tales and found they had thirty-one common narrative 'functions' (units of action, identified as units by their repetition in a variety of narratives). Within these he identified seven common character roles:

1. villain

2. donor/provider (of magical item for protection or of the quest mission)

3. helper

4. princess/sought-for person/object of quest

5. dispatcher

6. hero

7. false hero.

While we could identify some of these roles by their name, for example 'princess', most are identifiable by their role, a function discernible through a sequence of actions. In structuralist terms, then, characters are predominantly seen as agents of narrative action or actants, operating within a sequence of actions.

Critical Activity 3

Working with the list of character types you compiled, analyse a contemporary narrative you are familiar with and identify the structural relations between the characters. Can you identify any patterns you have seen elsewhere? Are any of the structures familiar to you? Do they connote archetypal relations? How are they being used? Do they say something new or different about a particular structural relationship? Or do they reaffirm existing conceptions of a relationship? Discuss your ideas with a group or write your responses in your journal.

Discussion

From a structuralist perspective, relations between characters occur within a context provided by common narrative structures – for example, the 'cliff-hanging' ending of soap opera episodes: the 'red herrings' of detective narratives; or the reiteration of a moral or ethical point in the conclusions of American family sit-coms. Narratives which commonly repeat such structural features are called formulaic narratives. As our examples might suggest, much writing for serialized television programmes is formulaic.

A vivid example of formulaic narrative occurs in the conclusion of the film *Wayne's World*, which, through mimicry, lampoons the formulaic episode endings of the television serial *Scooby Doo*. Here, the screenplay highlights, through parody, the formulaic nature of the final expository sequences of much American popular television. In such sequences, characters frequently give a résumé of the plot, generally concluding with an explanation of the moral point of the episode or an explanation of how a mystery was solved or a villain caught. For such formulaic narratives to work, there have to be correlative formulaic, or archetypal, character roles.

Although it can be argued that most writers in most historical periods have made use of known archetypes when writing characters, there is a major distinction to be made between these and the structuralists' reductive analysis of character as archetype. In the latter approach, character is specifically analysed in terms of how it relates to the internal world of a text rather than to the external world beyond the text. In other words, structuralists were concerned to examine how characters, as 'actants' or 'agents' of narrative, relate to the structural frame of a generic, or formulaic, plot structure rather than in terms of how they might reflect real people fitting into a social structure beyond the text.

For example, in the James Bond series of novels by Ian Fleming, characters are schematically evaluated in terms of their archetypal roles – the hero, the villain, the *femme fatale* – within the frame of a formulaic narrative such as that of the quest myth ('Eco', in Waites, Bennett and Martin, 1982). By analogy, we might view the film narrative of *Pretty Woman* as an interpretation of the Cinderella story, while the film *Apocalypse Now* can be seen as an adaptation of the structural features of Joseph Conrad's *Heart of Darkness*, relocating the basic narrative elements of a story set in the Belgian Congo at the end of the nineteenth and beginning of the twentieth centuries to the Vietnam war.

Some structuralists developed more complex models of literary study by asserting that it was through analysing the reader's experience of a text rather than studying its author or its characters as 'real' people, that we could arrive at a method for connecting a text with the 'real' world. As we shall see in the next section, this produced a different set of strategies for thinking about the representation of character. But before we study this second area of structuralist thought, let us look at how the conception of characters as actants or agents of the plot can be used in relation to creative work.

As the examples we have been looking at indicate, one of the major ways in which writers can make use of structuralist insights into stock (or structural) relations between characters and stock (or structural) elements of narrative is through adaptation. We would therefore like you to try the following exercise.

Writing Activity 4

You may find it useful to refer back to and draw on the work you did for Writing Activity 3 in chapter 2 and to the Preparatory Research Activity for chapter 3 in order to do this exercise.

Identify and summarize the basic elements of a well-known film. Try and highlight the basic or indispensable units of the plot, those which you feel characterize its formulaic nature. Similarly, identify the main character types and their basic relationships – those which seem to you to be essential to the plot.

Take this structural frame and rebuild it by adding your own choice of details, changing the times and locations and shifting the emphasis of narrative perspective. Before you begin writing, experiment with a variety of options based on changes you have made.

The idea of reducing narrative to its most basic units, such as the relations between characters and their relation to 'spheres of action', then, was a strong feature of structural analysis. In one sense this reductive distillation of the elements of character into archetype posed one problem which was never satisfactorily resolved: how were the structuralists to deal with 'subjectivity' or the representation of a psychological self? The analysis of characters as actants or agents of narrative can be seen as a marked flaw in structuralist method. This mode of analysis fails to address adequately many of the complexities of characterization in modern fiction – for example, attempts to represent psychological depth.

Barthes' Five Codes

Theorists such as Roland Barthes offered a way of supplementing this lack. Identifying the relationships between the characters not only helps to establish their function in relation to the development of the plot but also helps to place a character within a matrix of received cultural expectations for the reader. By approaching character as a 'grammatical (and not psychological) person' (1977 [1968], p.109), Barthes' theorizing of reader response was based on a post-structuralist premise, which saw both character and human identity as constructed in discourse. Through focusing on readers' experiences and examining how texts trigger their responses, he explored the relationship between readers' cultural knowledge and their capacity for understanding a text. His notion of the shared cultural code by which readers interpret texts was analogous to post-structuralist writers' ideas of discourse, a concept indicating the various language, symbolic and knowledge systems we learn according to the culture we live in.

In *S/Z* (1990 [1973]), Barthes focused on the importance of the reader in generating the meaning of texts and suggested that the signification (potential meanings) of any narrative could be analysed in terms of five codes. As we describe these codes to you, we would like you to imagine horizontal and vertical lines intersecting each other. Two of these codes, the code of enigmas (the hermeneutic code) and the code of actions (the proairetic code), are seen as present syntagmatically – or horizontally – in the text, while the remaining three, the code of symbols (the symbolic code), the code of signs or images (the semic code) and the code of cultural knowledge (the reference or cultural code), are seen as present in paradigmatic – or vertical – relations to the text.

The two syntagmatically placed codes are concerned with the patterning of enigmas and actions within a text. Enigmas are all the questions, puzzles and riddles which a text sets up and their eventual answers, solutions and resolutions. According to Barthes, we can track the opening up of a mystery, or enigma, in a narrative and plot how the eventual resolution is arrived at, including all the ways in which the resolution is deferred or delayed through false answers and equivocation. Enigmas are the hooks which make the reader want to read on; they include any narrative feature which generates a question in the mind of the reader. The introduction of a character in a narrative can generate questions such as: who is this? how do they relate to the plot and the other characters? why have they been introduced now? We have to read on in order to search for the solutions to these mysteries.

Actions, in Barthes' sense, are the sequential units which comprise a 'sphere of action', that is, the series of actions which make up one generic and recognizable whole. An example would be that 'answering the telephone' might comprise a generic sphere of action since it could be broken down into a series of actions such as: 'the phone rings', 'character picks up the receiver', 'conversation', 'character puts down the receiver'. This is the minimal number of units into which we could break down this action. How these are described and whether all the actions within the sequence are completed might radically affect the plot.

Generic spheres of action include a vast range of possibilities, from 'taking a stroll' to 'murder'. Most structuralists grouped this vast range into three categories relating to three types of relationship between characters, upon which action could be based: desire, communication and participation (or help). Desire is exemplified in the quest/questor relationship we discussed earlier.

This level of analysis might seem over-detailed but it is a useful way of thinking about the internal consistency, or continuity, within a piece of writing. We said that syntagmatically placed codes are present in a text as horizontal units of narrative. As we re-read a piece of writing we can check if all the questions arising in the narrative have been answered. Are there minor characters who are introduced and then forgotten about? Did a character begin a sequence of actions and end up in limbo because an important aspect of the sequence was not completed? What was the function of introducing a particular character or a character's account of an event into the narrative? How did that character or retelling of an event link to the rest of the events in the narrative?

In Toni Morrison's *Beloved* (1987) the gradual piecing together of an event, through the perspectives of several characters' versions of Sethe's murder of her baby, is introduced into the narrative as an enigma, a mystery which we have to read on to uncover. 'Every dawn she saw the dawn, but never acknowledged or remarked on its color. There was something wrong with that. It was as though one day she saw red baby blood, another day the pink gravestone chips...' (p.39). Not only do the enigmas arising from this extract compel the reader to continue reading in terms of the plot – what happened to the baby? is it dead? did it survive? who injured it? – they also function as part of the characterization of Sethe. What is wrong with Sethe? Why is she numb to the world around her? Why does she see the colour of a morning sky in terms of a baby's blood and gravestones? Is she ill? Is she mad? Is she bereaved? Why is she acting like this? The enigmas function to construct Sethe as a disturbed character and as someone burdened with a secret or traumatic past.

Writing Activity 5

Either: Write a short story which has a twist in the tail. You could use the technique of an unreliable narrator's characterization to effect the twist. As you plan the narrative try to plot it in terms of Barthes' idea of enigmas, which compel the reader to read on, and in terms of sequences of character action, which can be either completed, disrupted or left unresolved for dramatic effect. Make sure that you re-read your work several times, checking its consistency in terms of the completion of action sequences and in terms of the enigmas it contains. Are they all resolved? If not, why not?

Using ambiguity over the origin and completion of any given sequence of action is one way of creating the 'red herrings' which outwit the reader in twist-in-the-tail narratives. For example, in the genre of the murder mystery, the detective who finally solves the case is represented throughout as analysing chains or sequences of action, to determine the identity of the murderer. Often, many characters, linked by the similarity of the chains of action they are involved in, start out as suspects.

Or: Write a short story in which one central enigma is never resolved. For example, in his short story 'Hills like White Elephants' (1928), two of Ernest Hemingway's characters are represented as discussing an event for the duration of the story, an event which is never directly named throughout the narrative. Think of as many ways as you can of incorporating such an ellipsis (a missing event/detail/piece of information) into a narrative. Having written a story, think about how many ways an unresolved enigma can be used strategically in character construction.

In contrast, the remaining codes through which Barthes suggests we can decipher and analyse narrative are paradigmatically or vertically placed in relation to the narrative. In other words, these codes refer to aspects which are present in culture as well as in the text itself. They refer to the symbolic vocabulary on which the reader can draw in order to interpret a text.

The symbolic code is the code of antitheses through which we can analyse the major dichotomies traditionally inherent in western thinking – for example, good/evil; parent/child; nature/culture – and suggest how these inform the structural relations between major symbols in western literature. Such dichotomies may be represented simply as given, or they may be inverted, reversed, challenged or completely collapsed in a text for dramatic effect. For example, characters may be set up in binary relationships to one another, through the symbolic codes of colour (black/white) or gender (male/female), and then this relation may be inverted, as in both Joseph Conrad's *Heart of Darkness* (1902) and Toni Morrison's *Beloved* (1987). In *Beloved* the symbolic codes of colour are relied upon in rewriting white western versions of the colonization of Africa and the American slave trade. The strategy of binary reversal and inversion becomes significant in writing about cultural difference and in cross-cultural studies of literature, especially since – as we saw in chapter 2 in the contrast between Chinua Achebe's and Charles Dickens' uses of the colour white – the signification of colour can vary according to cultural expectations.

In both Conrad's and Morrison's texts, the western symbolic correlation of white with good and black with evil is reversed, as the symbolic status of white as a positive image is inverted and recontextualized as a source of evil in black culture. This is implied in Baby Suggs' comment in *Beloved*, '"There is no bad luck in the world but white folks"' (p.89). In Conrad's text, the figure of the white sepulchre becomes a symbol of the hypocrisy of white moral degeneracy endemic in the ivory trade (p.35). It is the first sign of symbolic inversion which continues with the contrasts between the dying black labour force and the fat, white company accountant dressed in starched white linen:

> ...in the great demoralization of the land he kept up his appearance. That's backbone. His starched collars and got-up shirt-fronts were achievements of character...I could not help asking him how he managed to sport such linen. He had just the faintest blush, and said modestly, "I've been teaching one of the native women about the station. It was difficult. She had a distaste for the work." Thus this man had verily accomplished something. And he was devoted to his books which were in apple-pie order.
>
> Everything else in the station was a muddle...Strings of dusty niggers with splay feet arrived and departed; a stream of manufactured goods, rubbishy cottons, beads, and brass-wire sent into the depths of darkness, and in return came a precious trickle of ivory. (p.46)

The contrasts between the detailed description of an individual white man, the overweight accountant, and the collective description of the Africans highlights the incongruity of whiteness in this African setting, either as a skin colour or, as signified by the starched linen, as a cultural practice. The symbolic colour binary of black versus white, which dominates European literary traditions, is thus inverted. This serves to highlight one of the major moral inversions of the novel, whereby the 'white' civilizing and enlightening missions of colonialism, assumed by western societies to be good, are shown instead to be evil and immoral. Here, this is represented by the association of the white-clothed, white-skinned accountant with the ivory, a tarnished white, which is described as a 'precious trickle', connoting both the blood and money associated with the ivory trade.

Through the inversion of a pre-existing colour dichotomy, the colour 'black' is used, not to connote the association of evil with black, but to confirm the association of evil with white. Through the commoditization of human life, 'Strings of dusty niggers' are seen as the equivalent of 'a stream of rubbishy goods'. Indigenous black Africans are presented as commodities, strung together like 'beads', in a white economic system. Their representation, as such, functions as an indictment of the white colonialists' greed and moral indifference in allowing such a macabre exploitation to continue.

The semic code is a developed version of Barthes' notion of indices, which we discussed earlier – see Writing Activity 1 in chapter 3 – and refers to how signifiers cluster together in texts to construct telling representations of people or places. You may have been told in previous literary studies to consider characterization through a close examination of how the language – the controlled use of rhythm, diction, imagery and symbolism – has been very carefully selected in order to describe to best effect a character's appearance, speech and actions in various contexts throughout a particular work. To some extent, in structuralist analysis, such an approach involves examining the connotative functions of the 'indices' as opposed to the 'informants' which, as we saw earlier, only give basic information about a character or place.

David Lodge's characterization of Vic in *Nice Work* (1988), which we discussed earlier in this chapter, offers informants (unequivocal details which give basic information about him) – 'Ten stone, two ounces. Quite enough for a man only five feet, five and a half inches tall' (chapter 1). On the other hand, Conrad's characterization of the accountant in *Heart of Darkness* relies on indices – the figurative, metaphorical and connotative functions of language. The accountant is not merely described in denotative language, he is also characterized through the additional connotative functions of language: 'His starched collars and got-up shirt-fronts were achievements of character.' (p.26). The connotations of 'starched collars', in Conrad's text, characterize the accountant as someone who is both stiff and intractable, someone prepared to give greater importance to the trivia of an incongruously imported etiquette and sense of social propriety than to the hideous genocide surrounding him.

Writing Activity 6
Write two pieces describing the same person – a member of the group, or someone you know well. In the first piece, use informants; in the second, indices. What are the strengths and weaknesses of each mode of representation? Which do you find the most effective and which the most literary? Write a third piece in which you combine what you feel are the most effective aspects of the first two descriptions.

You may like to base this piece on a 'brainstorming' session using the suggestions below, which will help you to generate an interesting vocabulary to write from. Describe the person via a list of objects or sensations such as: colour, smell, sound, taste, sight, memory, ambition, clothes, food, record, event, newspaper, occupation, person (adult/child/friend/relative/enemy/lover/stranger). Which would most typify them? What would be their favourite version of the things on the list? How would other people see them in terms of this list?

You may add or subtract from this list, of course. When you have completed it, re-read it carefully to see if you can exchange some of the words for ones which connote more about the character than your first choices.

Barthes' fifth code, the referential or cultural code, refers to a body of knowledge which forms the discourse – that is, all the cultural knowledge – at the time when a text is read by any given reader. This body of knowledge forms the common fund of knowledge of any given society at a particular point in time, and includes a plurality of sub-divisions, for example, 'physical, physiological, medical, psychological, literary, historical [codes]' (Barthes, 1990 [1973]).

In other words, the cultural code – or discourse – refers to all the knowledge which exists in a particular culture at a given time and which is available to a reader as the resource through which they may interpret a text. Of course, authors also have such codes available to them when they write. However, as we have seen before, a text is capable of generating new meanings for readers centuries after the author's death who bring to it interpretations that would not have been possible when the author was alive.

An example of this is Derek Jarman's contemporary interpretation of Christopher Marlowe's play *Edward II* (1591–2), in his film of the same name.

Jarman's film follows the dialogue of Marlowe's text quite faithfully, but sets the action in Britain under Margaret Thatcher. Scenes are enacted by actors dressed as gay rights campaigners protesting against Clause 28, a piece of legislation which restricted the publication and performance of gay literature and art. Thus Jarman's specific 'reading' of *Edward II* refers to cultural codes which were not present at the time Marlowe wrote the play.

The work of Roland Barthes forms a bridge between structuralist and post-structuralist approaches to character. Like the post-structuralists, he came to see readers' responses to texts as constructed out of the discourse of the particular era in which they were readers, but he went on to take the view that human subjectivity itself was constructed from discourse.

Writing Activity 7

Either: Adapt a piece of renaissance drama by recontextualizing it in the present day. Incorporate contemporary settings and topical themes. Make use of set design, props and non-speaking parts to help you. Try to keep the original dialogue but, if this proves impractical, you may translate the language into contemporary idiom.

Or: Working with a group, play some audio recordings of characters' voices. These may be from a radio broadcast, or better still, recordings made by members of the group of people they know. As you are listening, write down notes about the person – for example, details such as name, appearance, age, occupation, regional and ethnic origin, class, political persuasion, whether they are married or single, personality, biography, and so on. Use these notes and the content of what the recorded voices are saying as the basis for a short story or poem.

Critical Activity 4

After hearing the voices compare your initial impressions with those of other members of the group. Did everyone visualize the person in the same way?

Any points of agreement indicate a shared cultural context through which we interpret the signs we receive. Any points of disagreement indicate the significance of the 'reader' – the individual listener – in bringing meaning to the 'signs' or 'texts' we receive (visual, textual or aural). This example illustrates that no 'text' (textual, visual or aural) has a fixed meaning.

Post-Structuralism and Character

If we return to the definition of 'character' given at the beginning of this chapter, we see that character can mean, on the one hand, a mark – as in the characters of the alphabet or the typeface of this book – and, on the other hand, a 'personality', either of a real person or of a fictional representation in a novel or play. To some extent post-structuralist ideas of character are based on a conflation of these meanings. In chapter 2 we saw that, from a post-structuralist perspective, language does not just represent the world, it also simultaneously constructs it.

Similarly, language does not just construct the world for us as we know it, it also constructs us, the people in it. This reverses many of the common-sense assumptions we have of character, language and ourselves that we began to piece together in our opening examination of the word 'character'.

Our common-sense assumption is that, as people, we exist as solid, physical and recognizable objects with unique, individual and recognizable personalities which are stable, fixed, unchanging, and which pre-exist our knowledge of language. From this perspective, language only comes in at a secondary level: we use it after we have experienced something to describe what we know already exists.

The post-structuralist reversal of this seemingly logical explanation is to suggest that, as the French philosopher Jacques Derrida has said, 'there is nothing outside the text' ('il n'y a pas de hors-texte' or 'there is no outside text') (1974 [1967], p.158). In other words, you cannot know who you are, or possibly even experience anything, without first acquiring a language in which to think, experience and name yourself.

Derrida's idea is that, in becoming participants in and users of a language, we can only use a symbolic system which was there before us. We cannot speak or think unless there is already a language for us to speak and think in, and to name things in. 'Consciousness' is a word in the system of the English language. Until we learn this word and the whole conceptual and linguistic context within which it takes its meaning, we cannot have a consciousness. Similarly, the word (or sign) 'consciousness' could not have the meaning English speakers ascribe to it without it being part of a pre-existing system in which it makes sense.

Thus, it is through our encounter with language, through learning to speak, that we come to understand the concept of consciousness. Everything we can think of to 'say', 'think', 'name', 'describe' or 'know' about ourselves and our sensations, our experiences or the world we live in, is a word. Through language we learn to map out who we are, and to measure the distinctions between ourselves and others. We might think we choose how to use the system of language which we inherit from others, but it is already charged with ideas which precede us and thus did not originate with us.

For example, just as a whole spectrum of different objects can be classified as 'red', so, in English, the whole spectrum of humanity was for a long time reduced to broad generic classifications such as 'male' or 'female', 'black' or 'white'. Language's capacity for broad classification and labelling tends to obscure, to habitual language users, the fact that there are many shades of 'black' and 'white', many ideas of what it is to be a man or a woman, across different cultures and in different historical periods.

Through our acquisition of language, then, not only do we learn to name things, we also learn to classify by dividing similarity or by homogenizing difference. Invested in these processes of grouping and dividing through language is the power to divide or group, to include or exclude, one racial or cultural group from another. Similarly, a language's systemic classifications function to classify men and women as similar or different. Thus language not only names us, it places or positions us in groups in relation to others and, from a post-structuralist perspective, mediates every aspect of our relationship to the world.

Critical Activity 5

Think of the different ways your identity is mapped and documented by official regulations and legislation. Explore the way in which official versions of identity might be incorporated in, or form the basis of, a piece of characterization. Some examples can be found in *Nice Work* by David Lodge (1988. p.17), *Lucy* by Jamaica Kincaid (1994, pp.148–9) and in *Beloved* by Toni Morrison (1988, pp.154–6).

Discussion

The three texts we suggested you look at indicate the way in which official or publicly documented versions of identity can be used to construct character. David Lodge uses the format of a curriculum vitae to describe his central male character, Vic Wilcox, in *Nice Work*:

> Who am I?
> He grips the washbasin, leans forward on locked arms, and scans the square face, pale under a forelock of lank brown hair, flecked with grey, the two vertical furrows in the brow like a clip holding the blunt nose in place, the straight-ruled line of the mouth, the squared-off jaw. You know who you are: it's all on file at Division.
> Wilcox: Victor Eugene. *Date of Birth*: 19 Oct. 1940. *Place of Birth*: Easton, Rummidge, England. *Education*: Endwell Primary School, Easton; Easton Grammar School for Boys; Rummidge College of Advanced Technology. MI Mech. Eng. 1964. *Marital Status*: married (to Marjorie Florence Coleman, 1964). *Children*: Raymond (*b*.1966), Sandra (*b*.1969), Gary (*b*.1972). *Career:* 1962–64, apprentice, Vanguard Engineering; 1964–66, Junior Production Engineer, Vanguard Engineering; 1966–70, Senior Engineer, Vanguard Engineering; 1970–74, Production Manager, Vanguard Engineering; 1974–78, Manufacturing Manager, Lewis & Arbuckle Ltd; 1978–80, Manufacturing Director, Rumcol Castings: 1980–85. Managing Director, Rumcol Castings. Present Position: Managing Director. J. Pringle & Sons Casting and General Engineering.
> That's who I am.
>
> (Chapter 1)

Here the c.v. sets up an introductory description of the Vic character, while also introducing details of further characters, suggestions of social class and social mobility, age, personal history and some sense of the representation of personal values. The format of the c.v. not only provides the information that Vic has a wife and three children but also suggests that work is placed above personal relationships in his value system, since this is how we as readers are introduced to the domestic and personal side of Vic's life. It also functions to show not only the significance of work to Vic but also that Vic's identity is inextricably bound up with work roles. Conversely, we also perceive that the c.v. format only gives a partial insight into a character, as Vic is also shown as feeling unfulfilled and on the brink of an identity or mid-life crisis – having little else in his life but work.

Earlier in this chapter (pp.137–8) we examined a passage from Jamaica Kincaid's *Lucy* which, too, makes reference to official documents in relation to the construction of a character. Within the narrative, official documents mapping Lucy's identity as a migrant are of crucial importance at one level – for they secure her the rights to residency and employment – but, as we saw, they say nothing of who she is. Again, details from official documents provide basic information about Lucy, but this is balanced by the implicit recognition that such information is sketchy and selective.

Kincaid, like Lodge, takes the idea of official versions of the self functioning as a kind of mask which conceals other selves. There is an irony in both writers' use of references to official, public documentation of identity, which casts doubt on the authority of public records generally. Since this kind of documentation often names us within a social network, it often relates to our ability to access power. Yet in both cases such information is so partial as to be fallible to the point of uselessness.

The third example we suggested you look at was Toni Morrison's use, in *Beloved*, of a newspaper clipping through which Stamp Paid finds out the details of Sethe's act of infanticide. There are several ironies about this reference to a newspaper report, not least the fact that Morrison took the idea of the story she recounts from an American resource book called *The Black Book*, an anthology of news reports on black people from the beginnings of slavery to the civil rights movements in the 1960s. The unreliability of the news report Stamp Paid reads is exposed through its juxtaposition with the rest of Morrison's narrative, in which several perspectives are given describing the act of infanticide and the motives behind it. Thus, 'authoritative' accounts of the character of Sethe are thrown into doubt when placed against alternative versions of her character.

Each of these constructions of character acknowledges the impossibility of mapping a single version of identity and is particularly sceptical about the authority of official documentary accounts. The extracts are examples of contemporary writers' attempts to write character while simultaneously engaging with the insight that this is no longer either a clear or easy project.

Writing Activity 8
Describe the same character in the following different formats:

1. curriculum vitae
2. love letter
3. newspaper or television report
4. school report
5. job reference/assessment report
6. friend's letter
7. diary entry
8. neighbour's description

9. stranger's description
10. police report
11. poem

Select your most interesting accounts and use them as the basis of a short story.

Cultural determinism, cultural essentialism and social constructionism are all terms which relate to the idea that everything we know about the world and ourselves we have learned through language, including our sense of who we are as unique, individual, human beings. Thus, at one level, we are invented: invented by the ideas and beliefs of what it is to be a person – female, male, child or adult – within the particular culture into which we are born and at the particular time we are born into it.

Since ideas about what men and women are, and what their roles and rights are believed to be, can change over time and across cultures, identity is seen as neither permanently stable nor universally fixed. This view of identity was highlighted by the work of Jacques Lacan, a French psychoanalyst, and supplemented by the insights of Jacques Derrida, a French philosopher. It is also informed by the work of other French critics, such as Roland Barthes, Michel Foucault, Julia Kristeva, Hélène Cixous and Luce Irigaray.

The post-structuralist view can be seen as a reaction against the history of dominant western cultural ideas about the human being. Although the post-structuralist view radically challenges these ideas, many of them still have currency – either they are still supported or are being reacted against. The theologically-inspired idea of divine essence, spiritual essence, or a human soul at the core of human identity and experience, which informed medieval and renaissance views of the world, still exists within religious discourses and has its equivalence in some senses in secular ideologies – certain ecological groups have stressed pantheistic tendencies, which can be allied to this idea.

The scientific and philosophical rationalism of the seventeenth and eighteenth centuries prompted ideas about individuals and societies, through the application of logic and rational thinking, moving towards developed morality and intellectual enlightenment. Such thinking is dominant in western society in the present era. These ideas, known in sum as Enlightenment thinking, are based on the premise that the insights of science and the application of reason and rational thought can be used to develop ways of making the world a better place to live in for everyone. Enlightenment thinking has been prescriptively applied to explanations of social order and to ideas about the individual moral and intellectual development of society's members. These ideas are important since they have helped to shape both readers and writers of literature through their influence on literary form and content. Think how many novels are concerned with representing the intellectual and moral development or decline of an individual in their construction of character.

Enlightenment thinking has been radically criticized in post-war French philosophy, notably in the work of Jacques Derrida and Jean François Lyotard. One of Lyotard's key examples to show that scientific and rational thought leads neither to the betterment of society nor to the intellectual enlightenment or moral development of humans is that the application of rational thought and scientific insights led to the creation of the Nazi death camps.

Part of Derrida's critique of Enlightenment thinking is that it presumes there is some point at which the moral progression of either individuals or societies can stop, having arrived at an ideal state of moral development, fixed knowledge and truth. It is this investment in an idea of truth or certainty which is ultimately criticized by both Derrida and Lyotard. As we shall see, their insights have radically challenged common-sense assumptions about the individual's relationship to the world, supporting the idea that human identity is culturally constructed and that it is determined by the limits of what we know at any given time.

Biological explanations about human experience and identity, particularly theories which informed Social Darwinism, were popular in the nineteenth century and remain significant today. Social Darwinism subscribed to the idea that social inequality could be explained by biological inequality. Men and women of different races were all assumed to be progressing, from their non-human origins, along an evolutionary scale towards higher intellectual and rational states of enlightenment, and thus towards 'civilization'. White European middle-class males were seen as being the morally, physically and intellectually superior social grouping, at the forefront of evolutionary progression, with all other members of the human species ranked at various levels behind them. Two of the arguments against biological explanations of identity are that they have been used to validate sexist and racist ideologies and to justify the *status quo* in unequal societies.

Finally, the Romantics' insights into human experience and identity remain influential, particularly with regard to creative writing, through the idea of expressive realism. At one level, their interventions helped to sustain the idea of individual human essence and, at another level, they were influential in promoting the idea that literature was about the expression of the 'truths' of emotional, passionate and intuitive experience. This carried the implication that an individual was capable of providing an authentic testament to emotional as well as intellectual experience.

A synthesis of the ideas outlined here leads us to the common-sense idea of human identity as one which is rooted in a coherent, consistent, unique experience of innate individuality, which might at some level be influenced by God, biology, free will or society. It is this assumption of stable identity which post-structuralists challenge. The challenge to conventional ideas about people and their identities has led to new kinds of characterization in contemporary literature, particularly in postmodern literature.

Postmodern literature, for our purposes, is literature which engages with the post-structuralist insights to which we have drawn attention throughout this chapter. Predominantly, these are the ideas that a single view of reality or identity is no longer viable; that the classic realist view of representation is problematic; and that the idea of people having a fixed, unchanging essence at the core of their personality is unreliable.

Critical Activity 6

How many social roles can you think of in describing yourself? To what kind of networks do they connect? Do you think your identity changes in relation to the different networks and social contexts of which you are part? Or are you always the same? If you feel your social roles compel you to act and speak differently, in which context could we find the real you? Where do you feel the most like you, and the least? How do you think other people see you in these different roles? What would someone think of you if they could see you all the time? Can you think of ways of incorporating the idea of different social roles into a narrative character?

Discussion

In William Goldman's *Marathon Man* (1974) the opening chapters juxtapose what are the apparently unconnected parallel narratives of two completely different characters, a young history student, Thomas Babington Levy, and a secret agent known as Scylla. Through contrasts in description and dialogue Goldman's narrative conceals the relationship between the two characters – that they are brothers.

As the two narratives converge through this revelation, the boundaries between the two spheres of action become blurred. The domestic world of the younger brother, Babe, is threatened by the dangers in the second narrative (which involves the exposure, pursuit and capture of an ex-Nazi war criminal), while the clinically rational, amoral and impersonal sphere of the secret agent is invaded by the ethics and emotional involvement of kinship ties.

The different social roles of the Scylla/older brother figure in *Marathon Man* are described separately to add mystery, tension and suspense to the narrative's structure. Another example of this kind of technique, where the vastly different social roles of one character are employed for dramatic and comic effect, may be found in the film *True Lies*. Here, a marriage is rejuvenated after a wife discovers that her boring and unexciting husband has another role in life, as a secret agent, in which he is dynamic and exciting.

In Margaret Atwood's *Cat's Eye*, the idea of one person having many different roles, and thus many different identities, is explored throughout the text to question how identity is formed and whether it is stable or indeterminate. We need to understand some of the current philosophical debates about the instability of identity before considering some alternative models of character and characterization.

In chapter 2, as we saw, structuralists embraced the premise that the link between *signifier* and *signified*, between words and the things they describe, was arbitrary. For post-structuralists Saussure's insight did not go far enough. Post-structuralists have subsequently adopted the idea that, having exposed this arbitrary link, it is important to add that the nature of this arbitrariness is likely to change.

For example, structuralists embraced Saussure's notion that the word 'woman' was an arbitrary choice of marks to signify the object woman – that is, an actual or 'real' woman. They would follow the argument that the printed word 'woman' took its meaning not from any direct or logical relation to any actual woman (the word doesn't look like a woman, sound, smell, feel, act or think like a woman, in fact it is 'nothing like a dame'!), but from its relationship to the other parts of an existing system of words.

Identity, Language and Knowledge

'Woman' only begins to mean 'woman' when it is related to the rest of the system of words of which it is a part, in this case the English language. For example, 'woman' is more likely to mean woman when it is placed within a system of words which includes 'man' rather than into a system which includes, say, 'hombre', 'homme' or 'anthropos'.

Post-structuralists take these ideas further. Assuming that to make sense and generate meaning, words have to operate within a given system in which they make sense, we must also realize that the rules governing the identified system are subject to change. Therefore the meaning of the word 'woman' is not only *not* linked by any logical system to the material object it seeks to describe (a 'real' woman), it is also only temporarily linked to the system which validates it.

This conception of the instability of the meanings behind words is the idea known as 'différance' which was theorized by Jacques Derrida. In addition to highlighting the indeterminacy of meaning, Derrida developed his insight as part of a philosophical critique of western notions of presence and essence. Derrida's major argument is that in the West we have been obsessed with looking for the source of things and with the truth of things, and his insight is that basically there is no such thing.

Most people would assume that a person actually describing an event which happened to them would be the source of truth about that event. A man knocked down by a laundry van, providing he survived, should surely be the eyewitness to that experience. If he was sitting in front of us he could give us his personal testimony in his own voice; we could question him to make sure that we absolutely got to the source of what happened.

Derrida's argument is that we are under an illusion in this scenario because we think that a human voice is a manifestation of our inner self, our personality, our experience, our consciousness. As we suggested above (p.150), language always pre-exists us and we are restricted and limited by the existing parameters of that language. Crucially, in learning how to operate and understand a language system, we are similarly encoded and shaped within its inscriptions.

Jacques Lacan, a French psychoanalyst, gave one explanation of the thesis that language encodes us within its systems, drawing concepts from Freud's theory of identity formation and from linguistics. Initially, a small baby cannot distinguish between its own body and the rest of the world. Eventually, the baby learns, before it can speak, to do so. At this point, a division between the senses of inner and outer self is first apprehensible. Later, as a child learns language, this idea of having two selves is reinforced in language as the 'I' who speaks as opposed to the 'I' who is spoken about. Thus the Freudian idea of split self is affirmed and named in language.

Lacan went on to show how language systems were quite sexist, or ideologically biased, in favour of white, middle-class males. In the West, until recently, language systems were commonly built on words, cliches and phrases – such as 'chair*man*' and 'police*man*' – which differentiated between the sexes, and on vocabularies which held far more pejorative words to describe women than men. Lacan concluded that the 'I' position of language systems was male. His insights were radical at the time but have become more popular since they expose that personality is not inborn, but is constructed through language.

Furthermore, if girls and boys are placed differently within a language system, Lacan's work shows a cultural rather than biological explanation for sexual inequality. Three French feminist writers, Julia Kristeva, Hélène Cixous and Luce Irigaray, amplified Lacan's ideas by developing a genre of women's writing known as 'writing the body'. Following Lacan's insight that language was constructed from a male ideological viewpoint, these writers experimented with versions of writing developed to express women's experience and women's different relationship to language.

Michel Foucault suggested that human identities, or personalities, are constructed from discourse. Discourse generally means communication through speech. However, Foucault extended the meaning of the word with his concept of 'discursive fields'. Discursive fields are the conceptual and linguistic parameters of any given body of knowledge. Since discourse, at its fundamental level, is always constructed in and by, as well as communicated through, language, then by extension so is knowledge.

Hence, all the problems examined in this book in relation to the indeterminacy and unreliability of language as a system of communication and a form of representation can, by extension, be applied to all forms of knowledge. In post-structuralist theory, all knowledge systems come to be seen as indeterminate, partisan, partial and unreliable.

Alternative Models of Character

In the light of these philosophical debates about the instability of identity and the impossibility of representation, how do contemporary writers construct character?

Reading Activity

Read the following extracts and note your responses to each, including any questions you may have about each extract.

1.   "She's learning her Bible, Grace tells me," Mrs. Smeath says, and then I know it's me they're discussing...

"They'll learn all that," says Aunt Mildred. "Till you're blue in the face. But it's all rote learning, it doesn't sink in. The minute your back is turned they'll go right back the way they were."

The unfairness of this hits me like a kick. How can they say that, when I've won a special mention for my essay on temperance...I can recite whole psalms, whole chapters, I can sing all the coloured-slide white-knight Sunday School songs without looking.

"What can you expect, with that family?" says Mrs. Smeath. She doesn't go on to say what's wrong with my family. "The other children sense it. They know."

"You don't think they're being too hard on her?" says Aunt Mildred. Her voice is relishing. She wants to know how hard.

"It's God's punishment," says Mrs. Smeath. "It serves her right."

(Margaret Atwood, *Cat's Eye*, pp.179–80)

[approximately ten years later]

"What'd she use, a knitting needle?" one says. His tone is accusing: he may think I was helping her.

"I have no idea," I say. "I hardly even know her." I don't want to be implicated.

"That's usually what it is," he says. "Stupid kids. You'd think they'd have more sense."

I agree with him that she's been stupid...But there is also another voice; a small, mean voice, ancient and smug, that comes from somewhere deep inside my head: *It serves her right.*

(*Cat's Eye*, p.321)

2.   Inside two boys bled in the sawdust and dirt at the feet of a nigger woman holding a blood-soaked child to her chest with one hand and an infant by the heels in the other...Two were lying open-eyed in sawdust; a third pumped blood down the dress of the main one – the woman schoolteacher had bragged about, the one he said made fine ink, damn good soup, pressed his collars the way he liked besides having at least ten breeding years left. Now she'd gone wild, due to the mishandling of the nephew who'd overbeat her and made her cut and run.

(Toni Morrison, *Beloved*, p.149)

Paul D slid the clipping out from under Stamp's palm. The print meant nothing to him... "But this ain't her mouth," Paul D said. "This ain't it at all."...So Stamp Paid did not tell him how she flew...how her face beaked, how her hands worked like claws, how she collected them every which way: one on her shoulder, one under her arm, one by the hand, the other shouted forward into the woodshed...

(*Beloved*. p.155)

The best thing she was, was her children. Whites might dirty *her* all right, but not her best thing, her beautiful, magical best thing – the part of her that was clean. No undreamable dreams about whether the headless, feetless torso hanging in the tree with a sign on it was her husband or Paul A; whether the bubbling-hot girls in the colored-school fire set by patriots included her daughter; whether a gang of whites invaded her daughter's private parts, soiled her daughter's thighs and threw her daughter out of the wagon...

And no one, nobody on this earth would list her daughter's characteristics on the animal side of the paper.

(Beloved, p.251)

3. Why is it that the most unoriginal thing we can say to one another is still the thing we long to hear? 'I love you' is always a quotation. You did not say it first and neither did I yet when you say it and when I say it we speak like savages who have found three words and worship them. I did worship them but now I am alone on a rock hewn out of my own body.
CALIBAN You taught me language and my profit on't is
        I know how to curse. The red plague rid you
        For learning me your language.
...It is no conservationist love. It is a big game hunter and you are the game. A curse on this game. How can you stick at a game when the rules keep changing? I shall call myself Alice and play croquet with the flamingoes. In Wonderland everyone cheats and love is Wonderland isn't it? Love makes the world go round. Love is blind. All you need is love. Nobody ever died of a broken heart. You'll get over it. It'll be different when we're married. Think of the children. Time's a great healer. Still waiting for Mr Right? Miss Right? And maybe all the little Rights?

(Jeanette Winterson, Written on the Body, pp.9–10)

4. Ambrose was "at that awkward age." His voice came out highpitched as a child's if he let himself get carried away; to be on the safe side, therefore, he moved and spoke with *deliberate calm* and *adult gravity*. Talking soberly of unimportant or irrelevant matters and listening consciously to the sound of your own voice are useful habits for maintaining control in this difficult interval. *En route* to Ocean City he sat in the back seat of the family car with his brother Peter, age fifteen, and Magda G—, age fourteen, a pretty girl and exquisite young lady, who lived not far from them on B—Street in the town of D—, Maryland. Initials, blanks, or both were often substituted for proper names in nineteenth-century fiction to enhance the *illusion* of reality. It is as if the author felt it necessary to delete the names for reasons of tact or legal liability. Interestingly, as with other aspects of realism, it is an *illusion* that is being enhanced, by purely artificial means. Is it likely, does it violate the principle of verisimilitude, that a thirteen-year-old boy could make such a sophisticated observation?

(John Barth, Lost in the Funhouse, (reprinted in Charters, 1987, pp.10–18)

5. You are about to begin reading Italo Calvino's new novel, *If on a winter's night a traveller.* Relax. Concentrate. Dispel every other thought. Let the world around you fade. Best to close the door; the TV is always on in the next room. Tell the others right away, "No, I don't want to watch TV!" Raise your voice – they won't hear you otherwise – "I'm reading! I don't want to be disturbed!"... It's not that you expect anything in particular from this particular book. You're the sort of person who, on principle, no longer expects anything of anything. There are plenty, younger than you or less young, who live in expectation of ordinary experiences: from books, from people, from

journeys, from events, from what tomorrow has in store.

(Italo Calvino, *If on a winter's night a traveller.* pp.3–4)

Discussion

The five methods of representing character used by the contemporary writers quoted above show examples of character construction written in the light, or shadow, of contemporary philosophical and theoretical ideas.

1. The Unreliable Character

To a great extent the unreliable character is also the unreliable narrator. Given the frequent conflation of the unreliable character with the unreliable narrator, much of our earlier discussion of the unreliable narrator (chapter 5) bears relevance here. Quite unreliable is the central character in Ambrose Bierce's short story 'An Occurrence At Owl Creek Bridge' (1891) and the subsequent film version (1964). In this story the central character, Peyton Farquhar, is about to be hung but manages to escape death and return to his family. The twist in the tail is that most of Bierce's narrative is revealed as a fantasy occurring in the seconds during which Farquhar is hung.

The textual strategy of the unreliable narrator is a well-used literary convention. The Farquhar character and correlative narrative perspective (or dominant focalization) is a fairly conventional use of the unreliable character/narrator for surprise effect. Similar effects are achieved in detective or thriller narrative genres such as Agatha Christie's *The Murder of Roger Ackroyd* (1926).

However, unreliable characters are also used in contemporary fiction as textual strategies to represent the indeterminacy of identity. In the Atwood extracts given above, the anachronies in the narrative ordering of events and the disruption to linear chronology allow for various constructions of the character of Elaine Risley: as child, adolescent, young adult and mature adult. In some instances, details about the child Elaine are filtered through the focalization of the older Elaine and, by these various juxtapositions and shifts in focalization, her character is constructed as fluid, inconstant, contradictory and ambivalent. Apparent shifts in Elaine's moral position represent how identity is socially constructed – that is, how we learn to be who we are from other people.

Texts such as *Cat's Eye* show how the construction of character can be more complex in the contemporary novel than in the canonical, moral-development novel. Character construction is used here to suggest that identity is constructed in language and learned by mimicking other people's speech and behaviour patterns. Thus, at different times in the novel, the central character, Elaine Risley, is a victim of peevish, uncharitable hypocrisy. At other times she herself has learned to be a peevish, uncharitable hypocrite towards others. Atwood has constructed a contradictory and ambivalent character to suggest that the inscription of female identity is always problematic.

2.   The Choral Narrative

If the unreliable narrator has been revived in contemporary fiction since it so aptly addresses the contemporary sense of doubt about the coherent unity of anything, an alternative strategy for negotiating the truth of events is the choral narrative. By this term we mean to suggest a narrative in which a number of characters participate in, and narrate through various means, the same story. Examples of this kind of narrative can be found in two texts which we discussed in chapter 4: Michael Carson's short story 'Peter's Buddies' and Toni Morrison's novel *Beloved*, from which the three extracts under 2 on pp.158–59 are taken. The novel's major dramatic event, an act of infanticide by the child's mother, is told several times by different characters.

The three accounts quoted here describe the same event. The first gives the perspective of the white schoolteacher who has brutalized Sethe in the past and whose appearance as the leader of the posse which has come to take her back into slavery initiates her attempt to kill her children. The second perspective is that of two black male slaves, Stamp Paid and Paul D, who are friends of Sethe. Stamp Paid offers a news clipping to Paul D which gives an account of Sethe's arrest. Although Paul D cannot read, his response to the photograph of Sethe indicates a problem with representation and, within the context of Morrison's text, also functions as a critique of white versions of black experience. The third version is Sethe's own account of what happened and why. Although each character's account contributes something to the representation of the event, no single view gives all its aspects, which indicates that there is no fixed version of an event in the 'real' world.

3.   The Genderless Character

Previous writers have used the technique of the *unreliably gendered* narrator to effect a 'twist in the tail', but Jeannette Winterson in her novel *Written On The Body* (1993) – from which extract 3 on p.159 is taken – is the first writer we know of who has attempted to represent an *ungendered* narrator. To evade identifying the gender of her central character Winterson had to leave out many of the features of a realist characterization: the framework of socio-historic and personal history, and the detailing of lifestyle, personal interests, dress and appearance. Having read extract 3, how successful do you think Winterson has been in creating a genderless character?

The idea of playing with the gender identity of characters has also been used by the playwright Caryl Churchill. In *Cloud Nine* (1979) Churchill indicates the artificiality of gender identity, given that gender is socially constructed, by having two female characters, a Victorian woman and a young girl, who are played by adult male actors, and an adolescent boy who is played by a woman. Other writers who have employed this technique include William Shakespeare in, for example, *Twelfth Night* (1599–1600) and Virginia Woolf in her novel *Orlando* (1928).

The indeterminacies of the way gender is characterized in these narratives represents the indeterminacies of personal identity exposed by contemporary critical insights. They serve as reminders of the way gender and social identity within cultural experience are now seen as constructed and variable over time and across cultures rather than as innate or fixed.

4.   Metafictive Characters

'Metafiction' has been identified as one of the most typifying features of postmodern literature. It describes techniques in fiction which draw self-reflexive attention to a text's fictional status, and through this strategy highlights the problems and politics involved in representation. Postmodernist literature is eschewed by some critics for resorting to endless game-playing with language, while others see postmodern literature as capable of engaging with political issues. Two examples of characterization which to some extent illustrate the controversies within debates on postmodernism include John Barth's short story 'Lost in the Funhouse' (1968) and Angela Carter's *Nights at the Circus* (1984). In Barth's text – extract 4 on pp.159–60 – an adolescent boy's trip to the coast with his family is described through shifting registers, styles and focalization, and in shifting narrative perspectives, in such a way that the text is reduced to game-playing with the techniques of defamiliarization. Carter's text – an account of the adventures of a female trapeze artist working her way through a variety of Victorian entertainment circuits in the nineteenth century – uses metafictive techniques to challenge ideas about gender roles.

5.   The Reader as Character

Perhaps the most extreme form of metafictive elision between real person and character, effected through the idea that both are constructed in language, can be seen in a text which includes its reader as a character in the text. Roland Barthes (1977 [1968]) suggested that most texts give indications of 'signs of reception', suggesting that readers, as well as narrators, are *always* signified throughout a narrative:

> At first sight, the signs of the narrator appear more evident...than those of the reader...in actual fact the latter are simply more oblique...each time the narrator stops "representing" and reports details which he knows perfectly well but which are unknown to the reader, there occurs, by a signifying failure, a sign of reading, for there would be no sense in the narrator giving himself a piece of information. (p.110)

Such 'oblique' 'signs of reception' are dispensed with in the work of such writers as Italo Calvino – extract 5 on p.160 – which deliberately places the reader as a character in the text. Calvino sustains the consistency of the reader-as-character technique by repeated interjections of collusive or direct address to the reader: for example, on page thirty, the reader is reminded that they have arrived at   page   thirty.

Calvino's technique seems to have brought us full circle in its return to the reader-character elision discussed at the outset of this chapter. However, the circle is an illusory one, since the reader-character elision of realist literature presupposed that characters were the equivalents of real people, whereas the presuppositions of post-structuralist theories bring us to the insight that people, as fictional constructs, are the equivalents of characters.

Writing Activity 9

Either: Use one of the above five methods of post-structuralist characterization as the basis for a short story.

Or: Write a science fiction piece in which a character in the future finds a piece of text, or simply a word, and recontextualizes it in such a way as either to give it a new meaning or to void its current meaning.

In sum, contemporary writers use a variety of strategies for constructing character in relation to late twentieth-century critical thinking. These strategies are often antithetical to the conventions of realism and are frequently related to three areas of critical insight. Firstly, they relate to an increasing belief in the unreliability of modes of representation. They can be seen to acknowledge the insight that all representation is only arbitrarily linked to the world it seeks to represent. Secondly, they can be related to a collapse of faith in singular or fixed notions of truth and a loss of belief in the possibility of a single, shared view of reality. As such they can be seen as acknowledging reality as either indeterminable or comprising a plurality of views and perspectives simultaneously. Thirdly, they can be related to the loss of faith in the idea that personal identity is constant, fixed, permanent or innate, and can be seen as acknowledging that personal identity is indeterminate, variable, fluid or constructed from various discourses (which themselves are indeterminate, variable, fluid...).

Further Reading

Aston, E. and Savona, G. (1991) *Theatre as a Sign-System: A Semiotics of Text and Performance*. London: Routledge.

An interesting semiological and structuralist approach to dramatic texts and performance. See chapter 3 for an accessible discussion of character from the perspective of structuralism, specifically in relation to theatre production and play texts.

Chatman S. (1978) *Story and Discourse: Narrative Structure in Fiction and Film*. Ithaca and London: Cornell University Press.

An extensive introduction to narrative analysis which should be accessible to both students and tutors. See chapter 3, in particular, for a focused discussion of literary theory and character.

Rimmon-Kenan, S. (1983) *Narrative Fiction: Contemporary Poetics*. London: Methuen.

This is an accessible and informative introduction to all aspects of narrative theory which also includes a chapter (5) on characterization and a useful analysis of the modes for writing characters' speech.

Tallack, D. (1991[1987]) *Literary Theory at Work – Three Texts*. London: Batsford.

This edited collection contains a selection of useful essays on a range of literary theoretical perspectives including feminist, structuralist and post-structuralist approaches to character. The second chapter on structuralism by Bernard McGuirk is particularly interesting since it deals with structuralist approaches to character and gives useful suggestions for further reading. The essays will be more accessible to tutors than to students.

Watt, I. (1957) *The Rise of the Novel*. London: Hogarth Press.

Belsey, C. (1980) *Critical Practice*. London: Methuen.

Both include accounts of realism which are informative on the conventions of realist characterization. Watt provides a useful socio-historical account of the development of the novel as a form, although this should he supplemented by Dale Spender's *Mother of the Novel* (1986, London: Pandora Press). Watt also has a useful chapter on the rise of realism as a literary tradition. Belsey offers highly readable explanations of the conventions associated with both classic and expressive realism and perceptive critiques of them. Each of these texts should be accessible to students.

Postscript

In the Introduction, we referred to Wilson Harris's view of life as a series of infinite rehearsals and suggested that this might apply to writing also. If you have worked your way through this book, we hope you are able to think of it, too, as a rehearsal. Throughout, we have written from the premise that the process of writing is as important as the work we produce. In fact, unless you are very fortunate, you will probably only be satisfied with a small proportion of what you write. As you continue to write, we recommend that you think of your writings as part of a continuous process.

However, at some point you will probably want to evaluate your work. How should you go about this? The aim of our postscript is to suggest ways in which you might appropriate some of the theoretical ideas and writing techniques you have encountered in the book, in order to evaluate your own writing. It should be clear by now, given that there are many competing – and often conflicting – views about how to approach literature, that the methodology and mechanics of evaluating creative writing are no less areas of contention than critical theory itself. Below are some suggested criteria for evaluating your own writing which we hope will offer you useful guidance, whether you are reading this book by yourself or as a member of a writing group.

1. Controlled and Crafted Writing

Since creative writing is self-consciously constructed, it should show evidence of control, design, self-consciousness and critical selection in both its choice and use of language. Creative writing should be distinguishable by its inevitably controlled style and its inevitably literary use of language. Since it is a text-based and not an oral medium, creative writing, unlike everyday speech, can be planned, revised, edited and redrafted with the immense resources of a text-based culture's vocabulary to draw on. One way in which writing appears controlled and crafted is in its conciseness.

2. Conciseness and Precision

As you redraft your work, it should become increasingly more difficult to edit it. Aim for precision and conciseness. Imagine that you had only ten words to take with you to a desert island. Ten words in which to sum up your entire life. You probably would not choose phrases like 'it was a sunny day' or use 'he said' or 'she said' too many times, if at all! Try not to over-use adjectives or personal pronouns.

Setting a limit on what you write forces you to think carefully about which words you choose to include. You would probably choose indicial or connotative language, or arrange your choice of words into specific contexts within which they open up new chains of associations. Try to avoid convolution (long-windedness) and tautology (repetition). Remember the different ways of writing characters' speech you experimented with, and how the difference between telling and showing added to the immediacy of your writing.

3. Literary Writing

As we have seen, the Russian Formalists suggested that one way in which literary writing can be distinguished from everyday language usage is in its capacity to defamiliarize the reader from the taken-for-grantedness of the world. Avoid clichés and treat words as if they were objects of value: jewels or gold nuggets. Do not take words or their usage for granted. Pick up new words and find innovative contexts for familiar words. Use a dictionary and a thesaurus, and keep a vocabulary book.

4. Public vs Private Language

Your work should be accessible to other readers. The amount of introspection and privately understood allusion you can afford is minimal. Practice making your writing accessible to a silent reader; try to distance your own voice as you re-read your writing and imagine how it would read if you had never read it before. Remember that Roland Barthes' notion of the shared cultural code which readers draw on to make sense of a text did not include your own silent thoughts as you read back your own writing. You must place yourself in the role of the reader when you re-read work and defamiliarize yourself from your role as writer.

5. Internal Consistency

Finally, your work should be internally consistent. In other words, your writing should be consistent within its own frame of reference, in terms of style, register, logic, causality, tense and so on. The exercises in chapter 7 based on Barthes' notion of enigmas and sequences of action indicate two ways in which a work can be checked for its internal consistency. Other ways of monitoring the consistency of your work include: the accuracy of any research-based element and the consistency of your writing in relation to the conventions of the genre or form you are writing in.

A final point concerns 'designed inconsistency'. Most of the pitfalls we suggest you avoid in your writing can, conversely, be incorporated, providing that this occurs by design and not by accident. Your writing can thus be vague, employ shifts in register, break with genre, be convoluted or tautological and use clichés and everyday speech *provided this is for a specific purpose* which, again, should be evident from the internal consistency of your writing.

Biographies and Bibliographies of Major Literary Theorists

Many of the writers included in this section have written extensively in many areas. The bibliographies included here are a selection of the best-known works by each writer. An asterisk* has been included next to those texts we feel may be useful starting points for students. These texts are important within current English Studies at advanced and degree level.

Mikhail Bakhtin (1895–1975)

Mikhail Bakhtin was a Soviet literary theorist who, from the 1920s onwards, refined the same set of ideas, and who attracted the attention of Soviet intellectuals in the 1970s. Born in Lithuania, the son of a bank official, Bakhtin spent part of his childhood in Odessa before going to University in St. Petersburg. Here, from 1913–1918, Bakhtin was influenced by Classical and Germanic philosophical thinking and the Roman oratorical tradition. For most of his life Bakhtin was a teacher, a writer and a university lecturer, living in various parts of Russia, before becoming Chairman of the Department of Russian and World Literature at the University of Saransk in 1957.

In 1929, Bakhtin was arrested and sentenced to five years internal exile, but this was commuted due to ill health. From 1923, he suffered from a bone disease which resulted in his leg being amputated in 1938. Bakhhtin worked as a book-keeper in Kustanaj from 1929 until 1935, during which time he was supplied with books by friends and wrote some of his most influential essays.

Throughout his writing career Bakhtin's work was frequently lost, destroyed or the subject of controversy. His doctoral dissertation on the work of Rabelais, written between 1946 and 1949, was disallowed and not published until 1965. Some of his works are contentiously rumoured to have appeared under the names of his friends V.N. Volosinov and P.N. Medvedev during the period leading up to his arrest and exile.

Bakhtin had two key theses. The first was that art should enable the articulation of diverse points of view. He felt that the novel, in particular, was the form most capable of simultaneously expressing the pluralism and heterogeneity of linguistic and cultural systems within art, as opposed to conveying the absolutism of monological discourse. Secondly, Bakhtin felt that comedy, in the form of the 'carnivalesque' of folk-culture, could be seen as having cathartic, transformative and revolutionary powers, in its potential to expose the relativity of power hierarchies within society. Bakhtin's theories of literature and the novel have gained influence in English studies since their translation into English, firstly in the late 1960s and latterly in the mid to late 1980s.

Key Concepts:

Heteroglossia; polyglossia; dialogism; carnivalesque; centrifugal and centripetal.

Major Texts by Mikhail Bakhtin available in English translation

- (1968) *Rabelais and His World.* Trans. by Hélène Iswolsky. London: MIT Press. (First published in Russian, 1965)

- (1981) *The Dialogical Imagination. Four Essays.** Trans. by Michael Holquist and Caryl Emerson. Austin: University of Texas Press.

- (1984) *Problems of Dostoevsky's Poetics.** Manchester: Manchester University Press.

Roland Barthes (1915–1980)

Roland Barthes studied French Literature and Classics at the University of Paris. He also taught in universities in Romania and Egypt before joining the Centre Nationale de la Recherche Scientifique, where he pursued research in Sociology and Lexicology. Barthes also studied the sociology of signs, symbols and collective representations at the Ecole des Hautes Etudes, and from 1976 onward was Professor of Semiology at the Collège de France.

Barthes is famous for his ideological critiques of mass-culture, working from the premise that the mass media's 'collective representations' are the equivalent of a sign system; and for his attempt to analyse semiotically the mechanics of visual as well as textual language. In *Mythologies* (1973) Barthes attempted to analyse how one might go beyond simply unmasking ideologies, in order to account in detail for 'the mystification which transforms petit-bourgeois culture into a universal culture'.

Barthes is well-known as much for his conceptualization of 'The Death of the Author' (1977) and for his attempt to theorize a poetics of reading in *The Pleasure of the Text* (1975) as for his disciplinary eclecticism. Barthes was self-reflexive in his methodology, his work often being suggestive and open-ended. In its different eras, Barthes' work can be seen to share the features of both structuralist and post-structuralist literary criticism.

Key Concepts

The death of the author; the grammar of narrative/narratology/structuralism; the five codes.

Major texts by Roland Barthes available in English translation

- (1967) *Elements of Semiology*. Trans. by Annette Lavers and Colin Smith. London: Jonathan Cape. (First published in French, 1964)

- (1967) *Writing Degree Zero*. Trans. by A. Lavers and C. Smith. London: Jonathan Cape. (First published in French, 1953)

- (1973) *Mythologies*.* Trans. and edited by A. Lavers. London: Granada. (First published in French, 1972)

- (1977; reprinted 1982) 'Introduction to the Structural Analysis of Narratives'.* in Stephen Heath, editor and translator, *Image-Music-Text*. London: Fontana.

- (1976) *The Pleasure of the Text*. Trans. by Richard Miller. London: Jonathan Cape. (First published in French, 1975)

- (1977; reprinted 1982) 'The Death of the Author'* in S. Heath, editor and translator, *Image-Music-Text*. London: Fontana.

- (1990) *S/Z*. Trans. R. Miller. Oxford: Blackwell. (First published in French, 1973)

Hélène Cixous (b.1937)

Hélène Cixous was born in Oran, Algeria, of Jewish and Austro-German descent. Despite the fact that her first language was German, she first studied English within the French education system. Having previously taught at the University of Bordeaux and the Sorbonne, Cixous became Professor of English Literature at the University of Paris III (Vincennes) in 1968, at the age of 29. Here, in 1970, she was a co-founder and member of the editorial board of the journal *Poétique* and, in 1974, she established the Centre de Recherches en Etudes Féminines, in effect founding the first research group on the theory of femininity.

Since the 1960s, Hélène Cixous has written an extensive and impressive range of fiction, critical readings of modern writers, essays and writings on epic theatre. The range of her critical work includes readings of: Shakespeare, James Joyce, the German Romantics, Kafka, Clarice Lispector, Kierkegaard, Heidegger, Derrida, Freudian psychoanalysis and the poetry of, among others, Rimbaud, Rilke and Celan. Her plays have focused on South East Asia and the fate of Eastern Europe, and her recent essays discuss apartheid, nationalism and post-colonialism. Her work collapses the boundaries between politics and poetics, and combines interpretation with creation, particularly feminine creation.

Cixous' work is predominantly a search for new techniques of writing and in particular is concerned to ratify the status of feminine writing. Along with Julia Kristeva and Luce Irigaray, she is one of three French feminist critics attempting to theorize an *écriture féminine*. She is also known for her work on 'writing the body'.

Her contribution to English studies is largely related to theorizing relations between sexuality and textuality (gender and writing) in two mid-1970s essays in which she discussed the potentiality for writing to be transgressive. Cixous' written work often involves an experimental mix of the genres and registers of theory, memoir, narrative and lyric in order to resist what she has seen as the phallocentric oppression of women within received language systems.

Key Concepts

Ecriture féminine; writing the body; phallocentrism.

Major Texts by Hélène Cixous available in English translation

- (1972) *The Exile of James Joyce or the Art of Replacement*. Trans. by Sally Purcell. New York: David Lewis. (Also: London: Calder, 1976; and New York: Riverrun, 1980) (First published in France, 1968)

- (1974) 'The Character of "Character"'. Trans. by Keith Cohen. *New Literary History*, Vol. 5, Winter, pp.384–402.

- (1976) 'The Laugh of the Medusa.'* Trans. by Keith Cohen and Paula Cohen. *Signs*, Vol. I, Summer, pp.875–99. (First published in French, 1975)

- (1986) 'Sorties'* in Hélène Cixous with Catherine Clement *The Newly Born Woman*. Trans. by Betsy Wing. Minneapolis: University of Minnesota Press. (First published in French, 1975)

- (1992) *'Coming to Writing' and Other Essays*. Trans. by Deborah Jensen. Cambridge: Harvard University Press.

Jacques Derrida (b.1930)

Jacques Derrida is a philosopher and lecturer who was born in Algeria but who has lectured in Paris for over thirty years. His ideas have been among the most influential in the transformation of literary and cultural studies since the 1960s. Derrida's critique of western metaphysics has had a massive impact on all forms of knowledge – especially on previous concepts of reading, writing and speech.

His work has not only exposed, but also reversed, many of western society's taken-for-granted assumptions about the way language works, the formation of authoritative knowledge and ideas of truth.

Controversial ideas associated with Derrida are the process of deconstruction and the infamous statement that 'there is nothing outside the text'. Derrida was concerned to demonstrate the fallacy of believing that we can establish or arrive at the fixed truth of anything, particularly through language. Phonocentrism is Derrida's term to describe belief in the authority of the spoken word. We tend to believe that a speaking person, as an eyewitness to the events of their own life, can be the agent for establishing the truth of something that happened to them.

Logocentrism is Derrida's term for belief in the authority of the written word. We tend to assume that we can arrive at a finite point of understanding what a word 'really' means, just as we assume we can trace its origin. Thus we think that in words we can establish fixed meanings and through language we can arrive at the truth about an event or an idea.

Derrida suggests that all these assumptions are wrong. Speech cannot give us the truth, since to speak we have to borrow words and meanings which were in play before us, and we are limited by what these words allow us to say. For example, if we could only speak in one language in which there was no word for 'confusion', could we say that we 'felt confused'? From this we can begin to question the nature of what we have always taken for granted as our 'feelings', by seeing how what it is possible to 'feel' is at some point proscribed by what it is possible to say.

In words themselves, the search for truth – for the true meaning of a word – is also a lost cause, according to Derrida, since the meanings of words are always in flux and never fixed. Trying to find the origin of a word is like peeling the layers from an onion: when you take away the final layer there is nothing at the centre. Similarly, etymological investigations become like stripping wallpaper from the walls of an old house where the most recent design covers the previous ones, just as with words one (temporary) meaning is layered over a previous (temporary) meaning. Like compacted layers of wallpaper, words are continually being supplemented with a new version of what they mean. Even in their contemporary usage, the meaning of words is continually shifting, depending upon how they are contextualized against other words.

Derrida's ideas are seen as liberating by some critics, since freedom from the notion that words have fixed, stable meanings allows for pejorative meanings to be unhinged from particular words. However, other critics perceive Derrida's ideas as nihilistic, suggesting that we need to see words as having fixed meanings or we lose the power to communicate.

Following the successful reception of his paper, 'Structure, Sign, and Play in the Discourse of the Human Sciences', outlining many of his key ideas to an audience at Johns Hopkins University in 1966, Derrida was credited with initiating a new critical movement in the United States. He was offered a teaching post at Yale University and since the late 1960s has divided his time between the United States and Europe.

Key Concepts

Deconstruction; différance (a portmanteau term coined by Derrida bringing together the senses of difference and deferment); logocentrism; phonocentrism; supplement.

Major texts by Jacques Derrida available in English translation

- (1968) *Writing and Différance*. Trans. by Alan Bass. London: Routledge.

- (1973) 'Différance'* in *Speech and Phenomena, and other Essays on Husserl's Theory of Signs*. Trans. by David B. Allison. Evanston, Illinois: Northwestern University Press.

- (1974) *Of Grammatology*. Trans. and introduced by Gayatri Chakavorty Spivak. London: Johns Hopkins University Press. (First published in French, 1967)

- (1981) *Dissemination*. Trans. by Barbara Johnson. London: Athlone Press.

- (1982) *Margins of Philosophy*. London: Harvester Wheatsheaf. (First published in French, 1972)

- (1991) *Between the Blinds: A Derrida Reader.* Trans. and edited by Peggy Kamuf. London: Harvester Wheatsheaf.

Michel Foucault (1926–1984)

The son of a surgeon, Paul-Michel Foucault was born in Poitiers, where he was educated in Catholic schools before moving to Paris in 1946. Later educated at both the prestigious Ecole Normale Supérieure and the Centre Nationale de la Recherche Scientifique, Foucault initially studied psychology but switched to psycho-pathology in 1952.

As a student Foucault was a member of the Communist Party in 1950–51. After graduating, he taught at universities in Uppsala, Warsaw and Hamburg before returning to work in France in 1960. In the late 1960s, Foucault returned to Paris where he taught philosophy at the University of Vincennes before becoming Professor of the History of Systems of Thought at the Collège de France. Michel Foucault died of a brain tumour in 1984.

In his major works, Foucault was concerned to map the development of our ideas about identity and knowledge. His view of identity was that it is constructed from a web of social relations which are organized in the interests of power. Foucault charted the way in which subjectivities are constructed from specialized areas of knowledge, or discourses. Discourse, on the one hand, means to communicate through language but, in Foucault's sense, it also refers to any body of knowledge which comes to be seen as authoritative, and which thus comes to dominate and construct our conceptions of truth or reality at any given time.

Foucault's work showed that ideas about truth and reality are often related to and transmitted by institutional structures in society. He also showed that such ideas are historically specific – i.e. linked to the beliefs of a particular historical period – rather than universally and timelessly consistent. Thus, at a given moment in the history of, say, Europe or Africa, there will be a particular discourse of medicine, governing how the body, illness and treatment are perceived. Foucault was especially interested in the procedures by which discourses are controlled and organized. For him, dominant bodies of knowledge, particularly when people believe in them, are the source of power and control in a society.

Key Concepts

Discourse; discursive fields; discipline.

Major Texts by Michel Foucault available in English translation

- (1970) *The Order of Things: an Archaeology of the Human Sciences.* Trans. by Alan Sheridan Smith. New York: Random House. (First published in French, 1966)

- (1971) *Madness and Civilization: a History of Insanity in the Age of Reason.* Trans. by Richard Howard. New York: Mentor Books. (First published in French, 1964)

- (1972) *The Archaeology of Knowledge.* Trans. by Alan Sheridan Smith. New York: Harper and Rowe. (First published in French, 1969)

- (1977) *Discipline and Punish: the Birth of the Prison.** Trans. by Alan Sheridan Smith. New York: Pantheon. (First published in French, 1975)

Gérard Genette (b.1930)

In 1970, French critic and rhetorician Gérard Genette founded the journal *Poétique,* along with Hélène Cixous and Tvetzan Todorov. Since then, Genette has taught at Columbia University and New York University. In *Narrative Discourse: An Essay in Method* (1980) Genette developed a model of analysis combining literary theory with literary criticism which exposed, quite radically, how the disrupted chronologies of time are used structurally within European novelistic literature. Genette's model is exemplified through an analysis of a Proust novel, but his observations can be applied to the work of many other European prose writers.

Genette's analytical model can be seen as an example of narratology, an analysis of literary texts which combines structuralist methods with the premise that a narrative can be systematically broken down into units for the purposes of close (and almost scientific) analysis. His model also includes: a foundational analysis of narrative levels; analysis of the varieties of narratorial perspective and positioning within the levels of narrative he identifies; and an analysis of focalization, a term employed ubiquitously to map the complexities of possible shifts in narratorial point of view throughout a narrative.

Like Roland Barthes (who, in his *Introduction to the Structural Analysis of Narrative,* draws an analogy between the structure of a sentence and a corresponding potential for seeing that narrative is comprised of identifiable component parts or units), Genette draws an analogy between the expansion of narrative action and the expansion of a verb, naming the units of his model for narrative analysis after the linguistic terms for verbal expansion: *tense, mood* and *voice.*

Key Concepts

Narrative levels (diegetic, hypodiegetic, extradiegetic, intradiegetic): homodiegetic and heterodiegetic narrators; analepses; prolepses; tense; voice; mood; focalization; narratology; structuralism.

Major Texts by Gérard Genette available in English translation

- (1980) *Narrative Discourse: An Essay in Method.** Trans. by Jane E. Lewin. Ithaca and London: Cornell University Press. (First published in French, 1972)

- (1982) *Figures of Literary Discourse.* Trans. by Alan Sheridan Smith. Oxford: Blackwell.

Luce Irigaray (b.1939)

A former member of the Ecole Freudienne de Paris and a practising psychoanalyst, Luce Irigaray is also Director of Research in Philosophy at the Centre Nationale de Recherche Scientifique, Paris, where she has held a research post since 1964.

Key Concepts

Writing the body; *écriture féminine;* phallocentrism.

Major Texts by Luce Irigaray available in English translation

- (1985) *Speculum of the Other Woman.* Trans. by Gillian C. Gill. Ithaca and London: Cornell University Press. (First published in French, 1974)

– (1985) *This Sex Which is Not One.** Trans. by Carolyn Burke and Catherine Porter. Ithaca: Cornell University Press. (First published in French, 1977)

– (1993) *Je, tu, nous: Toward a Culture of Difference.* Trans. by Alison Martin. London and New York: Routledge.

Roman Jakobson (1896-1982)

Roman Jakobson was born in Russia where in 1915, along with Petr Bogatyrev, he became a founder-member of the Moscow Linguistic Circle, a group of writers responsible for developing Russian Formalism, which disbanded in 1930 owing to government pressure. Jakobson moved to Czechoslovakia in 1920 where he helped to establish Czech formalism, an important antecedent of structuralism, by founding the Prague Linguistic Circle, a group disbanded in 1939 when Germany invaded Czechoslovakia.

Following this, Jakobson moved to North America where he published further work, taught at Columbia, Harvard and MIT, influenced the development of New Criticism in the 1940s and 1950s, and where he died in 1982. Fuelled by an interest in the techniques and ideas of Russian futurist poets, Jakobson and the Russian Formalists developed a theory of literary production which focused on the analysis of a writer's technical and stylistic skills, based on the premise that an artist was a technician with trained skills developed to produce a crafted object.

The Formalists, preoccupied with the technical aspects of language usage, were interested in the distinctive nature of literary language, that is, its 'literariness'. Jakobson used his research into 'aphasia' – speech defects – to argue that metaphor and metonymy could be identified as the two poles between which literary language and style traditionally moved. Jakobson also suggested that all cultural production could be analysed through a model developed from his analysis of these two aspects of literature.

Key Concepts

Metaphor and metonymy; literariness.

Major Texts by Roman Jakobson

– (1960) 'Linguistics and Poetics'* in Thomas A. Sebeok, ed., *Style in Language.* Cambridge, Mass.: The Technology Press/MIT, and New York: John Wiley.

– (1971) 'The Metaphoric and Metonymic Poles,'* extract from 'Two Aspects of Language and Two Types of Aphasic Disturbances' in Roman Jakobson and Maurice Halle, *Fundamentals of Language.* Second revised edition. The Hague: Mouton. (First edition, 1956)

Extracts from both articles are reproduced in David Lodge, ed., *Modern Criticism and Theory: A Reader.* (1988) London and New York: Longman, pp.32–61.

Julia Kristeva (b.1940)

Julia Kristeva was born in Bulgaria and went to Paris in 1966 where she has since worked as a university lecturer, writer and psychoanalyst. After researching the restricted language usage of psychotics and the pre-linguistic stage of children's language development, Kristeva supplemented her linguistic-based work with psychoanalytical approaches, in order to address the methodological problems of the effects of subjectivity (of both observer and observed) on her findings. She has drawn eclectically on ideas from Marxism, psychoanalysis, phenomenology and literary theory to theorize an understanding of sexual difference.

Key Concepts

Significance; the semiotic; semiotic flux; the symbolic.

Major Texts by Julia Kristeva available in English translation

– (1980) *Desire in Language: A Semiotic Approach to Literature and Art.* Leon S. Roudiez, ed. Trans. by Thomas Gora, Alice Jardine and Leon S. Roudiez. Oxford: Blackwell.

– (1984) *The Revolution in Poetic Language.** New York: Columbia University Press. (First published in French, 1974)

– (1986) *About Chinese Women.* London: Marion Boyars. (First published in French, 1974)

Jacques Lacan (1901–1981)

Jacques Lacan was born and educated in Paris. He was a psychoanalyst who trained at the Paris Medical Faculty. In developing his views of identity formation, Lacan drew on the insights of the psychoanalyst Sigmund Freud (1836–1939) and the linguistic theorist Ferdinand de Saussure.

Lacan's ideas were fundamental in the development of structuralism, and have been widely drawn on by subsequent feminist critics, as they opened a route for the development of an explanation of gender difference which was not rooted in biological difference. If identity is shaped in language then it can be unshaped or reconstructed.

The two stages of identity formation Lacan detailed were the mirror stage and the entry into the symbolic order. The mirror stage refers to the sudden insight a baby experiences when it realizes its separate embodiment in the world of things. This insight can be noted as the infant recognizes that its reflection in a mirror is different from the self it experiences through embodiment. Later, as the child learns language (in Lacan's phraseology, language and cultural sign systems are referred to collectively as 'the symbolic order'; thus learning a language is known as 'entering the symbolic order'), a division between the senses of inner and outer self is named in language as we come to recognize two aspects to ourselves, the 'I' who speaks as opposed to the 'I' who is spoken about. Thus the Freudian idea of split self is affirmed and named in language.

Lacan's work has subsequently been used to show how males and females enter language differently, since Lacan pointed out that language systems are constructed so that what was previously assumed to be a shared position of 'I', which could be used by both men and women, was implicitly a male 'I' position. Feminist theorists have adapted Lacan's model, suggesting that because language systems were created from a male perspective they reinforce the assumption that male experience is the norm. Thus women, on learning a language, have to learn a male way of looking at things and have much of their own female experience and perspective on things silenced.

Lacan's insights were radical since they broke with the tradition of American psychology at the time, and because they allowed for the insight that identity, or personality, is not inborn, being constructed through language. In showing a cultural rather than biological explanation of identity formation and social relations, Lacan's work has been drawn upon and interrogated in subsequent theories of gender identity and gender difference.

Key Concepts

The law of the father: the symbolic order.

Major Text by Jacques Lacan available in English translation

– (1977) *Ecrits. A Selection.** Trans. by Alan Sheridan Smith. London: Tavistock.

Ferdinand de Saussure (1857-1913)

Ferdinand de Saussure, a Swiss linguist, was educated in Germany and France. He was a professor at the University of Geneva from 1891 until his death in 1913. Between 1906 and 1911 Saussure gave a series of lectures (1906–7; 1908–9; 1910–11) at the University of Geneva in which he described his ideas on linguistics. Following Saussure's death, his theoretical ideas were reconstructed from students' lecture notes and published in Paris in 1915 by a group of his colleagues (Charles Bally, Albert Sechehaye and Albert Reidlinger) under the title, *Course in General Linguistics*.

Saussure is seen as the founder of modern linguistics and the inaugurator of semiology, a general science of signs. His ideas formed a crucial foundation for the development of structuralism and have since become influential in the analysis of all forms of human communication, including art, literature and social anthropology. Before Saussure, language was studied as a diachronic system in terms of its chronological process – in other words, analysed and charted in terms of its historical change. After Saussure, language has been studied as a synchronic system – in other words, in terms of all the elements and rules available at any given time.

Saussure's main arguments were that:

- Literary texts should be seen as part of a literary system, and that it should be possible to identify, analyse and ultimately understand such a system;
- Historical explanations of literary phenomena and their sources of meaning were suspect;
- Theories of realism were naive;
- Theories of literature should emphasize the social and cultural dimension of the generation of meaning in the production and reception of literary texts.

To support his thesis that language was a synchronic system, Saussure identified *langage* as the universal phenomenon of language within which he distinguished two elements: *langue* – a particular language system (such as English); and *parole* – speech, that is, language in use. He also identified that all linguistic signs had two aspects: the 'signifier' (an actual word, printed or spoken) and the 'signified' (the thing the word describes or the meaning associated with a word) which were arbitrarily linked. It was because of this arbitrary link that language needed a systematic structure.

Key Concepts

Langue and *parole;* sign; signified and signifier.

Major Text by Ferdinand de Saussure available in English translation

- (1983) *Course in General Linguistics*. Trans. and annotated by Roy Harris. Edited by Charles Bally and Albert Sechehaye with the collaboration of Albert Reidlinger. London: Duckworth.

Victor Shklovsky (1893-1984)

Victor Shklovsky was influential in the development of Russian Formalism and, with Yury Tynyanov and Boris Eikhenbaum, founded the *Opoyaz* group – a society for the study of poetic language. The *Opoyaz* group, along with members of the Moscow Linguistic Circle (see Roman Jakobson, p.176), developed the fundamental ideas for the theory known as 'Russian Formalism', which itself is fundamental to the development of structuralism.

The major concept associated with Shklovsky is that of *ostranenie* (making strange) or 'defamiliarization' as it has become known in English translation. This is the idea that the purpose of art is to make strange to us the world we live in. According to Shklovsky, in everyday life we tend to take things for granted, and, as we do, our perceptions tend to become lazy, automatic or habitual responses which lapse into uncritical and unquestioning modes of awareness.

What literary or poetic language has the facility to do is to disturb this common-sense or taken-for-granted and lazy way of perceiving things by making them strange to us. In making the familiar world strange, art has the capacity to resensitize us to the world we are perceiving as well as to draw attention to our faculties of perception.

Thus, for Shklovsky, the purpose of art is to change our mode of perception from an automatic, uncritical minimalist form of awareness to a heightened artistic and questioning mode: 'art exists that one may recover the sensation of life; it exists to make one feel things, to make the stone *stony*. The purpose of art is to impart the sensation of things as they are perceived, and not as they are known...because the process of perception is an aesthetic end in itself and must be prolonged' (Shklovsky, 1917). In doing this, art allows us to see the world in fresh terms. For example, in defamiliarizing the world to us, an object of art could lead to our taking up a new perspective on the social world and a questioning of the way it is ordered.

Key Concepts

Defamiliarization: literariness.

Major Text by Victor Shklovsky available in English translation

– (1965) 'Art as Technique'* in, translators and editors, Lemon, Lee T. and Reis, Marion J., *Russian Formalist Criticism: Four Essays*. Lincoln: University of Nebraska Press. (First published in Russian, 1917)

Select Bibliography

Primary Material

Extracts from the following editions have been used in the principal critical activities:

Alther, Lisa (1975; reprinted 1977) *Kinflicks*. Harmondsworth: Penguin.

Atwood, Margaret (1988) *Cat's Eye*. London: Virago.

Barth, John (1967) 'Lost in the Funhouse' reprinted in Charters, Ann (ed.) (1987) *The Story and Its Writer: An Introduction to Short Fiction*. New York: St. Martin's Press.

Bloch, Robert (1961; reprinted 1977) *Firebug*. London: Corgi.

———————— (1959; reprinted 1962) *Psycho*. London: Corgi.

Brodber, Erna (1988) *Myal*. London: New Beacon Books.

Calvino Italo (1981; reprinted 1992) *If on a winter's night a traveller*. London: Minerva.

Carter, Angela (1984; reprinted 1985) *Nights at the Circus*. London: Picador.

Chisholm, Matt (1978) *The Indian Incident*. Feltham: Hamlyn.

Christie, Agatha (1937; reprinted 1954) *Murder in the Mews*. London: Pan Books.

Clarke, Gillian (1985) *Selected Poems*. Manchester: Carcanet.

Conrad, Joseph (1902: reprinted, Penguin Classics, 1985) *Heart of Darkness*. Harmondsworth: Penguin.

Cross, Melinda (1989) *A Defiant Dream*. Richmond: Mills and Boon.

Curtis, Tony (1993a) 'Dedicating the House of Art', *Poetry Wales,* 29 (2), 33.

Defoe, Daniel (1722; reprinted 1965) *Moll Flanders*. London: Pan Books.

Dickens, Charles (1861; reprinted 1965) *Great Expectations*. Harmondsworth: Penguin.

Goldman, William (1974) *Marathon Man*. London: Macmillan.

Hardy, Thomas (1891; reprinted 1957, 1960) *Tess of the D'Urbervilles*. London: Macmillan.

Hulse, M., Kennedy, D. and Morley D. (Eds) (1993) *The New Poetry*. Newcastle: Bloodaxe Books.

Joyce, James (1922; reprinted 1960) *Ulysses*. London: The Bodley Head.

Kay, Jackie (1991) *The Adoption Papers*. Newcastle: Bloodaxe Books.

Kincaid, Jamaica (1991; reprinted 1994) *Lucy*. London: Picador.

Lawrence, D.H. (1913; reprinted 1948) *Sons and Lovers*. Harmondsworth: Penguin.

Lodge, David (1988; reprinted 1989) *Nice Work*. Harmondsworth: Penguin.

Mo Timothy (1982: reprinted 1983) *Sour Sweet*. London: Sphere Books.

Morrison, Toni (1987; reprinted 1988) *Beloved*. London: Picador.

Rendell, Ruth (1973) *Some Lie and Some Die*. London: Arrow Books.

Reynolds, Oliver (1985) *Skevington's Daughter*. London: Faber.

Riley, Joan (1985) *The Unbelonging*. Harmondsworth: Penguin.

Salinger, J. D. (1951; reprinted 1958) *The Catcher in the Rye*. Harmondsworth: Penguin.

Strange, Oliver (1933; reprinted 1961) *Sudden*. London: Corgi Books.

Thomas, Dylan (1940; reprinted 1979) *Portrait of the Artist as a Young Dog*. London: Dent.

Weale, Anne (1987) *Night Train*. Richmond: Mills and Boon.

Winterson, Jeanette (1993) *Written on the Body*. London: Cape.

Secondary and Critical Reading

Abbs, P. (1989) *A is for Aesthetic: Essays on Creative and Aesthetic Education*. London: The Falmer Press.

Abbs, P. (1990) *The Forms of Narrative: A Practical Study Guide For English*. Cambridge: Cambridge University Press.

Aston, E. and Savona, G. (1991) *Theatre as Sign System: A Semiotics of Text and Performance*. London: Routledge.

Bakhtin, M. M. (1981) *The Dialogic Imagination: Four Essays*. Trans. Emerson, C. and Holquist, M. Austin: University of Texas Press.

Barber, C. (1993) *The English Language: A Historical Introduction*. Cambridge: Cambridge University Press.

Barthes, R. (1977; reprinted 1982) *Image-Music-Text*. Trans. Heath, S. London: Flamingo.

Barthes, R. (1974; reprinted 1990) *S/Z* Trans. Miller, R. Oxford: Blackwell.

Barthes, R. (1964; reprinted 1970) *Writing Degree Zero and Elements of Semiology*. Boston, Mass.: Beacon Press.

Baxter, J. (1989; reprinted 1992) *English for GCSE: a Course for Further Education*. Cambridge: Cambridge University Press.

Belsey, C. (1980) *Critical Practice*. London: Methuen.

Bonnycastle, S. (1991) *In Search of Authority: An Introductory Guide to Literary Theory*. Peterborough, Ontario: Broadview Press.

Booth, W. (1961) *The Rhetoric of Fiction*. Chicago: University of Chicago Press.

Buck, L. and Dodd, P. (1991) *Relative Values or What's Art Worth?* London: BBC Books.

Butler, S. (1985) *Common Ground: Poets in a Welsh Landscape*. Bridgend: Poetry Wales Press.

Carr, H. (Ed.) (1989) *From My Guy to Sci-Fi: Genre and Women's Writing in the Postmodern World*. London: Pandora.

Charters, A. (1987) *The Story and Its Writer: An Introduction to Short Fiction*. New York: St. Martin's Press.

Chatman, S. (1978) *Story and Discourse: Narrative Structure in Fiction and Film*. Ithaca and London: Cornell University Press.

Coxon, R. and Baker, M. (1983) *A-Level English: Course Companion*. London: Letts.

Curtis, T. (1993b) 'In Different Voices', *Poetry Wales*, 29 (2), 29-31.

Derrida, J. (1974; reprinted 1976) *Of Grammatology*. Trans. Spivak, G. C. Baltimore: The Johns Hopkins University Press.

Dipple, Elizabeth (1988) *The Unresolvable Plot: Reading Contemporary Fiction*. London: Routledge.

Doyle, B. (1989) *English and Englishness*. London: Routledge.

Durrant, A. and Fabb, N. (1990) *Literary Studies in Action*. London: Routledge.

Eagleton, T. (1983) *Literary Theory: An Introduction*. Oxford: Basil Blackwell.

Easthope, A. and McGowan, K. (1992) *A Critical and Cultural Theory Reader*. Milton Keynes: Open University Press.

Forster, E.M. (1927; reprinted 1971) *Aspects of the Novel*. Harmondsworth: Penguin.

Fowler, R. (1973; reprinted 1987) *A Dictionary of Modern Critical Terms*. London: Routledge.

Genette, G. (1972; 1980) *Narrative Discourse: An Essay in Method*. Trans. Lewin, J. and Culler, J.. London: Cornell University Press.

Gordon, G. and Hughes, D. (Eds) (1991; reprinted 1992) *The Minerva Book of Short Stories 4*. London: Minerva.

Hall, E., Hall, C., and Leach, A. (1990) *Scripted Fantasy in the Classroom*. London: Routledge.

Harland, R. (1987) *Superstructuralism: The Philosophy of Structuralism and Post-Structuralism*. London: Routledge.

Hawthorn, J. (1992) *A Concise Glossary of Contemporary Literary Theory*. London: Arnold.

Hawkes, T. (1977) *Structuralism and Semiotics*. London: Routledge.

Hemingway, E. (1947; reprinted 1972) *The Essential Hemingway*. Harmondsworth: Penguin.

Horstmann, R. (1991; reprinted 1993) *Writing For Radio*. London: A. C. Black.

Jefferson, A. and Robey, D. (1982: reprinted 1993) *Modern Literary Theory: A Comparative Introduction*. London: Batsford.

Lodge, D. (1990) 'The Novel as Communication' in Mellor, H. (Ed.) *Ways of Communicating*. Cambridge: Cambridge University Press.

Lodge, D. (1988) *Modern Criticism and Theory: A Reader*. London: Longman.

Lodge, D. (1981; reprinted 1991) *Working With Structuralism: Essays and Reviews on Nineteenth and Twentieth-Century Literature*. London: Routledge.

Lodge, D. (Ed.) (1972) *20th Century Literary Criticism: A Reader*. London: Longman.

Margolies, D. (1982/83) 'Mills & Boon: Guilt without Sex', *Red Letters* **14**, 5-13.

Monteith, M. and Miles, R. (1992) *Teaching Creative Writing: Theory and Practice*. Milton Keynes: Open University Press.

Moss, G. (1989) *Un/Popular Fictions*. London: Virago.

Palmer, J. (1991) *Potboilers: Methods, Concepts and Case Studies in Popular Fiction*. London: Routledge.

Parker, S. (1993) *The Craft of Writing*. London: Chapman.

Peck, J. (1983; reprinted 1993) *How to Study a Novel*. London: Macmillan.

Peck, J. and Coyle, M. (1984; reprinted 1993) *Literary Terms and Criticism*. London: Macmillan.

Peim, N. (1993) *Critical Theory and the English Teacher: Transforming the Subject*. London: Routledge.

Prince, G. (1987; reprinted 1988) *Dictionary of Narratology*. Aldershot: Scolar Press.

Propp, V. (1968) *Morphology of the Folktale*. Ed. Wagner, L. Trans. Scott, L. Austin: University of Texas Press.

Rice, P. and Waugh, P. (1989) *Modern Literary Theory: A Reader*. London: Arnold.

Rimmon-Kenan, S. (1983) *Narrative Fiction: Contemporary Poetics*. London: Methuen.

Rylance, R. (Ed.) (1987; reprinted 1992) *Debating Texts: A Reader in 20th Century Literary Theory and Method*. Milton Keynes: Open University Press.

Sapir, E. (1949) *Selected Writings in Language, Culture and Personality*. Trans. Mandelbaum G. Berkeley: University of California Press.

Selden, R. and Widdowson, P. (1993) *A Reader's Guide to Contemporary Literary Theory*. London: Harvester Wheatsheaf.

Sellers, S. (Ed.) (1991) *Taking Reality by Surprise: Writing for Pleasure and Publication*. London: The Women's Press.

Stibbs, A. (1991) *Reading Narrative as Literature: Signs of Life*. Milton Keynes: Open University Press.

Tambling, J. (1991) *Narrative and Ideology*. Milton Keynes: Open University Press.

Tate, C. (Ed.) (1985) *Black Women Writers at Work*. Harpenden: Old Castle Books

Thomas, M. Wynn (1994) 'Anglo-Welsh poets and the Welsh language during the '80s' in Davies, J.A. and Pursglove, G. (Eds) *Writing Region and Nation*. Swansea: University of Wales Press.

Thompson, J. (1985) *Orwell's London*. New York: Shocken Press.

Waites, B., Bennett, T. and Martin, G. (1982; reprinted 1983) *Popular Culture: Past and Present*. London: Croom Helm/Open University Press.

Watson, C. (1971: reprinted 1987) *Snobbery with Violence: English Crime Stories and their Audience*. London: Methuen.

Watt, I. (1957) *The Rise of the Novel*. Harmondsworth: Penguin.

Webster, R. (1990) *Studying Literary Theory: An Introduction*. London: Routledge.

Index